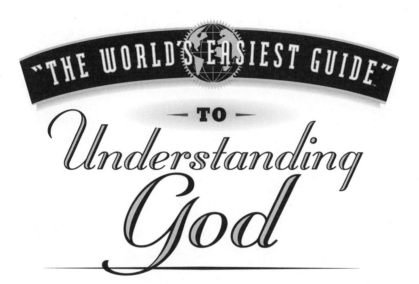

"THE WORLD'S EASIEST GUIDE"

— TO —

Understanding God

"THE WORLD'S EASIEST GUIDE"

— TO —

Understanding God

RANDY SOUTHERN

NORTHFIELD PUBLISHING
Chicago

Scripture taken from the Holy Bible, *New International Version*®. NIV®. Copyright © 1973, 1978, 1984 by International Bible Society. Used by permission of Zondervan Publishing House. All rights reserved.

Scripture quotations marked NASB are taken from the New American Standard Bible®, © Copyright The Lockman Foundation 1960, 1962, 1963, 1968, 1971, 1972, 1973, 1975, 1977, 1995. Used by permission.

Library of Congress Cataloging-in-Publication Data

Southern, Randy.
    "The world's easiest guide" to understanding God / by Randy Southern.
        p. cm.
    Includes index.
    ISBN 1-881273-84-9
    1. God. I. Title

BT103.S68 2003
231--dc21   2002044861

ISBN: 1-881273-84-9

1 3 5 7 9 10 8 6 4 2

Printed in the United States of America

Table of Contents

"THE WORLD'S EASIEST GUIDE"

PART ONE

God's Identity

God Who?

UNDERSTANDING VARIOUS BELIEFS ABOUT GOD

SNAPSHOT

"Grandpa, are you going to come see my Easter play at church?" Brittany asked.

"I don't think your church has enough insurance coverage for that to happen," Joe replied. Then he turned and gave a smile and wink to his daughter and son-in-law.

"What do you mean, Grandpa?" Brittany asked.

"Well, if I ever stepped foot in a church, I'm afraid the walls would crumble and the roof would come crashing down," Joe said with a grin. "Plus, everyone who knew me would be having heart attacks in the aisle."

"Why?" Brittany asked with a look of alarm. "Don't you like church, Grandpa?"

Joe looked at his daughter, then back at Brittany.

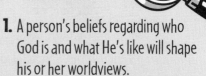

SNEAK PREVIEW

1. A person's beliefs regarding who God is and what He's like will shape his or her worldviews.

2. The Bible is our primary source of information about who God is and what He's like.

3. The Bible tells us that God alone is the Creator and sustainer of the universe, an awesome, invisible Spirit who makes Himself known to us in a personal way.

His grin faded. "I don't know how to answer that, Brit," he began, "except to say that there are certain things I don't believe in."

"Honey, we'll talk about this later," her mother interrupted. "Why don't you go next door and see if Kate wants to play?"

Joe put his hand over his face as Brittany headed out the door. "I'm sorry," he said. "I didn't mean to open a can of worms. I guess that's what happens when you invite your old atheist father to Sunday dinner."

"What were you going to tell her, Dad?" Brenda asked as she collected the silverware from the table.

"The truth," Joe shrugged. "That I don't believe in things I can't see or things that can't be proved."

"And you put God in that category?" Dave asked as he helped his wife clear the dinner plates.

"That's generally how atheism works," Joe replied with a sly smile.

"The thing is," Dave said, "I don't believe in atheists."

"I beg your pardon?" Joe said.

"I think everyone believes in some kind of God," Dave explained. "It's just a matter of how you define the word."

Joe stared at his son-in-law but didn't say anything.

"What if I said that God is simply that which created itself or that which has existed forever?" Dave asked.

"I'd say it sounds like something you read in a book and that it doesn't change anything for me," Joe replied.

"Okay, then let's talk about the beginning of the universe," Dave said.

"This is where you're going to try to tell me that God created everything," Joe predicted.

"Right," Dave replied. "And you're going to try to tell me that the Big Bang created everything."

"Yep," Joe said, "and from what I read in the Tribune this week, scientists are finding more and more evidence to prove it."

"We can talk about that another time," Dave said. "What I want to know is, what caused the Big Bang?"

"What caused it?" Joe asked. "Well, as I understand it, it was a gas cloud that became unstable and exploded."

"Okay," Dave acknowledged. "And where did the gas cloud come from?"

"Well, I haven't seen any video footage of it," Joe said, "but I suppose it was made up of random molecules that came together."

"And where did those molecules come from?" Dave pressed.

"Boy, you're just full of questions, aren't you?" Joe said. "Where did the molecules come from? I don't know. I suppose they've always been floating around in space somewhere."

"Then, congratulations, you have a god," Dave said with a smile. "You're no longer an atheist."

"I'm not?"

"No, remember?" Dave asked. "We said God is that which has existed forever or that which created itself. If you believe that certain random molecules have always been around, then that qualifies them to be gods."

Joe furrowed his brow but said nothing.

"So the question isn't 'Does God exist?'" Dave explained. "It's 'What is He like?' You picture God as a bunch of random molecules; I picture Him as a perfect Being."

Joe shook his head. "Suddenly I feel like I've lost my identity," he said with a laugh. "If I'm not an atheist, what do I call myself now?"

"How about a seeker?" Brenda offered.

"Don't press your luck," Joe replied with a wink.

* * * * * * * * * * * * * *

You don't have to be a theologian to have a fully formed opinion of who God is and what He's like. In fact, you don't even have to know much about religion. All you have to do is keep your eyes and ears open to the entertainment media around you.

Think about how many times you've seen God depicted or referred to on TV, in music, and in the movies. Among countless other things, He's been portrayed as . . .

➤ a slightly imperfect taskmaster who can't remember what a "cubit" is (in a classic Bill Cosby comedy routine),

➤ a mute, female flower child (by singer Alanis Morissette in the movie *Dogma*),

➤ a George Burns-like comedian (by—who else?—George Burns in the *Oh God!* movie trilogy),

➤ an impatient grouch who can't stand His worshipful followers (in *Monty Python and the Holy Grail*), and

➤ a "slob like one of us" (in the 1995 Joan Osborne hit song "One of Us").

Charlton Heston, James Garner, Val Kilmer, Robert Mitchum, and Sandra Bernhard have all been cast as God. Some of the portrayals are reverent, some are less so, and some are offensive.

But are any of them accurate? Are any of them even in the ballpark?

Who's Right?

The diversity of Hollywood portrayals of God reflects the diversity of beliefs about Him among the major religions and belief systems. For example . . .

NOTABLE QUOTABLE

God is that than which nothing greater can be conceived.

—ANSELM

14

➤ Muslims believe that God (Allah) is unapproachable by sinful humans, that love and compassion are not among his strong suits, and that his deity makes him too mighty to interact personally with mere humans.

➤ Mormons believe that God was once a man and that he still has a physical body made of flesh and blood.

➤ Many followers of New Age philosophies believe that God is an impersonal force that pervades all creation, and that everyone and everything is ultimately God.

➤ Scientologists believe that God is found within the "divine nature" of the person doing the searching, that humans are actually part god and can attain a more godlike nature.

➤ Christian Scientists believe that God is an abstract concept, synonymous with such terms as *Life, Truth, Love, Principle, Mind, Substance, Intelligence,* and *Spirit.*

➤ Many Hindus believe that there are hundreds, thousands, even millions of different gods in existence.

➤ Buddhists believe that there is no such thing as a personal God.

➤ Deists believe that God created the world and then left it alone to operate on its own, without any guidance, direction, or intervention from Him.

The inclusive-minded might suggest that there is no right or wrong when it comes to God, that what we believe about Him ultimately doesn't matter as long as we're sincere in that belief.

But that's simply not true. If belief dictated reality, Santa Claus would be alive today, based on the number of kids who think he's real. In fact, he'd probably be a fixture on the TV talk-show circuit, along with the Easter bunny and the tooth fairy.

Accurate beliefs are particularly important where God is concerned. Our views of God will strongly influence the way we . . .

➤ approach life,

➤ treat others,

➤ deal with tragedy, and

➤ make sense of the world.

For example, a person who believes that God is unapproachable will likely live his life in fear and unease, unsure of how to please his deity. A person who believes that God is found within human nature would have no reason to think about atoning for her sins. A person who believes that God is an abstract concept is unlikely to pursue a personal relationship with Him.

That's why it's vitally important that we not fall for "stories" or "rumors" about God. That's why we must go straight to the source—the Book He Himself authored (using human writers)—for information. That's why our beliefs about God must come from the Bible.

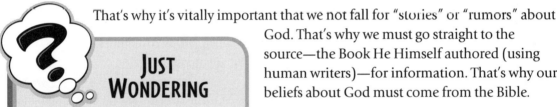

JUST WONDERING

How do we know that Christian teachings about God are correct?

Such teachings are based on information from God's own Word, which means it can be trusted completely. Second Timothy 3:16 tells us that everything in Scripture comes from God Himself. Hebrews 6:18 emphasizes that it is impossible for God to lie. Proverbs 30:5 says, "Every word of God is flawless." (If you're interested in more information regarding the trustworthiness of the Bible, check out chapter 7.)

Source Material

The Bible is chock-full of passages that describe God's characteristics and attributes. What's more, it contains hundreds of eyewitness accounts of the Lord in action—documented evidence of His dealings with human beings.

We'll explore God's individual attributes and characteristics in detail in chapter 3. In this chapter, we're going to concentrate on six truths that identify who He is and set Him apart from the deities of other religions. Those truths are as follows:

1. God alone is God.

2. God is the Creator.

3. God is the sustainer of the universe.

4. God is a spirit.

5. God is personal.

6. God is worthy of reverence, awe, and fear.

The Solo Act

The God of the Bible is not a deity among deities; He is the *only* Deity. In theological terms, the belief that there is only one God is called *monotheism*. The Bible certainly supports a monotheistic view. The fact that there is no other God but God is affirmed throughout Scripture:

➤ "Who among the gods is like you, O LORD? Who is like you—majestic in holiness, awesome in glory, working wonders?" (Exodus 15:11).

➤ "Hear, O Israel: the LORD our God, the LORD is one" (Deuteronomy 6:4).

➤ "This is what the LORD says—Israel's King and Redeemer, the LORD Almighty: I am the first and I am the last; apart from me there is no God" (Isaiah 44:6).

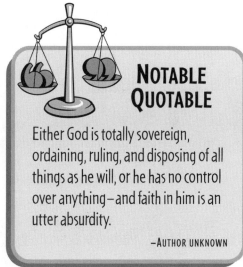

NOTABLE QUOTABLE

Either God is totally sovereign, ordaining, ruling, and disposing of all things as he will, or he has no control over anything—and faith in him is an utter absurdity.

—AUTHOR UNKNOWN

Not only does God's singularity as Deity run counter to the polytheistic beliefs of Hindus and others, but it also negates the possibility of people becoming gods (or even "godlike"), as is taught by Scientologists and others.

The Bible leaves little room for flexibility on the issue of monotheism. God is not keen on sharing His glory with imaginary deities. In fact, in Exodus 20:5 God Himself says, "I, the LORD your God, am a jealous God."

Unlike human jealousy, which often results from insecurity and is considered a character flaw, God's jealousy is perfectly justified. Because He alone is God, He

alone deserves all honor and praise. That's why He zealously protects what is rightfully His—namely, all human worship. God hammers the point home in Isaiah 48:11 when He says, "I will not yield my glory to another."

The Israelites learned that lesson the hard way—time and time again—in the Old Testament. On numerous occasions, God demonstrated to His people just how strongly He felt about maintaining His monopoly on their worship.

Judges 2:10–15 demonstrates just how seriously God takes His exclusive worship. The events described in the passage took place after the death of Joshua, the godly leader who led the Israelites into the land that God had promised them.

> After that whole generation had been gathered to their fathers, another generation grew up, who knew neither the LORD nor what he had done for Israel. Then the Israelites did evil in the eyes of the LORD and served the Baals. They forsook the LORD, the God of their fathers, who had brought them out of Egypt. They followed and worshiped various gods of the peoples around them. They provoked the LORD to anger because they forsook him and served Baal and the Ashtoreths. In his anger against Israel the LORD handed them over to raiders who plundered them. He sold them to their enemies all around, whom they were no longer able to resist. Whenever Israel went out to fight, the hand of the LORD was against them to defeat them, just as he had sworn to them. They were in great distress.

Similar accounts can be found throughout the book of Judges—and much of the Old Testament. The one constant in every account is God's fierce protectiveness of His glory. The inescapable lesson to be learned from these accounts is that the Lord alone is God, and woe to anyone who believes otherwise.

God demonstrated the fruitlessness of believing in any other "god" but Himself in an incredible competition staged at Mount Carmel. According to 1 Kings

18:16–40, God instructed His prophet Elijah to challenge the prophets of Baal, a Canaanite god, to a contest.

The rules of the contest were simple. Elijah would build an altar and offer a sacrifice (a slaughtered bull) to God; the prophets of Baal would do the same for their god. The first deity to send fire from heaven to consume his sacrifice would be declared the God of Israel.

The prophets of Baal went first. They carefully prepared their altar and sacrifice and then called on Baal to accept it. When that didn't work, they began to dance and shout. When that didn't work, they slashed themselves with swords and spears to arouse Baal to action. Yet Baal remained silent and inactive, and their sacrifice remained untouched.

When Elijah's turn came, he dug a trench around his altar and then instructed spectators to fill four large jars of water and pour them all over the altar. Then he had them do it again—and again, until the water had drenched the wood, the sacrifice, and the altar, and filled the freshly dug trench.

While the crowd was still puzzling over Elijah's unusual "fireproofing" strategy, the prophet stepped away from the altar and asked the Lord to show Israel, once and for all, who the real God is.

As soon as the words left Elijah's lips, a roaring fire appeared and consumed his sacrifice . . . as well as the wood beneath it, the stone altar on which it set, the soil around it, and the water that filled the trench.

ON A PERSONAL NOTE

Interview some of your friends, family members, coworkers, neighbors, and acquaintances regarding their beliefs about who God is and what He's like. You don't have to get confrontational. Just start some dialogue about God's nature, and see where things go. Ask the people you talk to to share some of the life experiences that have influenced their beliefs about God. Be prepared to do the same for them.

NOTABLE QUOTABLE

It is necessary to apply to Scripture in order to learn the sure marks which distinguish God, as the Creator of the world, from the whole herd of fictitious gods.

—JOHN CALVIN

The demonstration was so overwhelming that, according to 1 Kings 18:39, "When all the people saw this, they fell prostrate and cried, 'The LORD—he is God! The LORD—he is God!'"

That acknowledgment is step one in discovering who God is and what He's like.

The Creative Director

The fact that you are a sentient being on a life-sustaining planet, able to ponder the nature of God, is due solely to the Lord's creative work. The first two chapters of Genesis make it clear that nothing in the universe is the result of random chance. God personally designed . . .

> ➤ the earth,
> ➤ the sky,
> ➤ the seas,
> ➤ vegetation,

> ➤ the sun, moon, and stars,
> ➤ birds and sea creatures,
> ➤ land animals,
> ➤ man and woman, and

> ➤ anything else in creation you care to name

. . . according to a specific plan and for a specific purpose.

God's master plan for creation is known only to Himself. (It's part of His "secret" will, which we'll discuss in chapter 13.) His *purpose* for creation is made clear in passages such as Isaiah 43:6–7, in which God refers to His human creation—His "sons" and "daughters" as those "whom I created *for my glory*" (italics added).

Revelation 4:11 echoes the theme of God's glory in creation: "You are worthy, our Lord and God, to receive glory and honor and power, for you created all things, and by your will they were created and have their being."

God alone is Deity, and God alone is responsible for the creation of the world. Our universe exists because God determined that it should. That makes Him worthy of glory.

Regardless of what we choose to believe about God, we must acknowledge that the only reason we're able to exercise our logic, deductive skills, and intelligence in reaching our conclusions is that God *created* us with logic, deductive skills, and intelligence.

The Sustainer

Contrary to the beliefs of many deists, God's involvement in the universe did not end at creation. He didn't wind the universe like a clock and then leave it to run down on its own. He didn't set the globe spinning and then turn His attention to other worlds. He didn't put the finishing touches on man and woman and then retire to a distant corner of the universe.

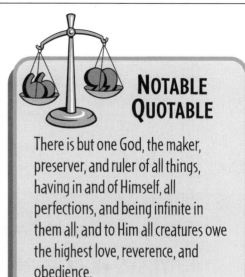

NOTABLE QUOTABLE

There is but one God, the maker, preserver, and ruler of all things, having in and of Himself, all perfections, and being infinite in them all; and to Him all creatures owe the highest love, reverence, and obedience.

—JAMES BOYCE

Colossians 1:17 says the Lord "is before all things, and in him all things hold together." The idea is that God keeps the universe functioning in the way He intended. That means His interest and attention is constant. He's not an "absentee landlord."

The book of Job confirms God's active involvement in the universe:

> *"God's voice thunders in marvelous ways;*
> *he does great things beyond our understanding.*
> *He says to the snow, 'Fall on the earth,'*
> *and to the rain shower, 'Be a mighty downpour.' . . .*
> *The breath of God produces ice,*
> *and the broad waters become frozen.*
> *He loads the clouds with moisture;*
> *he scatters his lightning through them.*
> *At his direction they swirl around over the face of the whole earth*
> *to do whatever he commands them" (Job 37:5–6, 10–12).*

Beyond that, Scripture indicates that God takes an even more hands-on approach to sustaining the life He created. Psalm 104 reads like a "to do" list on God's refrigerator. Among other things, God . . .

➤ "makes springs pour water into the ravines" (verse 10),

➤ gives "water to all the beasts of the field" (verse 11),

➤ "waters the mountains" (verse 13),

➤ "makes grass grow for the cattle" (verse 14), and

➤ makes "plants for man to cultivate—bringing forth food from the earth" (verse 14).

Implicit in these passages is the fact that none of the things described would happen without God's direct involvement. The world exists because God created it; the world continues to function because God sustains it.

That's the Spirit!

The Bible offers very little information about God's physical appearance—except for the fact that He has no physical appearance. In John 4:24, Jesus said that "God is spirit." That would indicate that He has no physical body (contrary to Mormon beliefs) or even any distinguishable features.

The word spirit invariably conjures up images of Hollywood ghosts and poltergeists. However, those images don't do justice to God's actual form. God is unlike anything else in creation, which means we have no context for understanding what His spiritual form is like. He is not made of matter, vapor, or energy.

Perhaps the best way to summarize God's spiritual form and nature is to say that He cannot be perceived by our human senses. John 1:18 tells us that "no one has ever seen God." The apostle Paul describes the Lord as "invisible" in 1 Timothy 1:17.

NOTABLE QUOTABLE

Any fool can count the seeds in an apple. Only God can count all the apples in one seed.

–ROBERT H. SCHULLER

God cannot be thought of in terms of size, shape, or dimension. In fact, the second of God's Ten Commandments in Exodus 20:4 ("You shall not make for yourself an idol in the form of anything in heaven above or on the earth beneath or in the waters below") warns that we shouldn't even try to put a form to Him.

To portray God's features in a physical form—whether it be as a golden calf (Exodus 32) or a modern Hindu idol—is to misrepresent Him. God's existence is infinitely more excellent than our mere flesh and blood. That's why He considers it a dishonor to be portrayed as something physical.

A Personal Deity

God could have chosen to remain a complete mystery to us, an invisible Creator-Sustainer too lofty to be detected—let alone known—by His human creation. Fortunately for us, that's not the way God operates. In fact, our heavenly Father wants us to learn everything we can about Him—and He's gone to great lengths to help us do that.

Though God's total being can never be perceived by human senses, God does make Himself known in a variety of ways. He does that first and foremost through His Word, the Bible, which contains everything we need to know about Him.

To help us make sense of who God is—to put His being into terms that we can understand—the Bible often uses anthropomorphic language in describing Him. That is, it assigns Him human characteristics in order to make a point or help us relate to Him more easily. For example, the Bible describes God as having . . .

> ➤ a heart (Genesis 6:6),

> ➤ arms (Numbers 11:23; Deuteronomy 33:27),

> ➤ hands (Exodus 15:6),

> ➤ fingers (Exodus 8:19; 31:18),

> ➤ a face (Exodus 33:20),

> ➤ eyes (Psalm 33:18; Hebrews 4:13),

JUST WONDERING

Will we be able to see God in heaven?

There's clear evidence in the Bible that we will. In Matthew 5:8, Jesus says, "Blessed are the pure in heart, for they will see God." First John 3:2 promises that "we shall see him as he is." Revelation 22:4 goes so far as to say that God's servants "will see his face." The Bible doesn't tell us exactly how we will be able to "see" our heavenly Father. It's quite possible, though, that the nature of that "sight" won't be revealed until we get to heaven.

➤ a mouth (Deuteronomy 8:3), and

➤ a tongue (Isaiah 30:27).

Yet we know from other passages that God does not have a physical body. These references to body parts are for our benefit. In order to teach us things about Himself that we've never experienced, God uses images that we are familiar with.

That's why you'll find descriptions of God . . .

➤ seeing (Genesis 1:31),

➤ hearing (Exodus 2:24),

➤ smelling (Genesis 8:21),

➤ sitting (Psalm 80:1), and

➤ walking (Leviticus 26:12).

Those are all activities and functions we can relate to. When we read them, we get an image of God that we can understand.

In addition to communicating information about Himself in identifiable terms, God—the all-powerful, all-knowing Creator-Sustainer of the universe—actually allows us to interact with Him on a personal level.

ON A PERSONAL NOTE

Here's a Bible study suggestion. Read Psalm 139:15–16 and Jeremiah 1:5. Spend some time thinking about these questions: How does it feel to know that the Creator of the universe is so personally interested in your life? What impact should that knowledge have on the way you think of yourself and your future?

The amazing truth is that God desires a personal relationship with each and every one of us. Toward that end, God demonstrated His personal nature once and for all two thousand years ago when He came to earth, as one of us, in the person of His Son, Jesus.

In chapter 9, we'll explore the specifics of what Jesus' coming and His work on earth mean to us. For now, though, we'll simply marvel at the prospect of a one-on-one relationship with the most powerful Being in the universe.

A Force to Be Reckoned With

The fact that the Lord relates to us personally does not mean that we're free to treat Him as we would another person. This is God we're talking about—not "the Man Upstairs" or "the Big Guy" or any other cliché or colloquialism you care to name. Any relationship we have with Him should reflect our understanding of exactly who He is.

The Lord is the Sovereign Deity whose intense hatred of sin and disobedience is seen throughout Scripture. We don't have to look hard to find descriptions and accounts that should disabuse us of any inclination to underestimate God or take Him lightly. Check out these startling passages:

NOTABLE QUOTABLE

The relationship between God and a man is more private and intimate than any possible relation between two fellow creatures.

–C. S. LEWIS

➤ "So the LORD said, 'I will wipe mankind, whom I have created, from the face of the earth—men and animals, and creatures that move along the ground, and birds of the air—for I am grieved that I have made them'" (Genesis 6:7).

➤ "They moved the ark of God from Abinadab's house on a new cart, with Uzzah and Ahio guiding it. . . . When they came to the threshing floor of Kidon, Uzzah reached out his hand to steady the ark, because the oxen stumbled. TheLORD's anger burned against Uzzah, and he struck him down because he had put his hand on the ark. So he died there before God" (1 Chronicles 13:7, 9–10).

➤ "Now a man named Ananias, together with his wife Sapphira, also sold a piece of property. With his wife's full knowledge, he kept back part of the money for himself, but brought the rest and put it at the apostles' feet. Then Peter said, 'Ananias, how is it that Satan has so filled your heart that you have lied to the Holy Spirit and have kept for yourself some of the money you received for the land?' . . . When Ananias heard this, he fell down and died. And great fear seized all who heard what had happened. . . . About three hours later his wife came in, not knowing what had happened. Peter asked her, 'Tell me, is this the price you and Ananias got for the land?' 'Yes,' she said, 'that is the price.' Peter said to her, 'How could you agree to test the Spirit of the Lord? Look! The feet of the men who buried your husband are at the door, and they will carry you out also.' At that moment she fell down at his feet and died" (Acts 5:1–3, 5, 7–10a).

➤ "Then I saw a great white throne and him who was seated on it. Earth and sky fled from his presence, and there was no place for them" (Revelation 20:11).

"The fear of the LORD is the beginning of knowledge," Proverbs 1:7 says. That doesn't mean we should spend our lives cowering from our heavenly Father; however, it does mean we should approach Him with genuine reverence, humility, and gratefulness.

David seems to have had a healthy attitude toward His relationship with the infinite Creator. You can almost hear the awe and wonder in David's words in Psalm 8:3–4: "When I consider your heavens, the work of your fingers, the moon and the stars which you have set in place, what is man that you are mindful of him, and the son of man that you care for him?"

NOTABLE QUOTABLE

The almighty and everywhere present power of God; whereby...he upholds and governs heaven, earth, and all creatures; so that herbs and grass, rain and drought, fruitful and barren years, meat and drink, health and sickness, riches and poverty, yea, and all things come, not by chance, but by his fatherly hand.

—HEIDELBERG CATECHISM

The Final Word

The God Christians worship is ...

➤ powerful enough to have spoken the universe into existence,

➤ active enough to maintain a constant presence in the world, sustaining the universe He created,

➤ mysterious enough to be undetectable to our human senses,

➤ caring enough to present Himself in terms we can understand and appreciate, and

➤ fearsome enough to have the earth and sky flee from His presence.

What's more, He is infinitely too complex for us to ever fully comprehend. But that shouldn't keep us from a lifetime of discovery. Lamentations 3:22–23 tells us that God's blessings are new every morning. That means we can look forward to learning more about Him every day of our lives!

Psalm 34:8 issues the invitation to try and discover His goodness: "Taste and see that the LORD is good."

 # Know What You Believe

How much do you know about God? Here's a quiz to test your knowledge.

1. Which of the following statements is not true of God?
   a. He is responsible for creation.
   b. He relates to us personally.
   c. His physical body is much larger than ours.
   d. He sustains the universe.

2. What is monotheism?
   a. The belief that there is only one source of knowledge regarding God—the Bible
   b. The belief that only one God exists
   c. The belief that God chose only one nation—the Israelites—to be His people
   d. The belief that mononucleosis is one of the plagues God sent to the Egyptians

3. Why does God prohibit people from making idols of Him?
   a. He likes to be present when people worship Him, and He doesn't want to have to send His presence to every little statue that people build of Him around the world.
   b. He hasn't yet decided which animal most closely represents Him.
   c. Most idols are designed by amateurs, and God only works with the top artists.

d. His existence is infinitely more excellent than anything that can be portrayed in physical form.

4. Which of the following is true of the anthropomorphic language found in the Bible?
   a. It gives us images of God we can understand and relate to.
   b. It derives from both the Latin and Greek languages.
   c. It was first introduced in the book of 1 Kings by the pagan Anthropomorph people.
   d. It is of no use to modern Christians.

5. Which of the following is not a proper response to God?
   a. Humility
   b. Awe
   c. Gratefulness
   d. Irreverence

Answers: (1) c, (2) b, (3) d, (4) a, (5) d

CHAPTER 2

That's Him –
I'd Recognize Him
Anywhere

UNDERSTANDING GOD'S REVELATION

SNAPSHOT

"What a beautiful sunset!" June declared as she cleared the dirty plates from the picnic table.

"God's really outdoing Himself with this one," Cliff agreed.

Bob laid his head on the table and groaned.

"Did I say something wrong?" Cliff asked.

"We were having such a nice cookout," Bob said. "And then you had to go and mention the 'G'-word."

"Does anyone else have a problem with talking about God?" Cliff asked.

"Not me," said Lisa.

"Not me," June chimed in.

Bob glared at Lisa, then at Cliff and June. "You guys

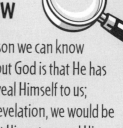

SNEAK PREVIEW

1. The only reason we can know anything about God is that He has chosen to reveal Himself to us; without His revelation, we would be clueless about His nature and His purposes.
2. God reveals Himself primarily in three ways–through creation, through personal experiences, and through His Word.
3. The fact that God reveals Himself demands an appropriate response from His people–that is, a commitment to discover everything we can about what He has revealed.

may have gotten to my wife," he said, "but you're not going to get to me."

"Don't be paranoid, dear," Lisa said. "Nobody *got* to me. It was my decision."

"Okay, it was *your* decision," Bob acknowledged. "But *they're* the ones who put those ideas about God and Christianity in your head."

"You make us sound dangerous," June said.

Cliff reached into his jacket and snarled, "Back off, man. I've got a pocket Bible in my hand and I'm not afraid to use it."

"You're not dangerous," Bob said. "Just . . . persuasive." Then he looked at his wife. "To *some* people, that is."

Lisa just rolled her eyes.

"So when you think of God—" June began.

Bob waved his hand. "No, no, no. I'm not going to get into a philosophical debate with you. I'm a simple guy; I deal in facts. So unless you can back up your words with evidence—*real* evidence, not churchy stuff—I'm not interested in hearing it."

"What kind of evidence are you looking for?" Cliff asked.

"Let me put it this way," Bob said. "When you can *prove* to me that God exists, we'll talk."

Cliff reached down, grabbed a leaf, and handed it to Bob.

"What's this?" Bob asked with a slight hesitation.

"That's the proof you asked for," Cliff replied.

Bob turned the leaf over. "I don't see God's signature on it anywhere," he said.

Cliff took the leaf from him and held it up for inspection. "It's there in every perfectly designed branch, every beautiful color, every—"

"Before you break into song," Bob interrupted, "let me remind you that not all of us view nature the way you do."

"Maybe you're just not looking close enough," Cliff suggested.

"Why do you say that?"

"The way I see it," Cliff said, "living in this world and asking for proof of God's existence is like standing at a Monet exhibit in an art museum and asking for proof of the artist's existence."

Bob turned and pointed at Cliff. "No, it's not, because a Monet exhibit would have pictures of the artist and eyewitness accounts of people who saw him and talked to him and watched him work. *That's* the kind of proof I'm talking about." With just the slightest hint of a smile, Bob bowed, nodded toward an imaginary judge, and said, "The prosecution rests, your honor."

"Hold on there, counselor," Cliff said. "What if you didn't know who the artist was? What if all you had to go on was the artwork itself?"

"What do you mean?" Bob asked.

"Let's say you're standing in a gallery filled with beautiful paintings that were . . . I don't know, discovered in storage somewhere hundreds of years ago. And let's say all of the paintings are masterpieces, the quality of Monet or da Vinci or Van Gogh."

"Or the guy who did the dogs playing poker," Bob added.

"Him, too," Cliff acknowledged. "And let's say these paintings were complete mysteries. No one knew anything about them—who painted them, where they came from, or when they were done. All you had were the works themselves. Would you agree that someone still had to have created them?"

Bob looked around at Lisa and June. "Will I get dessert faster if I say yes?" he asked.

* * * * * * * * * * * * * * *

We have a confession to make. This is a book about . . . theology. (Cue audience gasp and dramatic music.)

We've done our best to disguise it with an inviting cover, a clean layout, simple language, cool artwork, and an author's photo of a guy who doesn't look terribly academic (or even terribly bright, for that matter). However, there's no getting around the fact that this book is intended to introduce readers to a variety of *theological* concepts.

If you need some time to compose yourself or steel your nerves for what lies ahead, by all means do so. We'll wait for you at the next subhead.

God, I Presume

Theology—from the Greek words *theos*, meaning "God," and *logos*, meaning "rational expression"—may be the most audacious and presumptuous word in the English language. *Theology*, generally speaking, is the human study of God's truths.

Think about that definition for a moment. Fallible human beings of limited intelligence—a race of people who, until about five hundred years ago, believed that if a ship sailed too far on the ocean, it would fall off the edge of the world—presuming to understand something of the infinite, eternal, and perfect God of heaven. The whole notion is ludicrous.

Or, at least it would be, if it weren't for a wild card in the theological deck.

The Book on Revelation

As we alluded to earlier, our problem in trying to understand God is one of equipment. Our task involves an *infinite* Being, yet we have only *finite* tools with which to tackle it. The fact is, our brains aren't capable of the thought processes necessary for "solving" the mysteries of God.

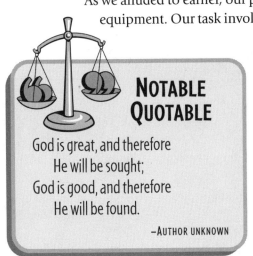

NOTABLE QUOTABLE

God is great, and therefore
He will be sought;
God is good, and therefore
He will be found.

—AUTHOR UNKNOWN

In order for us to understand God, we have to have help—not from other finite creatures, but from the only One who is infinite, God Himself. Fortunately for us, God is more than willing to provide that help in the form of *revelation*, a "revealing" of Himself to us.

Let's be clear about this. The only reason that knowing God is even a possibility for us is that God has *made* it possible. He has taken the initiative in making Himself known to us.

The Bible certainly makes no secret of God's revelatory nature. In Romans 1:18–19, the apostle Paul wrote, "The wrath of God is being revealed from heaven against all the godlessness and wickedness of men who suppress the truth by their wickedness, since what may be known about God is plain to them, because God has made it plain to them."

Jesus identified His own role in the revelation process when He told His disciples, "No one knows the Son except the Father, and no one knows the Father except the Son and those to whom the Son chooses to reveal him" (Matthew 11:27).

God's self-revelation represents the extent of our body of knowledge about Him. In other words, the only things we're capable of understanding about God are the things He makes known to us. When it comes to gaining insight into who He is, we are completely at His mercy. Fortunately for us, God is generous in sharing information about Himself.

ON A PERSONAL NOTE

Here's a "what if" scenario for you to think about: What if God had not revealed Himself to us? What if He had chosen to remain silent after creation and left us to our own devices in trying to reach some conclusions about Him? What do you think life would be like? Put some thought into your answers; then spend some time thanking God that we'll never have to face such a scenario and praising Him for His generous revelation.

To Know Him Is to ... Not Fully Comprehend Him

That's not to say God is an open book. The Lord communicates with His followers on a need-to-know basis. That is, He reveals those aspects of His nature or work that are necessary for our . . .

➤ salvation,

➤ understanding of Scripture,

➤ worship, and

➤ spiritual growth.

That which we don't need to know, He keeps hidden. In other words, God is at once knowable and incomprehensible.

The idea that God is knowable is affirmed in several Scripture passages:

➤ "This is what the LORD says: 'Let not the wise man boast of his wisdom or the strong man boast of his strength or the rich man boast of his riches, but let him who boasts boast about this: that he understands and knows me, that I am the LORD, who exercises kindness, justice and righteousness on earth, for in these I delight,' declares the LORD" (Jeremiah 9:23–24).

➤ "Now this is eternal life: that they may know you, the only true God, and Jesus Christ, whom you have sent" (John 17:3).

➤ "We know that we have come to know him if we obey his commands" (1 John 2:3).

These passages suggest that certain truths about God are available to us. We can discover, for example, that He is . . .

➤ loving,

➤ just,

➤ forgiving, and

➤ active

. . . to name but a few of His perfections. (For more information on the knowable qualities of God, take a look at chapter 3.)

Because of our finite-infinite compatibility problems, however, we can never fully comprehend God, in all of His infinite and eternal glory. The Bible writers certainly recognized the incomprehensibility of God. The psalmist wrote, "His greatness no one can fathom" (Psalm 145:3). The apostle Paul marveled, "Oh, the depth of the riches of the wisdom and knowledge of God! How unsearchable his judgments, and his paths beyond tracing out! Who has known the mind of the Lord? Or who has been his counselor?" (Romans 11:33–34).

The fact that God is *incomprehensible* does not simply mean that there are attributes and aspects of His nature that we're not aware of; it also means that we cannot fully grasp the attributes and aspects He *has* revealed about Himself.

For example, we know that God is loving, but we can't fully grasp what His perfect love is like. We know that God is just, but we can't fully understand the implications of His justice. We know that God is forgiving, but we're incapable of understanding the depths of His forgiveness. We know that God is active, but we're aware of only a fraction of the things He does.

NOTABLE QUOTABLE

When we speak of knowing God, it must be understood with reference to man's limited powers of comprehension. God, as He really is, is far beyond man's imagination, let alone his understanding. God has revealed only so much of Himself as our minds can conceive and the weakness of our nature can bear.

—John Milton

Stick with What You Know

Though it's tantalizing to theorize about the "mysteries" of God, we can't concern ourselves with the incomprehensible aspects of His nature. Instead, our best bet is to focus on the things He *has* revealed about Himself. To do that, we can look to three different areas: *creation, personal experience,* and *Scripture.*

Each of these areas reveals certain aspects of God's nature—if we look closely enough at them and recognize them for what they are.

And Heaven and Nature Sing

The universe is the handiwork of God. Genesis 1:1 makes it clear that He alone created it. No one else had input in its design. No one else was responsible for providing the building materials. God was not influenced by anyone else's work in His design; neither was He trying to impress anyone else with the finished product. He created every detail of the physical world according to His specifications and preferences.

Just as all great art reveals something about the artist, God's universe reveals something about its Creator. David captured that truth beautifully in Psalm 19:1–4:

> *The heavens declare the glory of God;*
> *the skies proclaim the work of his hands.*
> *Day after day they pour forth speech;*
> *night after night they display knowledge.*
> *There is no speech or language*
> *where their voice is not heard.*
> *Their voice goes out into all the earth,*
> *their words to the end of the world.*

By paying attention to the world around us, we can pick up clues as to what God, the Creator, is like. Consider these settings:

➤ The immensity of the Pacific Ocean and Mount Everest reveals the awesome power of God, especially in light of the fact that He simply spoke both geographical marvels into existence.

➤ The rich bounty of farmland throughout the world reveals God's work in providing for His people.

➤ The spectacle of the Northern Lights—or any given sunrise, for that matter—reveals God's love of beauty.

➤ The predictable rhythms of the physical world—the orbit of the planets, the rotation of the earth, the constancy of the laws of physics—suggest God's unchanging nature.

➤ The complexity of the human body, right down to the subatomic level, reveals the wisdom of God and the perfection of His design.

Obviously, there's a lot to be learned about God in His creation. However, creation is not God's *primary* means of revelation. Furthermore, it's an imperfect object of study. The curse that God handed down after Adam and Eve's sin in the Garden of Eden affected the earth itself as well as its inhabitants. (Check out Genesis 3:17–19 for more details.)

The result is that we now live in a fallen state. Much of what we see around us is not what God originally intended for His creation. That's why we must be careful not to make too many assumptions about God based solely on what we see in nature.

Experience Not Necessary, but Helpful

The second way God reveals Himself to us is through personal experiences. It's safe to say that everyone—believer and unbeliever alike—has encountered God in a personal way at least once in his or her life. Some people immediately recognize their encounters for what they are. Other people recognize their encounters only in retrospect. Still others fail to recognize their encounters at all.

Personal Encounters of the Divine Kind

Some personal encounters with God are quite obvious. The Bible is filled to the brim with such accounts. For example . . .

➤ Abraham was told by God that his descendants would be a great nation.

➤ Moses received traveling instructions from God, in the form of a burning bush.

➤ Solomon was given the chance to request anything he wanted from God and have it given to him.

➤ Shadrach, Meshach, and Abednego were protected by God from the flames inside a furnace.

➤ Daniel was protected by God from starving lions after being thrown in among them.

➤ Jonah was swallowed by a giant fish in his efforts to escape God's will.

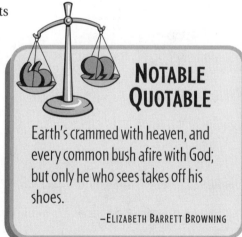

NOTABLE QUOTABLE

Earth's crammed with heaven, and every common bush afire with God; but only he who sees takes off his shoes.

–Elizabeth Barrett Browning

God's personal involvement in people's lives is not simply a biblical phenomenon, however. Listen closely to people at church or members of your Bible study when they talk about answered prayers, and you'll find that God continues to work in people's lives in unmistakable ways.

If you think hard enough, you can probably recall an experience in your own life that can only be explained as an act of God, whether it's . . .

➤ a job or source of income that came when you needed it most,

➤ a recovery from a serious injury or illness,

➤ a "near-miss" incident, or

➤ a significant change in attitude or perspective.

Regardless of the specifics, it's safe to say that there are times when God reveals Himself—that is, when He demonstrates His power, protection, and love for us—in ways that leave us slack-jawed. All we have to do is look for them.

NOTABLE QUOTABLE

God dwells in His creation and is everywhere indivisibly present in all His works. He is transcendent above all His works even while He is immanent within them.

–A. W. Tozer

Drawing Conclusions

As was the case with God's revelation through creation, we need to be careful about drawing too many conclusions about God based on our personal experiences. For one thing, we tend to place too much emphasis on big, obvious examples of God's work.

The Old Testament prophet Elijah learned that God doesn't always make Himself known in extraordinary ways. First Kings 19:9–13 relates the story of how the Lord announced to Elijah that He would appear to the prophet in person. While waiting, Elijah experienced . . .

➤ a wind powerful enough to tear apart a mountain and shatter rocks,

➤ a devastating earthquake that shook the mountain to its core,

➤ a roaring fire that consumed everything in its path, and

➤ a gentle whisper.

Understandably, Elijah looked for God first in the wind, the earthquake, and the fire. But God wasn't in any of them. First Kings 19:13 says, "When Elijah heard [the gentle whisper], he pulled his cloak over his face." Why? Because that's where God was.

There's a lesson to be learned from Elijah's experience. If we confine our search for God to the "big events," we're going to miss a lot of "gentle whispers"—quiet, low-key opportunities to find out more about Him. A better strategy is to concentrate on looking for God's work in the small things of life—the well-timed compliment or word of encouragement, for example—and let the big things take care of themselves.

NOTABLE QUOTABLE

People see God every day. They just don't recognize Him.

—PEARL BAILEY

Another risky aspect of relying too heavily on personal experience for our information about God is that we often have difficulty separating our actual experiences from what others tell us we *should* be experiencing. For example, some pundits suggest that God's justice and judgment for sin are outdated notions, the products of a more superstitious and less informed time. They argue that anyone who feels guilt or shame about a sinful lifestyle is simply unenlightened or struggling with deep-seated emotional issues.

People who experience guilt and shame as part of God's redeeming work in their lives, then, may not recognize His work for the healthy process it is. Instead, they may end up twisting His work or His attributes into something they are not intended to be.

Rather than experiencing and responding to God in a way that honors Him, many people interpret His work and respond to Him in a way that honors their preconceived notions. The resulting attitude can be seen in statements like these:

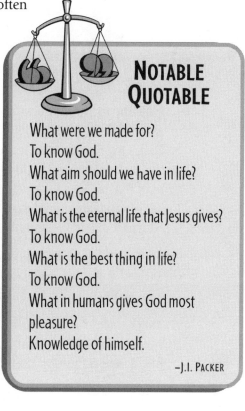

NOTABLE QUOTABLE

What were we made for?
To know God.
What aim should we have in life?
To know God.
What is the eternal life that Jesus gives?
To know God.
What is the best thing in life?
To know God.
What in humans gives God most pleasure?
Knowledge of himself.

—J.I. PACKER

➤ "God wants us all to be who we are, whether it's heterosexual or homosexual."

➤ "God wants me to be happy, whether it's with my wife or someone else."

➤ "God is not going to send someone to hell just for believing the wrong thing."

Our personal preferences and biases have no place in our efforts to understand God. We must remind ourselves that believing in something doesn't make it true. If our perceptions of what God is like don't match the reality of His being, we are the ones who will suffer for it.

A third reason that our personal experiences are untrustworthy when it comes to understanding God is that our perspective is limited. To give you an idea of what we're talking about, we'll refer to a well-known Indian folktale.

Six blind men wanted to discover for themselves what an elephant was like. One man felt the pachyderm's massive side and concluded that an elephant is like a wall. One man felt the animal's trunk and concluded that an elephant is like a snake. One man felt its tusk and concluded that an elephant is like a spear. One man felt its legs and concluded that an elephant is like a large cow. One man felt its ears and concluded that an elephant is like a large fan. One man felt its tail and concluded that an elephant is like a rope.

Each man based his conclusion on his own limited perspective and expressed it in a way that made sense to him. None of the men, however, even came close to accurately describing what an elephant is like.

That same principle applies to people who try to pigeonhole God based on personal experience. The truth is, our perspective is every bit as limited as the blind men standing next to the elephant. What appears to us to be reality concerning God may actually be every bit as ridiculous and far from the truth as someone mistaking an elephant for a rope.

That's why we need something . . .

➤ solid,

➤ dependable,

➤ all-encompassing, and

➤ with an accurate perspective

. . . to tell us what God is like. That's why we need the Bible.

The Source: Scripture

Nature won't give us an accurate picture of what God is like, and neither will our personal experiences. They can give us glimpses of Him, and perhaps encourage us to seek out more information about Him, but that's it. If we want absolutely trustworthy information about who God is, we need to go straight to Scripture.

Keep in mind that the Bible isn't the result of a bunch of guys sitting around a table, saying, "Hey, what should we tell people about God?" The Bible is the result of God directing specific people to write specific things about Him and His work in the world. God dictated precisely what would and wouldn't be in His Word. When He had said everything He wanted to say, the Bible was finished.

That's why we can say with certainty that *everything* God wants us to know about Him can be found in His Word. That makes the Bible the best-stocked supplier of godly information available to us.

JUST WONDERING

God used to reveal Himself in dreams to people in the Bible. Does He still use means like that to make Himself known? The last thing we want to do is suggest any restrictions on God's ability to reveal Himself to us. Having said that, we must be cautious about assigning supernatural significance to things that may or may not deserve it. Keep in mind that God's revelation will never contradict or add something new to His Word. Therefore, if a dream or any other "revelation" doesn't agree with the Bible, it's not from God. The best strategy for making that call, though, is prayer. Ask the Lord to give you a sense of peace or further direction regarding a potential "revelation."

The Bible is the last word and ultimate authority on God's . . .

➤ attributes or "perfections"

➤ laws

➤ work in creation

➤ work in salvation

➤ work in the lives of His people

➤ expectations

➤ will

➤ plan for the church

➤ plan for the future

All of these topics are explored in detail elsewhere in this book, so we won't rehash them here. What we *will* do is celebrate the fact that the Bible says anything at all about our heavenly Father.

Remember, God didn't *have* to reveal anything about Himself. (He's God; He doesn't *have* to do anything.) He could have . . .

➤ left His nature a complete mystery to us,

➤ forced us to guess at what He's like, based on nature and our personal experiences, and then punished us for getting it wrong, and

➤ had us walking around on pins and needles, always worried about offending Him.

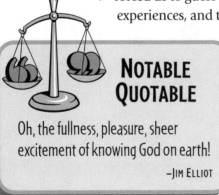

NOTABLE QUOTABLE

Oh, the fullness, pleasure, sheer excitement of knowing God on earth!

–JIM ELLIOT

But that's not what God chose to do. Instead, He gave us a guidebook, a written document that contains everything we need to know in order to develop a growing, personal relationship with Him.

That should make the Bible our first stop for all things God. If, for example, we . . .

➤ have a question about His holiness,

➤ are struggling with doubts about His goodness, or

➤ need to know how to explain His justice and righteousness to someone else,

. . . the Bible is the place to go. If we *don't* have a question, struggle, or need . . . the Bible is still the place to go.

If God is willing to devote Himself to the creation of a Book that contains every piece of information about Him that is relevant to our lives, we have a responsibility to learn everything we can about that Book. To do anything else would be like telling God that we're not interested in what He has to say about Himself.

Our Life's Mission

The fact that God is knowable means that we can (and should) learn essential truths about who He is and what He does—and then allow those truths to change our lives. The fact that He cannot be fully comprehended means that we will never run out of new things to discover about Him. Therefore, our life's mission is set: to continue to learn everything we can about God, His work, and His will.

Or, as the apostle Paul puts it in Colossians 1:10, to "live a life worthy of the Lord and . . . please him in every way: bearing fruit in every good work, growing in the knowledge of God."

ON A PERSONAL NOTE

Understanding God's revelation of Himself in His Word is not an easy task. The Bible can be an intimidating Book for people who aren't familiar with it. If you don't have a lot of experience in studying God's Word, here are a few tips you might want to consider:

➤ **Find a translation of the Bible that you can understand.** Many people prefer the *New International Version* (NIV) or the *New American Standard Bible* (NASB).

➤ **Invest in a study Bible.** Study Bibles contain helpful notes, cross-references, and information that bring passages into sharper focus.

➤ **Build a study library.** In time, you may also want to invest in a Bible concordance, dictionary, atlas, and other reference books, all of which can add new elements to your study.

Know What You Believe

How much do you know about God's revelation of Himself? Here's a quiz to test your knowledge.

1. Which of the following is not true of theology?
   a. The word comes from two Greek words, meaning "God" and "rational expression."
   b. It has not been an active field of study since the fall of the Greek dynasty.
   c. It is dependent on God's revelation of Himself.
   d. Generally speaking, it is the human study of God's truths.

2. Which of the following aspects of creation does not reveal something about God's nature?
   a. The bounty of the world's farmlands
   b. The beauty of the Northern Lights
   c. The immensity of the Pacific Ocean
   d. The pollution of the Atlantic Ocean

3. Which of the following statements does not reflect a problem in relying too heavily on personal experience in determining what God is like?
   a. God does not work directly in people's lives anymore.
   b. We tend to place too much emphasis on big, obvious examples of God's work.
   c. We often have difficulty separating our actual experiences from what others tell us we *should* be experiencing.
   d. Our perspective is limited.

4. Which of the following is not true of the Bible?
   a. It should be our primary source of information about God.
   b. It contains everything God wants us to know about Him.
   c. It is not completely trustworthy because it was written by humans.
   d. It is evidence of God's love and concern for us.

5. Which of the following is not part of the apostle Paul's instructions for Christians in Colossians 1:10?

a. To grow in the knowledge of God
b. To trust nothing but our personal experience of God
c. To bear fruit in every good work
d. To live a life worthy of the Lord

Answers: (1) b, (2) d, (3) a, (4) c, (5) b

What's He Like?

UNDERSTANDING GOD'S ATTRIBUTES

SNAPSHOT

"Who's up for a game of Password?" Kent asked in his best game-show-host voice.

The partygoers looked around at each other, shrugged their shoulders, and nodded their heads. "Sure, why not?" Marty said, speaking for the seven visiting couples in the Nelsons' living room.

"Those of you who were at our New Year's Eve party already know the rules," Kent explained. "Each couple plays as a team. One person gives the clues, and the other has to guess what's being described."

"One-word clues, right?" Marty called out.

"That's right," Kent said. "Each clue must be one word, and the clue can't have a form of the word you're trying to describe in it. If your partner can't guess it, then the turn goes to the next couple. For

SNEAK PREVIEW

1. God's attributes exist as perfections, which means He is the standard of every characteristic applied to Him (e.g., He is not just loving; He **is** love).
2. God's attributes may be divided into two categories: His incommunicable attributes, which belong only to Him, and His communicable attributes, which can be found, to some degree, in humans.
3. All of God's attributes exist in perfect harmony; none of them ever negate another.

you rookies, Darla and I will play a round to demonstrate." He held up a glass bowl containing dozens of folded pieces of paper.

"Wait a minute," Marty said. "If this is your house and your party and your game, aren't they your answers, too?"

"We haven't even started the game, and I've already been accused of cheating," Kent said with a grin. "Actually, our next-door neighbors were good enough to come up with words for us to guess."

"Well, that's *your* story," Marty replied in mock seriousness. "But if I lose, I'll be filing an official protest with the Password league commissioners."

"If there are no further interruptions," Kent said, giving Marty a long look, "Darla and I will begin our exhibition round."

Darla walked to the front of the group and drew a slip of paper from the bowl. She looked at it for a moment, squinted her eyes in thought, and then nodded her head. "Loving," she finally said to Kent.

"Me," Kent guessed.

The partygoers hooted and groaned in equal measure. Darla rolled her eyes and then looked back at her slip of paper. "Peaceful," she said.

Kent furrowed his brow. "Hmm, loving and peaceful," he repeated. "Gandhi?"

Darla shook her head. "Wise," she said.

"Loving, peaceful, and wise," Kent muttered. "I've got it—the Dalai Lama."

Darla shook her head again. "Godly," she said slowly and meaningfully. But as soon as the word was out of her mouth, she slumped her shoulders, lowered her head, and moaned.

"What?" Kent asked.

"I think she just gave away the answer," Marty suggested.

Darla looked at Kent and nodded. "The word was *God*," she explained.

"God?!" Kent roared. "You used *loving, peaceful,* and *wise* to describe *God?*"

"I suppose you could have come up with something better," Darla challenged.

"How about *vengeance* or *judgment* or *wrath?*" Kent offered. "If you'd given clues like those, anyone would have guessed God."

"Anyone with a little too much pent-up aggression," Darla responded.

Kent started to reply but then noticed that his party guests were all staring at him. "I guess . . . we'll have to agree to disagree about our Deity," he said to Darla.

* * * * * * * * * * * * * * *

"He's a thoughtful guy."

"She's a petty person."

"They're the most competitive couple I've ever met."

On the surface, these are relatively simple, easy-to-understand sentences. They contain terms similar to those most people use to describe friends and acquaintances. *Thoughtful. Petty. Competitive. Selfish. Cheerful. Vain.* When we hear adjectives such as those, we get a pretty good idea of what the people being described are like, and we know what to expect when we encounter them.

When the conversation turns to God, however, our regular methods of description prove to be woefully inadequate.

The problem is that our means of description are extremely *subjective.* We filter everything through the lens of our personal preferences and experience. For example, when we say someone is funny, it usually means they make us laugh. If we say someone has a great sense of humor, it usually means we make *them* laugh.

When it comes to God, however, our personal preferences, experiences, and opinions mean absolutely nothing. When the subject is Deity, we have no authority—or even the necessary perspective—to determine what is good or loving or just. Only God has that authority and perspective. God's actions define pure goodness, love, and justice. If God does something, it's automatically good (or loving or just or whatever) *because* He does it.

JUST WONDERING

I know that God loves me. Why do I need to know any more than that about Him?

Have you ever heard the expression "A little knowledge is a dangerous thing"? That principle certainly applies to our efforts to understand God. By focusing on a single attribute, such as love, we run the risk of reducing God to a stereotype and responding to Him as such. For example, if all we know about God is that He is loving, how can we properly worship and adore His omnipotence and omniscience? How can we take comfort in His omnipresence? How can we show proper respect and "fear" for His holiness and justice?

God is perfect. That's important to keep in mind because it means His goodness, love, justice, and any other attribute you care to name are perfect too. We don't look to Him to see if He's really good or loving or just. We look to Him to see what goodness, love, and justice really are.

Getting to Know Him

There is no master list of God's attributes in the Bible. Over the past few millennia or so, Bible scholars have identified several characteristics of God based on descriptions and accounts in His Word.

Depending on who's doing the counting and sorting, God's attributes can be grouped under a half-dozen or more categories and can include more than three dozen attributes. In this chapter, we're going to narrow our focus to fourteen characteristics, divided into two categories: incommunicable attributes and communicable attributes.

God's Incommunicable Attributes

At first glance, it may seem oxymoronic to attempt to describe, or communicate, God's incommunicable perfections. However, the term *incommunicable*, in this context, refers to attributes that belong *only* to God (as opposed to those that can be found—to some degree, at least—in humans).

Let's take a look at seven incommunicable attributes of God.

Eternality

God has no beginning and no end. There's never been a time when He did not exist. Psalm 90:2 puts it this way: "Before the mountains were born or you brought forth the earth and the world, from everlasting to everlasting you are God."

The name God used to identify Himself to the people of Israel, "I AM" (Exodus 3:14), expresses His eternal nature. He is constant existence. Before the universe was created, God is. After the universe has passed away, God is.

Simply acknowledging that God is everlasting doesn't go far enough in expressing His eternality, though. The fact is, God exists completely outside the boundaries and limitations of time. Passages such as Psalm 90:4 and 2 Peter 3:8 express this truth by suggesting that a thousand years are like one day to God.

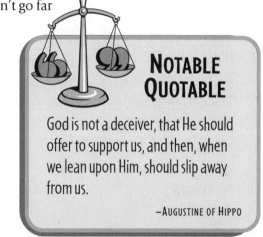

NOTABLE QUOTABLE

God is not a deceiver, that He should offer to support us, and then, when we lean upon Him, should slip away from us.

—AUGUSTINE OF HIPPO

As far as God is concerned, time—past, present, and future—is like a scroll rolled out on a table in front of Him. He can see everything that's already happened, everything that's happening now, and everything that's going to happen, because He is above it all.

A term closely related to God's eternal existence (and His independence, which we'll explore later in the chapter) is His *self-existence,* which emphasizes the fact that He owes His being to no one and nothing. God exists because He wills Himself to exist. In fact, He is existence. Apart from Him, nothing can exist.

The fact that God is eternal means that we never have to contemplate a time when He won't be around. He will always be present to sustain us and the world around us.

Immutability
God is unchangeable and unchanging. He does not learn, grow, age, mature, or develop. He is now as He always has been and as He always will be.

God Himself seems to leave little room for argument on this point. In Malachi 3:6 He says, "I the LORD do not change."

Psalm 102:25–27 puts God's immutability in a poetic light: "In the beginning you laid the foundations of the earth, and the heavens are the work of your hands. They will perish, but you remain; they will all wear out like a garment. Like clothing you will change them and they will be discarded. But you remain the same, and your years will never end.

The fact that God is unchanging makes Him perfectly reliable. We never have to worry about Him, say, changing the plan of salvation on a whim or requiring us to perform a thousand acts of charity before we can enter heaven. God is not affected by moods. We don't have to hope that He's in good spirits when we pray. We know He will always respond to us as He promises. In other words, He is worthy of our complete trust.

Independence

Strictly speaking, God does not need anything. He is not dependent upon anyone for any reason. Not only is He self-existent (as we saw in His eternal nature), but He is entirely self-sufficient. Nothing can add to or take away from who He is.

Here's how the apostle Paul explained God's independence to the people of Athens: "The God who made the world and everything in it is the Lord of heaven and earth and does not live in temples built by hands. And he is not served by human hands, as if he needed anything, because he himself gives all men life and breath and everything else" (Acts 17:24–25).

The fact that God does not need anyone is sobering news for people who take seriously their role as the crown of God's creation. Contrary to popular

JUST WONDERING

How do you explain a passage like Genesis 6:6, which says, "The LORD was grieved that he had made man on the earth"? Doesn't that suggest that His feelings had changed since the time of creation, when He was pleased with everything He had made?
Genesis 6:6, like 1 Samuel 15:10–11 and Jonah 3:4, 10, records God's response to a particular circumstance. The fact is, God responds differently to different situations. Why would anyone expect Him to do otherwise? He doesn't react to evil in the same way He reacts to righteousness. When the world was untarnished by sin, God responded to its goodness. After it became infested with evil, He responded to its sinfulness. That doesn't reflect inconsistency on His part; it reflects His perfect discernment.

opinion, God did not create the human race because He was lonely or bored or because He needed fellowship or worship. Passages such as John 17:5 indicate that God had perfect fellowship within the Trinity for an eternity before humans came on the scene.

That's not to say that we are worthless, or even unimportant, to God. The prophet Isaiah offers this remarkable promise to God's people:

> *You will be a crown of splendor in the LORD's hand,*
> *a royal diadem in the hand of your God. . . .*
> *For the Lord will take delight in you,*
> *and your land will be married.*
> *As a young man marries a maiden,*
> *so will your sons marry you;*
> *as a bridegroom rejoices over his bride,*
> *so will your God rejoice over you* (Isaiah 62:3–5).

We can bring delight and joy to God, and we can cause Him to rejoice. However, we can add nothing to His existence or His being.

Closely related to God's independence is His *transcendence*. This term refers to the fact that God is separate from His creation. This truth runs counter to the teachings of Hinduism and other Eastern religions, which claim that God is everywhere *and* everything (also known as *pantheism*).

It's true that God's Spirit permeates the world. It's also true that there is nowhere we can go where God is not. That does not mean, however, that God is the universe. Creation is God's work. It also serves as evidence of His existence. But it is *not* God.

God *transcends* His creation. He is above the world. He is independent of everything and everyone.

NOTABLE QUOTABLE

If God was small enough for us to understand, He wouldn't be big enough for us to worship.

—AUTHOR UNKNOWN

Infinity

God has no boundaries or limits. He is not subject to or bound by . . .

➤ the laws of physics,

➤ the law of gravity,

➤ the law of averages,

➤ the properties of science, or

➤ the dictates of reason and logic.

Concepts such as space and dimension have no relationship to Him. Our heavenly Father cannot be measured or quantified.

King Solomon was careful to acknowledge God's infinity during his dedication of the temple in Jerusalem. Solomon did not want the Israelites to assume that God was somehow "bound" to their new place of worship. As part of his dedication prayer, Solomon offered these words of adoration: "But will God really dwell on earth? The heavens, even the highest heaven, cannot contain you. How much less this temple I have built!" (1 Kings 8:27).

God's infinity also applies to His attributes. For example, God is not just loving; He is *infinitely* loving. That is, His love extends beyond the scope of our imagination. It is without boundary and without limit, as are His holiness, goodness, wisdom, and every other attribute listed in this book.

Omnipresence

Omnipresence is an attribute that defies complete comprehension by our finite minds. The simple explanation is that God exists everywhere; there is no place where He isn't. However, that definition doesn't really do justice to God's infinite presence.

You see, God isn't spread out across the universe like butter on toast or a blanket on a bed. There's not a little of Him here and a little of Him there. The fact that God is omnipresent means that His *whole* Being is present *everywhere* in the universe at *all* times. If you care to ponder how, exactly, that's possible, we'd advise you to take a couple of aspirin first.

Nowhere is God's omnipresence addressed more dramatically than in David's words of adoration in Psalm 139:7–10:

> *Where can I go from your Spirit?*
> *Where can I flee from your presence?*
> *If I go up to the heavens, you are there;*
> *if I make my bed in the depths, you are there.*
> *If I rise on the wings of the dawn,*
> *if I settle on the far side of the sea,*
> *even there your hand will guide me,*
> *your right hand will hold me fast.*

NOTABLE QUOTABLE

O God within my breast,
Almighty, ever-present Deity!

–EMILY BRONTE

Closely related to God's omnipresence is His *immanence*, which might be described as the flip side of His transcendence. Though God is separate from His creation (transcendent), He is still intimately involved in it. Passages such as Matthew 10:29–31 inform us that God takes note of even the tiniest details of the physical world, from the death of a sparrow to the fullness of our hair.

God's omnipresence can serve as both a warning and a comfort to us. On the one hand, it means that nothing we do is hidden from God's sight, no matter how much we might wish it were. On the other hand, we never have to worry about "falling through the cracks," where God is concerned. No matter how anonymous or alone we may feel at times, God knows exactly who we are and He is always with us.

Sovereignty

The fact that God is sovereign means that He sits alone atop the chain of command in the universe. He answers to no one. He is beholden to no one. He needs no one's permission or approval to act.

The psalmist defined God's sovereignty in simple terms: "The LORD does whatever pleases him, in the heavens and on the earth, in the seas and all their depths" (Psalm 135:6).

Every aspect of our physical universe is subject to God's control. He does what He wants, when He wants, in the exact way He wants. He cannot be stopped or overruled. He can't even be legitimately questioned or challenged. The fact that

He is perfect means that everything He does is perfect simply because *He* does it.

Who can argue with or improve upon perfection?

Unity

Moses announced God's unity to the Israelites in no uncertain terms in Deuteronomy 6:4: "Hear, O Israel: The LORD our God, the LORD is one." In Old Testament times, such a revelation would have been a bombshell. The truth that God is absolutely unique—that He alone is indivisible and One—stood in stark contrast to the polytheism (the belief in multiple gods) that was prevalent in the ancient Middle East.

God's unity is especially important to emphasize in light of His triunity (or Trinity), the fact that He exists in three persons—the Father, Son, and the Holy Spirit. Though each person of the Trinity is distinct and performs unique ministries, God is never separated or divided. He always exists in perfect unity. He is always One. (If you're wondering how the three persons of the Trinity can be considered One, check out chapter 5.)

God's Communicable Attributes

God's communicable attributes are those that are found in humans—albeit in an extremely limited way—as a result of our being created in God's image (check out Genesis 1:27). While none of us has ever experienced even a moment of omnipresence or sovereignty (which are incommunicable attributes), we have experienced moments of goodness, love, and truthfulness (which are communicable attributes).

Let's take a look at seven of God's communicable attributes.

Goodness

Everything God is and everything God does is worthy of approval. The psalmists echo that sentiment throughout their writings:

> ➤ "Taste and see that the LORD is good; blessed is the man who takes refuge in him" (Psalm 34:8).

➤ "For the LORD is good and his love endures forever; his faithfulness continues through all generations" (Psalm 100:5).

➤ "You are good, and what you do is good; teach me your decrees" (Psalm 119:68).

Of course, not everyone sees God's goodness so clearly. Some people point to events such as . . .

➤ the flood that destroyed the earth,

➤ the destruction of Sodom and Gomorrah, and

➤ the plague that killed the firstborn male children in Egypt

. . . and ask, "Can those actions—not to mention the One who caused them—*really* be considered good?"

The answer is, *absolutely*. Those actions are good because they came from God, who *is* goodness. Let's keep our perspective clear here. We have no authority to determine good and bad as far as God is concerned. *Everything* we know about goodness comes from Him. (James 1:17 says so.) Therefore, we have no choice but to accept His Word on the matter, especially in circumstances in which His goodness is less than obvious to us.

Closely related to God's goodness are three other characteristics that are often listed as separate attributes: *grace, mercy,* and *patience.*

God's *grace* refers to the goodness He shows to people who deserve only His judgment and punishment. The fact that the human race has any

ON A PERSONAL NOTE

Try using the perfections of God as a basis for a week-long Bible study. Choose seven attributes that have special meaning for you and build a study and prayer time around each one. For example, if you choose omnipotence, you might read and meditate on Matthew 19:26 before spending some time in prayer, thanking God that no situation is ever hopeless where He is involved and taking to Him needs and requests that are beyond the scope of your abilities.

hope for salvation is due to God's grace alone. None of us have ever done anything to earn God's love or forgiveness.

The apostle Paul described that truth this way: "For it is by grace you have been saved, through faith—and this not from yourselves, it is the gift of God—not by works, so that no one can boast" (Ephesians 2:8–9).

God's *mercy* refers to the goodness He shows to people in need. Deuteronomy 10:18 tells us that God "defends the cause of the fatherless and the widow, and loves the alien, giving him food and clothing." That's mercy.

David often requested God's mercy in times of distress. Look at his words in Psalm 57:1, which were written when he was on the run from the murderous King Saul: "Have mercy on me, O God, have mercy on me, for in you my soul takes refuge. I will take refuge in the shadow of your wings until the disaster has passed."

God's *patience* refers to the goodness He shows to people who reject Him. The phrase "slow to anger" is used throughout the Old Testament (including passages such as Numbers 14:18 and Psalm 145:8) to describe God's attitude and response toward sinful people.

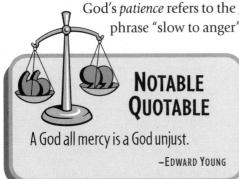

NOTABLE QUOTABLE

A God all mercy is a God unjust.

—EDWARD YOUNG

This "slowness" is certainly not the product of laziness or indifference toward sin. Instead, God's patience is the result of His desire to give people as many opportunities as possible to repent of their sins. Remember, God's ultimate judgment is final. After death, no one receives a second chance at salvation. That's why God's patience is so significant. Because of His goodness, He maximizes our opportunities to avoid judgment.

God aptly summarized the varied qualities of His goodness when He described Himself to Moses as a God "compassionate and gracious, slow to anger, abounding in love and faithfulness" (Exodus 34:6).

Holiness

God's holiness may be described as "a complete separateness from sin." It's not simply a matter of taking a strong stand against wrongdoing. Neither is it simply a matter of holding an eternal grudge against people who do evil. Holiness refers to an absolute *mutual exclusiveness.* Where God is, sin cannot be. In the same way that darkness cannot exist near the sun, sin cannot exist in the presence of God.

Biblical support for God's holiness can be found in dozens of direct quotations from God Himself—Leviticus 10:3 ("I will show myself holy"), for example—as well as in the refrain of Revelation 4:8, which will be repeated at the throne of God for eternity: "Holy, holy, holy is the Lord God Almighty, who was, and is, and is to come."

As we point out in chapter 9, God's holiness is what makes salvation necessary. Remember, God can have no interaction, no fellowship, with anything sinful or unclean. For people tainted by sin from birth, that's a problem. Only the perfect sacrifice of Jesus is sufficient to cover our sins and bridge the gap between God and those who repent and believe.

NOTABLE QUOTABLE

Oh Thou who art! Ecclesiastes names Thee the Almighty . . . the Psalms name Thee Wisdom and Truth; John names Thee Light; the book of Kings names Thee Lord; Exodus calls Thee Providence; Leviticus, Holiness; Esdras, Justice; Creation calls Thee God; Man names Thee Father; but Solomon names Thee Compassion, and that is the most beautiful of all Thy names.

–VICTOR HUGO

Passages such as 1 John 1:5–10 suggest that once we establish a relationship with God, the purity of His holiness serves as a kind of "spotlight," illuminating sin in our lives and urging us to seek forgiveness for it.

Justice

The fact that God is just means that He always does what is right. (In fact, another name for God's justice is *righteousness.*) The term *justice* conjures up images of a legal nature, and that's fitting. The Bible makes it clear that God is the supreme Judge:

➤ "Far be it from you to do such a thing—to kill the righteous with the wicked, treating the righteous and the wicked alike. Far be it from you! Will not the Judge of all the earth do right?" (Genesis 18:25).

➤ "But, O LORD Almighty, you who judge righteously and test the heart and mind, let me see your vengeance upon them, for to you I have committed my cause" (Jeremiah 11:20).

➤ "Then I saw a great white throne and him who was seated on it. Earth and sky fled from his presence, and there was no place for them. And I saw the dead, great and small, standing before the throne, and books were opened. Another book was opened, which is the book of life. The dead were judged according to what they had done as recorded in the books" (Revelation 20:11–12).

God's justice is what required Jesus to sacrifice His life for the sins of the world. God's righteousness demands that all sin be punished—by death. Perfect justice requires that there never be an exception to that fact. Jesus' death satisfied God's justice; therefore, anyone who claims Jesus as Savior is judged righteous by God.

Those who do not accept God's free gift of salvation are judged unrighteous by God and sentenced accordingly to eternity apart from Him. For God to do otherwise would not be just and, therefore, would be contrary to His nature.

Love

"Whoever does not love does not know God, because God is love" (1 John 4:8). Note the last three words of that verse: *God is love.* The point here is not that God shows affection to people. The point is that God *is* love.

ON A PERSONAL NOTE

God continues to demonstrate His love to us every day. Unfortunately, we don't always recognize that love when we experience it. You can correct that oversight by committing yourself to noticing and recording examples of God's love that you see in your life. Keep a journal of God's blessings, ways in which He makes His loving presence known to you. Your list may include everything from friends who support and encourage you to a church that enables your spiritual growth.

CHAPTER 3: What's He Like? Understanding God's Attributes

Some people may question that attribute, pointing to the abundance of suffering and pain in the world. But suggesting that God doesn't seem very loving is like saying water doesn't seem very wet. Not only is it absurd; it demonstrates a skewed perspective.

God's love is a perfect love. That means if our ideas and actions regarding love do not align with His, we cannot legitimately claim to love.

God's love means that He seeks the highest good for His creation. It is a selfless love, one that is concerned only with our ultimate well-being. We're not talking about a greeting-card sentiment. God's love is not a starry-eyed fixation based on emotion. Rather, it is a clear-eyed desire to bring about His perfect will in our lives, using whatever means necessary. Passages such as Hebrews 12:5–6 suggest that God's love involves chastising and discipline as much as it does happiness and blessing.

God demonstrated His love for us first by creating us. The fact that He has given us a chance to experience His creation shows just how much He loves us. And, if that isn't enough, John 3:16 reminds us that God demonstrated His love for us again, after we had rejected Him and turned to sin, by sending His only Son to die in our place so that we could have eternal life with Him.

Not only is it a mistake to underestimate or question God's love based on our own circumstances or feelings, but it's also damaging to our understanding of God to overstate His love at the expense of His other attributes. God's love never negates His holiness or justice.

Omnipotence
God is all-powerful; He is able to do anything that is consistent with His nature. However, to say that God is omnipotent is not to say that He can do anything. Strictly speaking, God's omnipotence is restricted by His natural limitations. For example, the Bible tells us that *God cannot lie, be tempted to sin, nor deny Himself* (see Titus 1:2; James 1:13; and 2 Timothy 2:13).

To do any of those things would be to go against His nature. And if God were able to go against His nature, He would not be God.

Having said that, we must emphasize that God is able to do anything and everything He wills Himself to do. The term "Almighty," which is used as a title for our heavenly Father throughout Scripture (from Genesis 17:1 to Revelation 19:6, actually), affirms His unimaginable power and might.

The Bible also reveals God's power over . . .

➤ creation (Psalm 33:6–9),

➤ human events, including the rescue of the Israelites from Egypt (Psalm 114), and

➤ death (2 Corinthians 13:4).

God's omnipotence allows us to rest secure in the knowledge that God can deliver us from any situation and can accomplish everything He has promised.

NOTABLE QUOTABLE

Can a mortal ask questions which God finds unanswerable? Quite easily, I should think. All nonsense questions are unanswerable.

–C. S. Lewis

Omniscience

God is all-knowing. His knowledge encompasses everything from the number of stars in the sky (Psalm 147:4) to the number of hairs on your head (Matthew 10:30). He knows the thoughts and actions of every living creature, as well as the design and inner workings of all creation.

God not only knows all things actual—that is, everything that has happened, is happening, and will happen—but also all things possible. He knows every possible outcome of every choice we don't make. For example, He knows how our lives would be different today if we had . . .

➤ married someone else,

➤ pursued another career, or

➤ said "Yes" instead of "No," or vice versa, at any point in our lives.

For those of us who struggle to remember our own anniversary or computer password, that scope of knowledge is incomprehensible. David, for one, was overwhelmed by God's omniscience. Look at his words in Psalm 139:1–4:

*O LORD, you have searched me
and you know me.
You know when I sit and when I rise;
you perceive my thoughts from afar.
You discern my going out and my lying down;
you are familiar with all my ways.
Before a word is on my tongue
you know it completely, O LORD.*

God's omniscience should impact our lives in at least two ways. First, it should inspire us to seek God's guidance, through prayer, in every decision we make. Since God knows every possible outcome available to us, He can and will steer us through the wisest course of action and prevent us from making potentially devastating mistakes.

Second, God's omniscience should motivate us to live a life that is pleasing to Him, knowing that one day we will stand before Him, and that He will be aware of everything we've ever done and everything we've ever thought.

Veracity

God is truth. John 17:3 tells us that our heavenly Father is "the only true God." Job 37:16 tells us that God is "perfect in knowledge." His perfect knowledge means that He is never mistaken in His perception or His understanding. He is the absolute standard of truth. Anything that doesn't comply with Him is false.

NOTABLE QUOTABLE

God is the God of truth; and every spiritual quality must live with that holy attribute.

—EDWIN HOLT HUGHES

Titus 1:2 emphasizes that God cannot lie, and that therefore His promise of eternal life is guaranteed. Indeed, God, in His truthfulness, is faithful to every one of His promises. Deuteronomy 32:4 refers to Him as "a faithful God." That means if He says something, we can bank on it.

As we mention in chapter 7, God's truthfulness extends to His written Word. The Bible is perfectly trustworthy because it is authored by a perfectly truthful God. God cannot lie, so His Word cannot contain misinformation.

OK, There Are Limits on Our Understanding

As we wrap up this chapter, we need to emphasize two points. First, as we pointed out in our discussion of God's love, all of God's attributes exist in perfect harmony. For example, God's love never cancels out His wrath, and His justice never interrupts His love. He is always completely loving, completely merciful, completely just, and so on.

If that seems impossible, it's because we don't have the brain power to understand God fully. That's one of the problems with being finite—we have no grasp of the infinite. Our only option, then, is to take God at His word when He describes Himself.

Second, we've only scratched the surface in discovering who God is. We identified fourteen of His attributes in this chapter. Some lists include as many as forty attributes. Regardless of how many characteristics of God we identify, though, we will never come close to understanding Him completely.

Words such as *holiness, omniscience,* and *veracity* give us handles with which to grasp basic truths about God, but they don't begin to define Him. We can approach God with the information we have, and even create an intimate relationship with Him, but we can never truthfully claim to fully understand Him.

Know What You Believe

How much do you know about God's attributes? Here's a quiz to test your knowledge.

1. Why are our human methods of description inadequate when the subject is God?
   a. The actual words that apply to God are found only in the ancient Hebrew language, which few people know.
   b. Our descriptions are tainted by our personal perspective, which makes it hard to communicate God's perfection.
   c. God often confuses our language, as He did at the Tower of Babel, because He does not want to be known by us.
   d. We invariably use terms that only theologians can understand.

2. Which of the following is true of God's incommunicable attributes?
   a. They belong to God alone.
   b. They are forbidden to be spoken of, under penalty of death.
   c. They cannot be described.
   d. They are more important than His communicable attributes.

3. What does it mean that God is immutable?
   a. He cannot be silenced.
   b. He cannot be described.
   c. He is unchangeable and unchanging.
   d. His Word is unintelligible.

4. Which of the following is not true of God's omnipresence?
   a. It is closely related to His immanence.
   b. It means that a small portion of God can be found at every point in the universe.
   c. It means that nothing is hidden from God's sight.
   d. It means that God is intimately aware of even the tiniest details of the physical world.

5. Which of the following is not a communicable attribute of God?
   a. Goodness
   b. Justice
   c. Holiness
   d. Fickleness

Answers: (1) b, (2) a, (3) c, (4) b, (5) d

Promise Keeper

UNDERSTANDING GOD'S COVENANTS

SNAPSHOT

"I think the Israelites got a bum rap," Ronny declared.

The rest of the Bible study group looked up from the Exodus passage in their Bibles. "Think about it," Ronny continued. "They were stuck out in the desert for decades. They never knew where they were going or how long it would take to get there."

"They had to walk hundreds of miles in wilderness conditions," Ken added.

Ronny nodded. "It was like a never-ending camping trip," he said. "Even if you like camping, you've got to admit that after a week or so, it gets pretty old."

"Plus, you know they had sand *everywhere*," Carl chimed in. "In their clothes, their blankets, their sandals."

SNEAK PREVIEW

1. The promises of God contained in Scripture are only as reliable as the One who makes them.
2. God has proven Himself to be faithful in His promises—or covenants—to Noah, Abraham, Moses, David, and others.
3. The fact that God kept His covenants in the past gives us assurance that He still can be trusted to keep His promises to those who are faithful to Him.

"That would be enough to make anyone a little squirrelly," Ronny offered.

"Yeah, but we're talking about making idols to worship," Steven pointed out. "I think that qualifies as something more than 'squirrelly behavior.'"

"I'm not saying that what they did was right," Ronny explained. "I'm just saying they had a reason."

"But they had an agreement with God," Steven said as he flipped through the pages of Exodus. "Look at . . . Exodus 24 . . . verse 7. After Moses read the conditions for God's covenant, the people said—quote—'We will do everything the LORD has said; we will obey.' They agreed verbally to God's conditions; then they turned around and broke the covenant."

"Thank you, Johnnie Cochran." Ronny chuckled. "But maybe if the Israelites had known what was in store for them, they wouldn't have been so quick to sign on the dotted line."

"It doesn't matter," Steven replied. "They made a promise to God. They had a responsibility to do what they promised."

"I know," Ronny acknowledged. "I'm just thinking that maybe God could have been a little more understanding."

"You mean, maybe He could have let them off the hook?" Steven asked.

"Yeah, something like that," Ronny said.

"What if the situation had been reversed?" Steven proposed. "What if the Israelites had been careful to obey every commandment that God gave them and hold up their end of the bargain, only to find out that God had changed His mind and chosen, say, the Philistines to be His people instead? Do you think that would have been fair?"

"Well, no," Ronny acknowledged.

"Of course not," Steven said. "A deal's a deal."

"What if the Israelites had refused to make a deal with God because it was just too much for them?" Ken asked.

"They probably would have faded into history, like the Amalekites and Ammonites and all those other 'ite' people," Carl said.

"That's a good question," Steven acknowledged. "But I don't know that they could have turned down God's deal."

"So you're saying God made them an offer they couldn't refuse?" Ronny asked.

Steven smiled. "Yeah, I guess I am."

* * * * * * * * * * * * * * *

Have you heard the expression "A man is only as good as his word"? The same principle applies to deity.

One of the purposes of this book is to acknowledge and explore the incredible promises of God contained in His Word. Before we put too much stock in those promises, though, we need to point out that they are only as reliable as the One who makes them. If it turns out that God isn't interested in keeping His promises, we're in trouble. We've certainly got no leverage on Him. We can't *make* Him be true to His Word. There is no higher authority that we can appeal to.

In other words, we're at His mercy where His promises are concerned. Fortunately for us, we have ample evidence in Scripture that God takes His promises *very* seriously. In order to better understand God's attitude toward binding agreements, we're going to look at five "special promises" that God made at various points in biblical history.

ON A PERSONAL NOTE

Here are some questions to get you thinking about the topic of covenants and promises:

➤ When was the last time someone broke a promise to you?

➤ How did you react?

➤ How did that incident affect the way you view that person?

➤ How seriously do you treat promises? Give an example.

➤ What difference does it make in your life to know that God is always true to His Word?

The Party of the First Part . . .

Actually, *promise* isn't the right word for the kind of word-giving we'll be talking about in this chapter—*covenant* is. A covenant is a pact or formal agreement between two or more parties. In biblical times, covenants were made between individuals of equal standing or power, as seen in the pacts made by . . .

➤ Laban and Jacob (Genesis 31:44–54),

➤ David and Jonathan (1 Samuel 18:3; 23:18), and

➤ Abner and David (2 Samuel 3:12–13, 21).

Covenants were also imposed by greater powers on lesser ones, as seen in the treaties involving . . .

➤ Israel and the Gibeonites (Joshua 9) and

➤ the Ammonites and the men of Jabesh Gilead (1 Samuel 11:1–2).

Generally, the greater power would vow to protect the lesser one and, in return, would demand complete loyalty. That is the covenant model that God used in establishing pacts with His people—including those He made with . . .

➤ Noah,

➤ Abraham,

➤ Moses,

➤ David, and

➤ the beneficiaries of His new covenant.

By examining the terms of these specific covenants, God's faithfulness to them, and His expectations of faithfulness on the part of the second parties involved, we can get a better sense of how He works and what He expects from His people today.

The Noahic Covenant

The first covenant we need to look at is the one God established with Noah. The events that led up to the covenant are familiar to anyone who ever stepped foot in a Sunday school class. In response to the wickedness He saw on the earth, God sent a judgment in the form of a catastrophic flood that covered the earth and killed almost everyone and everything on it.

The only survivors were Noah, who "found favor in the eyes of the LORD" (Genesis 6:8); his family; and one male and one female member of every species of animal. This small band of humans and creatures survived the Flood on the ark that God had instructed Noah to build.

NOTABLE QUOTABLE

Trust in yourself and you are doomed to disappointment.
Trust in your friends and they will die and leave you.
Trust in money and you may have it taken away from you.
Trust in reputation and some slanderous tongues will blast it.
But trust in God and you are never to be confounded in time or in eternity.

–DWIGHT L. MOODY

When the floodwaters subsided, Noah and the other passengers on the ark disembarked and began the work of repopulating the earth, according to God's instructions.

This was the setting for God's covenant with Noah. The specifics of the covenant can be found in Genesis 9:8–17:

> Then God said to Noah and to his sons with him: "I now establish my covenant with you and with your descendants after you and with every living creature that was with you—the birds, the livestock and all the wild animals, all those that came out of the ark with you—every living creature on earth. I establish my covenant with you: Never again will all life be cut off by the waters of a flood; never again will there be a flood to destroy the earth."
>
> And God said, "This is the sign of the covenant I am making between me and you and every living creature with you, a covenant for all generations to come: I have set my rainbow in the clouds, and it will be the sign of the covenant between me and

the earth. Whenever I bring clouds over the earth and the rainbow appears in the clouds, I will remember my covenant between me and you and all living creatures of every kind. Never again will the waters become a flood to destroy all life. Whenever the rainbow appears in the clouds, I will see it and remember the everlasting covenant between God and all living creatures of every kind on the earth."

So God said to Noah, "This is the sign of the covenant I have established between me and all life on the earth."

Look carefully at God's words in this passage, and you'll see that this is an unconditional promise on His part. He did not say, "I will never destroy the earth with the flood again—*if* you will do such and such." Noah had no responsibilities, no terms to abide by, in God's covenant with Him. God promised never to send such a judgment again, no matter how evil Noah's descendants became.

NOTABLE QUOTABLE

The main hinge on which faith turns is this: we must not imagine that the Lord's promises are true objectively but not in our experience. We must make them ours by embracing them in our hearts.

—JOHN CALVIN

Believers today can certainly take comfort in God's covenant with Noah. We never have to worry about facing the watery destruction that people of Noah's day experienced. However, it's safe to say that God's covenant meant much more to Noah and his family than it does to us today.

If we miss the personal aspect of the Noahic Covenant, we may miss some vital information about God and the way He cares for those who are faithful to Him. Noah certainly filled the bill, as far as faithfulness is concerned. Genesis 6:9 describes him as "a righteous man, blameless among the people of his time" and a man who "walked with God."

The fact that Noah and his family survived the Flood was only the beginning of God's blessings for Noah's faithfulness. Though the Bible does not mention anything about it, we can assume that Noah and his family experienced a certain amount of emotional trauma as a result of their flood experience. Imagine the horror they must have endured on the ark as they listened to everyone and everything outside the boat die.

Who knows what aftereffects they suffered? At the very least, their hearts must have skipped a few beats every time they saw a thunderstorm gather on the horizon. God's promise never to destroy the earth with a flood again probably went a long way toward easing their fears. The rainbow, though, must have been a source of *special* comfort and reassurance to them. Every time they saw it, they would have been reminded of God's promise to them.

The Abrahamic Covenant

God's covenant with Abraham (or Abram, as he was originally known) shares a common theme with His covenant with Noah in Genesis 9. For reasons that aren't made explicitly clear in the text, both men were considered righteous in God's eyes. God saw something in them that made them right for a covenant with Him.

The details of God's covenant with Abraham can be found in Genesis 15:7–10, 17–21:

> He also said to him, "I am the LORD, who brought you out of Ur of the Chaldeans to give you this land to take possession of it."
>
> But Abram said, "O Sovereign LORD, how can I know that I will gain possession of it?"
>
> So the LORD said to him, "Bring me a heifer, a goat and a ram, each three years old, along with a dove and a young pigeon."
>
> Abram brought all these to him, cut them in two and arranged the halves opposite each other; the birds, however, he did not cut in half. . . .
>
> When the sun had set and darkness had fallen, a smoking firepot with a blazing torch appeared and passed between the pieces. On that day, the LORD made a covenant with Abram and said, "To your descendants I give this land, from the river of Egypt to the great river, the Euphrates—the land of the Kenites, Kenizzites,

NOTABLE QUOTABLE

[God's promises] are a foundation of our faith, and we have them as such; and also of our hope. On these we are to build all of our expectations from God; and in all temptations and trials we have them to rest our souls upon.
–MATTHEW HENRY

Kadmonites, Hittites, Perizzites, Rephaites, Amorites, Canaanites, Girgashites and Jebusites."

One of the features of covenants in Old Testament times—particularly those involving kings or heads of state—was a self-introduction of the ruler proposing the covenant and a recounting of what he had done for the other party involved in it. God's covenant with Abraham followed that pattern. God referred to Himself as "the LORD" and reminded Abraham that it was He who brought Abraham to the Promised Land. The "smoking firepot with a blazing torch" symbolized God's presence. In other words, God came near to Abraham to announce His covenant.

NOTABLE QUOTABLE

God's lips know not how to lie, but He will accomplish all His promises.

—AESCHYLUS

As with the Noahic Covenant, God's pact with Abraham was unconditional. Abraham's descendants were guaranteed to take possession of the land no matter what Abraham did. Within that unconditional framework, though, God instructed Abraham to obey certain specific instructions. For example, God commanded Abraham to . . .

➤ leave his home and extended family to go to a strange land (Genesis 12:1),

➤ be a blessing to others (Genesis 12:2),

➤ walk before Him and be blameless (17:1), and

➤ circumcise—that is, cut off the foreskin of—every male in his camp (Genesis 17:10–11).

We get a glimpse of what God must have seen in Abraham in Genesis 17:23. According to the verse, Abraham responded to the Lord's instruction regarding circumcision "on that very day." Prompt obedience was a hallmark of Abraham's character.

The universal result of God's covenant with Abraham is pretty well-known to people who are familiar with God's Word. Abraham's descendants, the Israelites, were given the Promised Land in which to live.

As was the case with Noah, however, there's a personal element to God's covenant with Abraham that we must not overlook. At the time God established the covenant, the idea of Abraham having descendants with his wife Sarah (originally known as Sarai) was pretty far-fetched. Both of them were not only childless, but they were well past childbearing age (and *retirement* age, for that matter). The news from God that they would have descendants must have come as a wonderful surprise to them.

The Mosaic Covenant

God's covenant with Moses (also known as the Sinaitic Covenant because it was established on Mount Sinai) introduced the Ten Commandments and the rest of the laws that would feature prominently in Israel's history.

Exodus 19:3–8 records the general terms of God's covenant, as well as the people's response to it:

> *Then Moses went up to God, and the LORD called to him from the mountain and said, "This is what you are to say to the house of Jacob and what you are to tell the people of Israel: 'You yourselves have seen what I did to Egypt, and how I carried you on eagles' wings and brought you to myself. Now if you obey me fully and keep my covenant, then out of all nations you will be my treasured possession. Although the whole earth is mine, you will be for me a kingdom of priests and a holy nation.' These are the words you are to speak to the Israelites."*
>
> *So Moses went back and summoned the elders of the people and set before them all the words the LORD had commanded him to speak. The people all responded*

JUST WONDERING

If Abraham was so faithful, why did he sleep with his wife's servant to produce an heir in Genesis 16?

The thought of two people so old having children themselves must have seemed too incredible for Abraham and Sarah to believe, so they started second-guessing the Lord's intentions. Sarah apparently believed that the only way Abraham could produce an heir was through her servant, Hagar, who apparently was of childbearing age. Sarah didn't realize that God doesn't need any help in fulfilling His promises! Both Sarah and Abraham seem to have recognized the gravity of their mistake immediately after Hagar became pregnant, but by then it was too late.

together, "We will do everything the LORD has said." So Moses brought their answer back to the LORD.

Notice that God used an introduction in His covenant with Moses similar to the one He used with Abraham. He identified Himself as the One who had delivered the Israelites from slavery in Egypt and would lead them into a land of their own ("I carried you on eagles' wings and brought you to myself"). God's identity and His work on behalf of the Israelites in the past were part of the incentive package for entering into a covenant with Him. The people knew who God was and what He was capable of.

> ## NOTABLE QUOTABLE
>
> In God alone there is faithfulness, and faith is the trust that we may hold to Him, to His promise, and to His guidance. To hold to God is to rely on the fact that God is there for me, and to live in this certainty.
>
> –KARL BARTH

Unlike the covenants God made with Noah and Abraham, which were unconditional, the Mosaic Covenant was *conditional*. That means God agreed to uphold His end of the covenant *only* if the Israelites upheld theirs.

God certainly gave the Israelites every reason to agree to His terms. As part of the pact, God promised to . . .

➤ lavish special attention on Israel,

➤ make the nation holy and distinct from all other nations,

➤ use Israel—like "a kingdom of priests"—to teach other nations about the correct worship of the living God, and

➤ give the Israelites specific instructions on how they should live in order to achieve maximum fulfillment.

That last point also represents the Israelites' responsibility in the covenant. The general stipulations of the covenant are found in Exodus 20:3–17. In short, God demanded strict obedience to the Ten Commandments:

1. Do not place any other gods before God.

2. Do not make idols.

3. Do not misuse the Lord's name.

4. Remember the Sabbath by keeping it holy.

5. Honor your father and mother.

6. Do not murder.

7. Do not commit adultery.

8. Do not steal.

9. Do not give false testimony against a neighbor.

10. Do not covet.

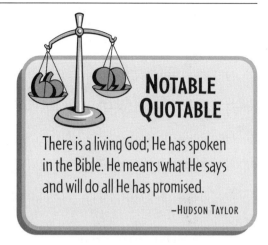

NOTABLE QUOTABLE

There is a living God; He has spoken in the Bible. He means what He says and will do all He has promised.

–Hudson Taylor

These Ten Commandments, or laws, are discussed in detail in chapter 6. Other specific stipulations of the covenant—laws regarding worship altars, servants, personal injuries, protection of property, justice and mercy, and festival celebration—can be found in Exodus 20:22–23:33. In all, there were dozens of rules for the Israelites to obey as part of God's covenant. Obviously, the privilege of being called God's people came with high expectations!

Israel's history after the covenant at Sinai is marked by periods of strict adherence to the terms of the covenant followed by periods of complete disregard for and rejection of God's commandments. Needless to say, Israel prospered during their periods of obedience and suffered during their periods of disobedience.

The New Covenant

The Law that God gave Moses as part of His covenant at Sinai was never intended as a means of *salvation* for the Israelites. Instead, it was intended as a "road map" of sorts to show the people how to walk with God. Unfortunately, the Israelites, more often than not, chose not to use it, preferring to "go their own way."

Many times in Scripture, God used His prophets and priests to call the people to repentance—that is, to leave their sinful ways of living and return to God's way. As we mentioned earlier, though, every act of repentance on the part of the Israelites proved to be short-lived. They temporarily adjusted their actions and lifestyle, but their hearts remained unchanged. Therefore, a new covenant was needed.

The details of this new covenant were given to the Old Testament prophet Jeremiah. God's revelation to His servant can be found in Jeremiah 31:31–37:

> *"The time is coming," declares the LORD, "when I will make a new covenant with the house of Israel and with the house of Judah. It will not be like the covenant I made with their forefathers when I took them by the hand to lead them out of Egypt, because they broke my covenant, though I was a husband to them," declares the LORD. "This is the covenant I will make with the house of Israel after that time," declares the LORD. "I will put my law in their minds and write it on their hearts. I will be their God, and they will be my people. No longer will a man teach his neighbor, or a man his brother, saying, 'Know the LORD,' because they will all know me, from the least of them to the greatest," declares the LORD. "For I will forgive their wickedness and will remember their sins no more."*

> *This is what the LORD says, he who appoints the sun to shine by day, who decrees the moon and stars to shine by night, who stirs up the sea so that its waves roar—the LORD Almighty is his name: "Only if these decrees vanish from my sight," declares the LORD, "will the descendants of Israel ever cease to be a nation before me."*

> *This is what the LORD says: "Only if the heavens above can be measured and the foundations of the earth below be searched out will I reject all the descendants of Israel because of all they have done," declares the LORD.*

One of the first provisions of this new covenant would be the "internalizing" of God's law. Instead of writing it on stones, a la the Ten Commandments, God would write His commandments in the minds and hearts of His people. In other words, God would cause His commandments to govern the lives of His people *internally*, rather than externally.

The reason for such a radical change in perspective is the presence of God's Holy Spirit in the lives of His people. As we mention in chapter 5, the Holy Spirit dwells within every believer. He's the One who empowers and encourages people to obey God.

A second provision of God's new covenant is the forgiveness of sins and God's promise to "remember [your] sins no more." This would be possible only through the sacrificial death of Christ. In fact, in Luke 22:20, Jesus announced to His disciples that the new covenant would be inaugurated through the pouring out of His blood. In other words, God can forgive and forget the sins of His people because Jesus paid the price for them. (For more information on the details of God's work of salvation, check out chapter 9.)

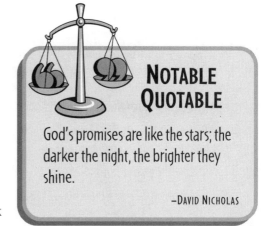

NOTABLE QUOTABLE

God's promises are like the stars; the darker the night, the brighter they shine.

–David Nicholas

Jesus, the Son of God, is the fulfillment of the new covenant. While He lived on earth, He instructed His followers in the ways of His Father. After He ascended to heaven, He sent the Holy Spirit to teach people the knowledge of God—a knowledge that would result in . . .

> ➤ faith,

> ➤ obedience, and

> ➤ devotion to the Lord

. . . for all who desired it.

Promises, Promises

The fact that God has taken the initiative in establishing covenants with His people demonstrates His amazing love and concern for us. Remember, He's the infinite, eternal Creator; we are His imperfect, finite handiwork. We have nothing to offer in a relationship with Him that He does not already have. He gains nothing by interacting with us on a personal level.

Yet still He does it. He graciously commits Himself to us though His new covenant. And the benefits are all ours.

The fact that God has proven Himself perfectly faithful to His past covenants means that we can trust Him to make good on all of His promises to us in Scripture. That's good news for those of us banking on such guarantees as . . .

JUST WONDERING

Does the new covenant cancel out the "old" Mosaic Covenant?

The new covenant doesn't cancel out the Mosaic Covenant, but it does supersede it, by virtue of the fact that the new covenant fulfills the requirements of the "old system" and achieves its purposes. Jesus Himself said, "Do not think that I have come to abolish the Law or the Prophets; I have not come to abolish them but to fulfill them" (Matthew 5:17).

➤ "You will keep in perfect peace him whose mind is steadfast, because he trusts in you" (Isaiah 26:3).

➤ "I will never leave you nor forsake you" (Joshua 1:5).

➤ "Delight yourself in the LORD and he will give you the desires of your heart" (Psalm 37:4).

➤ "If we confess our sins, he is faithful and just and will forgive us our sins and purify us from all unrighteousness" (1 John 1:9).

➤ "But the Lord is faithful, and he will strengthen and protect you from the evil one" (2 Thessalonians 3:3).

➤ "Cast all your anxiety on him because he cares for you" (1 Peter 5:7).

If you remember only one thing from this chapter, make it this: God will never renege on His Word.

Being Faithful

Faithfulness. That's the common factor in the covenants we've explored in this chapter. Noah and Abraham were chosen to enter into covenants with God because of their faithfulness. The stipulations of the Mosaic Covenant required faithful obedience on the part of the Israelites. The new covenant involves faithfulness on the part of those who enter into it.

The fact is, God *delights* in the faithful obedience of His people. That's not to say He still makes personal covenants with those who obey Him. (He doesn't need to; we have everything we need in the new covenant.) However, God still showers His blessings on lives lived according to His Word—to those who are faithful to Him.

ON A PERSONAL NOTE

Which Biblical promise of God has special meaning to you right now, considering the situations you're facing in your life and the specific needs you have? Write that promise in a personal journal, along with an honest evaluation of what it means to you. After you've done that, write a prayer of thanksgiving to God for His faithfulness to His promises.

Know What You Believe

How much do you know about God's covenants? Here's a quiz to test your knowledge.

1. What did God designate as a sign to Noah that He would never destroy the earth with a flood again?
   a. A rainbow
   b. A sponge
   c. The sun
   d. A dove

2. Which of the following is not true of the Abrahamic covenant?
   a. In it, God reminded Abraham that it was He who brought Abraham to the Promised Land.

b. It was established just before the American Civil War and involved freeing the slaves in the South.

c. It required Abraham to leave his home and extended family to go to a strange land.

d. It involved Abraham and his wife having a child when both were well into their senior citizen years (by today's standards, that is).

3. Which of the following is not an element of the Mosaic covenant?
   a. The Ten Commandments
   b. Obedience on the part of the Israelites
   c. A land co-op deal with the Philistines
   d. A reminder of God's work in rescuing the Israelites from Egypt

4. Which of the following did God not promise to do for the Israelites as part of the Mosaic covenant in Exodus 19?
   a. Lavish special attention on Israel
   b. Make the nation holy and distinct from all other nations
   c. Give them a human king to lead them
   d. Use Israel like "a kingdom of priests" to teach other nations about the correct worship of the living God

5. Which of the following is not a result of God's new covenant?
   a. Having God's law written on the hearts and minds of His people
   b. The fulfillment of the Mosaic covenant
   c. The complete forgiveness of sins
   d. The departure of God's Holy Spirit

Answers: (1) a, (2) b, (3) c, (4) c, (5) d

One Plus One Plus One Equals... One

UNDERSTANDING GOD'S TRINITY

SNAPSHOT

Jay checked his watch and stomped his feet impatiently on the platform. "Train's running late this morning," he said.

"Hmm?" Dan replied without looking up from his book.

"I said, the train's running late this morning," Jay repeated. Then he nodded toward Dan's book. "What've you got your nose in there?"

"It's a book on prayer," Dan explained.

"Prayer, huh?" Jay said. "Maybe you can explain something to me about that."

"What's that?" Dan asked as he closed his book and slipped it into his briefcase.

"Who are you talking to?" Jay asked.

"I'm talking to you," Dan replied. "Who else would

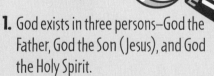

SNEAK PREVIEW

1. God exists in three persons–God the Father, God the Son (Jesus), and God the Holy Spirit.
2. God exists in perfect unity–not as three gods, but as One.
3. The three persons of the Trinity have distinct roles and ministries, yet are always in perfect agreement and harmony with each other.

I be talking to?"

"No, I mean when you pray," Jay explained. "Which God are you actually talking to?"

"Which God?" Dan repeated with a confused look on his face.

"Yeah, I always hear Christians saying things like, 'In the name of the Father and the Son and the Holy Spirit, blah, blah, blah,'" Jay explained. "So which One is it? Who are you talking to?"

"All of Them," Dan said.

"So your prayers automatically get forwarded to all three of Them?" Jay asked.

"No, just One," Dan corrected.

"Which One?"

"All of Them," Dan said.

Jay stopped and looked up at Dan. "Is this some kind of Christian 'Who's on First?' routine?" he asked. "Am I supposed to ask what's the name of the second baseman now?"

"It's not as confusing as it sounds," Dan assured him.

"Uh-huh."

"All you need to remember is that there's one God," Dan continued.

"Oh, so you don't consider Jesus to be a god," Jay offered.

"Oh, yes, I do," Dan emphasized. "Jesus is absolutely God."

"Absolutely God," Jay repeated. "And the Holy Spirit, what is He?"

"He's God too," Dan replied.

"All right," Jay said with a sigh. "So we've got the Father, who is God; Jesus, who is God; and the Holy Spirit, who is God. That adds up to—"

"One God," Dan finished.

Jay slapped his forehead. "Wait a minute. Are you talking about nicknames?" he asked. "Are God, Jesus, and the Holy Spirit all names for the same person?"

"No," Dan said. "Three persons."

"Three persons," Jay repeated.

"And one God," Dan added.

Jay just stared at him.

"Okay, maybe it is as confusing as it sounds," Dan acknowledged.

"No, I think I get it now," Jay said. "God is God, Jesus is God, and the Holy Spirit is God."

"Right!" Dan exclaimed.

Jay smiled. "And Who's on first, What's on second, and I Don't Know's on third."

* * * * * * * * * * * * * * *

If the Trinity is not the most confusing and least understood aspect of the Christian faith, it's easily in the top five. It's not that the subject is unfamiliar. Most Christians can tell you that the Trinity is made up of the Father, Son, and Holy Spirit. Beyond that, though, things get a little fuzzy.

The difficulties come in trying to piece together the seemingly disparate—even contradictory—truths that make up the doctrine of the Trinity. Compounding the problem is a difficulty in accurately communicating the truths of God's triune nature. The fact is, we don't have words in our language that satisfactorily convey what the Trinity is and isn't.

For example, when most people (theologians included) refer to the members of the Trinity, the word they use is persons—as in "The Father, Son, and Holy Spirit are the three persons of the Trinity." However, the word person suggests an individual. And it is inaccurate to say that the Trinity is made up of three individuals.

In this chapter, we're going to sort through these difficulties and discover what it means to serve a triune God. (In the absence of any better suggestions, we too will be using the word person in reference to the Trinity throughout this chapter.)

The Trinity Made Easy...
Er, Somewhat Understandable

To begin with, there are two sets of facts we need to understand about the Trinity. Here's the first one:

➤ God the Father is God.

➤ God the Son, Jesus, is God.

➤ God the Holy Spirit is God.

So far so good, right? None of these statements is particularly controversial or confusing to most Christians. Each one can be supported with several Bible passages. For example . . .

➤ John 6:27 uses the phrase "God the Father."

➤ John 1:1 refers to Jesus as "the Word" and says "the Word was God."

➤ In Acts 5:3–4 Peter makes it clear that to lie to the Holy Spirit is to lie to God.

Once we acknowledge the deity of the Father, Son, and Holy Spirit, we're faced with the second set of facts regarding the Trinity. They are:

➤ God the Father isn't Jesus or the Holy Spirit.

➤ Jesus isn't God the Father or the Holy Spirit.

➤ The Holy Spirit isn't God the Father or Jesus.

We're talking about three distinct persons (there's that word again) here. The Bible says so—again and again. For example, Isaiah uses the "LORD"—who is God the Father—to refer to the "Redeemer," who is Jesus, indicating that the two are distinct persons (59:20). Earlier, that book describes the "Sovereign LORD"—again God the Father—as sending His "Spirit," indicating that the two are distinct persons (48:16). Jesus' final command to His disciples instructed them to "go and make disciples of all nations, baptizing them in the name of the Father and of the Son and of the Holy Spirit" (Matthew 28:19).

If you're looking for something a little more concrete, check out the account of Jesus' baptism in Matthew 3:13–17. Matthew tells us that when Jesus came out of the water, "he saw the Spirit of God [Holy Spirit] descending like a dove." Furthermore, He heard a "voice from heaven" declare, "This is my Son, whom I love; with him I am well pleased."

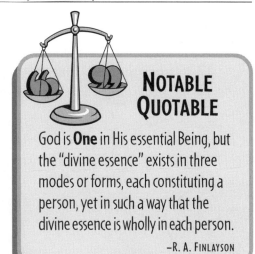

NOTABLE QUOTABLE

God is **One** in His essential Being, but the "divine essence" exists in three modes or forms, each constituting a person, yet in such a way that the divine essence is wholly in each person.

–R. A. FINLAYSON

There you have it: God the Father, Jesus the Son, and the Holy Spirit in the same place, at the same time, in three different forms.

When we combine the two necessary sets of facts about the Trinity, we're left with . . .

➤ God the Father, who is God and a distinct person;

➤ Jesus the Son, who is God and a distinct person; and

➤ the Holy Spirit, who is God and a distinct person.

Three different names. Three distinct persons. One God.

The Unity Handle

Here's where things start to get a little tricky, as far as our limited human comprehension is concerned. You see, one of God's perfections is unity (which you may recall from chapter 3). Deuteronomy 6:4 states this truth in the simplest and clearest terms possible: "Hear, O Israel: The LORD our God, the LORD is one." In the Old Testament, God repeatedly demonstrated His feelings about polytheism—the worship of many gods—in rather definitive ways.

In Numbers 25, God ordered Moses to execute every Israelite who worshiped Moabite idols. When that was finished, Moses was ordered to display the corpses of those who were executed as a warning to the rest of the Israelites. On top of that, God sent a plague that killed 24,000 Israelites—all because the Israelites refused to accept that He alone is God.

It goes without saying, then, that polytheism isn't an option when it comes to explaining the Trinity.

God is not . . .

➤ a group of three individual deities working together like a team of superheroes,

➤ one deity split into three separate parts, or

➤ a schizophrenic deity who appears as one of three different characters as the mood strikes.

God is the one true Deity, and He exists in three persons.

NOTABLE QUOTABLE

We define that there are two, the Father and the Son, and three with the Holy Spirit, and this number is made by the pattern of salvation [which] brings about unity in trinity, interrelating the three, the Father, the Son, and the Holy Spirit. They are three, not in dignity but in degree, not in substance but in form, not in power but in kind. They are of one substance and power, because there is one God from whom these degrees, forms, and kinds devolve in the name of Father, Son, and Holy Spirit.

—Tertullian

If that mathematical equation of the Trinity doesn't make sense, perhaps a scientific analogy will. The illustration of water is often used to explain God's triune nature. Water exists in three forms: solid, liquid, and gaseous—more commonly referred to as ice, water, and steam. Ice, water, and steam are all H_2O; likewise, God, Jesus, and the Holy Spirit are all God.

Furthermore, the solid form of ice is not the same as the liquid form or the gaseous form, even though they are all water. In correlation, God the Father is not the same as Jesus or the Holy Spirit, even though They are all God.

Unfortunately, the water analogy fails to fully capture the triune essence of God. Like most analogies, it breaks down if you try to push it too far. For example, God the Father does not change His form to become Jesus or the Holy Spirit the way ice changes to become water and then steam. (He also doesn't melt in temperatures over 32 degrees Fahrenheit, but that probably goes without saying.) Even with its limitations, though, the water illustration is helpful in giving us a handle with which to grasp the basic truths of the Trinity.

Why Three?

The question that inevitably arises is why. Why has God chosen to make Himself known in three persons? Why not two, or four, or twenty-six, for that matter? In answering this question, we need to carefully consider God's complex work in creation, His unique relationship with the Israelites, His work in providing a plan of salvation for the world, as well as His continuing presence in the lives of His people.

NOTABLE QUOTABLE

Holy Spirit of God, who prefers before all temples the upright heart and pure, instruct us in all truth; what is dark, illumine, what is low, raise and support, what is shallow, deepen; that every chapter in our lives may witness to Your power and justify the ways of God. In the name of Jesus, giver of all grace. Amen.

—JOHN MILTON

When those factors are carefully weighed, examined, and placed in the context of God's eternity and His innumerable perfections, the answer is perhaps best expressed . . . with an exaggerated shrug of the shoulders and a mumbled, "I dunno."

At the core of every theological discourse on the Trinity is the unknowable mystery of why God makes Himself known in three persons. God the Father is God; Jesus is God; the Holy Spirit is God. Period. No one else can make a biblically supported claim to deity, and no one can biblically support a challenge to the deity of any person of the Trinity.

God exists in three persons because He wills Himself to exist in three persons. Until we can discuss the topic in a heavenly setting, face-to-face with God, that answer will have to suffice.

Distinct Yet Equal

One thing we do know is that each person of the Trinity has unique responsibilities and ministries. However, in keeping with God's perfection of unity, no person of the Trinity ever acts independently of the others. In other words, there is never any conflict, opposition, confusion, or disharmony among God, Jesus, and the Holy Spirit. God is One not only in His Being, but in His purposes.

Along those same lines, we need to point out that all three persons of the Trinity are equal in Their importance, Their deity, and Their attributes, despite what we might assume based on Their titles. God the Father does not have seniority over Jesus the Son. The Holy Spirit is not a third wheel or a supporting player, regardless of His relative lack of "fame" compared to God and Jesus.

NOTABLE QUOTABLE

O Lord God almighty . . . I bless You and glorify You through the eternal and heavenly High Priest Jesus Christ, Your beloved Son, through whom be glory to You, with Him and the Holy Spirit, both now and forever.

—POLYCARP

The Originator

It's been said that God the Father originates, God the Son reveals, and God the Holy Spirit executes. Two of the most obvious examples of God's originating can be seen in creation and salvation.

The first verse of the Bible says, "In the beginning God created the heavens and the earth" (Genesis 1:1). The Latin term for the type of creation described in Scripture is ex nihilo, which means "out of nothing." This phrase is helpful in understanding the originating work of God because it emphasizes that nothing existed prior to God's creation.

God needed no raw materials or creative inspiration. The very *concept* of a physical universe and a human race originated with Him. A word from Him initiated the existence of all creation.

The second example of God's originating work is His plan of salvation for the human race. (The details of His plan can be found in chapter 9.) John 3:16 tells us that God *sent* His Son into the world to accomplish the work of salvation. God originated the plan; He set into motion the events that would result in a means of forgiveness and redemption for the sinful world.

We should emphasize that God the Father wasn't "bossing" Jesus around by sending Him into the world, and that Jesus wasn't a reluctant draftee. Each of Them was accomplishing His unique work. God originated the plan, and Jesus fulfilled it. Remember, the persons of the Trinity are *always* in complete agreement, harmony, and unity concerning Their work.

About Jesus

He Is God.

Let's move on to the second person of the Trinity, Jesus. We've already acknowledged that, as one of the three persons in the Trinity, Jesus is fully God. Jesus Himself claimed deity on several occasions:

> ➤ "I am the way and the truth and the life. No one comes to the Father except through me" (John 14:6).

> ➤ "The woman said, 'I know that Messiah' (called Christ) 'is coming. When he comes, he will explain everything to us.' Then Jesus declared, 'I who speak to you am he'" (John 4:25–26).

> ➤ "I and the Father are one" (John 10:30).

> ➤ "The high priest said to him, 'I charge you under oath by the living God: Tell us if you are the Christ, the Son of God.' 'Yes, it is as you say,' Jesus replied" (Matthew 26:63b–64a).

As deity, Jesus possesses the perfections of God. He is . . .

JUST WONDERING

Isn't the doctrine of the Trinity something best left to theologians? Is it really something average Christians need to know about?

It's safe to say that God won't issue a multiple-choice test on the subject when we die to determine our eternal destination. However, we should recognize that the Trinity plays a vital role in our daily Christian lives. Take prayer, for example. Traditionally, we direct our prayers to God the Father. We pray in Jesus' name because He made it possible for us to communicate with our heavenly Father. Our prayers are carried by the Holy Spirit, who even translates some of our poorly expressed requests and praise into a language that honors God the Father. Whether we realize it or not, we interact with all three persons of the Trinity every time we offer up a prayer.

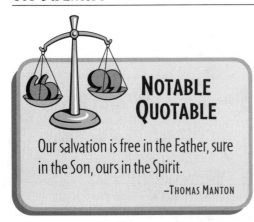

➤ eternal (John 8:57–58),

➤ omnipotent, or all-powerful (Matthew 28:18),

➤ omniscient, or all-knowing (Mark 2:8), and

➤ omnipresent, or everywhere (Matthew 28:20)

. . . to name but a few of His godly attributes.

We should point out that Jesus willingly laid aside His perfections in order to come to earth and dwell among us as a human. He gave up His autonomy and became a helpless baby, dependent on His human mother for care. He gave up His impassibility and made Himself vulnerable to pain, sickness, exhaustion, torture, and death. He submitted himself to physical restrictions like hunger and thirst. He squeezed His infinite presence into a human body.

But at no point did He ever become less than deity. Jesus has always been God and He will always be God.

He Was Human.

In addition to Jesus' deity, we're faced with the truth that when He came to earth, Jesus became fully human.

The New Testament certainly supports this view. Although His conception was miraculous, Jesus was born of a woman, just as all babies are born (Luke 2:6–7). Other passages tell us that Jesus . . .

➤ learned necessary life skills (Luke 2:52),

➤ got hungry (Matthew 4:2),

➤ got tired (John 4:6), and

➤ got thirsty (John 19:28)

. . . just as all humans do.

Through it all, though, Jesus never stopped being fully God.

Go ahead, ask the obvious question: How is it possible for Him to be fully God and fully human at the same time? Unfortunately, that query falls into the same category as why God has a triune nature. As finite human beings, we're simply not equipped to understand it.

He Is the Revealer.

As we mentioned earlier, Jesus' distinct work within the Trinity involves revelation. Specifically, Jesus reveals God the Father to us.

> **NOTABLE QUOTABLE**
>
> Nothing in the Trinity can be called greater or less, since the fountain of divinity alone contains all things by His word and reason, and by the Spirit of His mouth sanctifies all things which are worthy of sanctification.
>
> —ORIGEN

In John 8:19, Jesus startled the Pharisees by saying, "If you knew me, you would know my Father also." In John 14:9–10, in response to a request from one of His disciples to be shown God the Father, Jesus said, "Don't you know me, Philip, even after I have been among you such a long time? Anyone who has seen me has seen the Father. How can you say, 'Show us the Father'? Don't you believe that I am in the Father, and that the Father is in me? The words I say to you are not just my own. Rather, it is the Father, living in me, who is doing his work."

In effect, Jesus was saying, "If you want to know what God the Father is like, look at Me. If you want to know what God the Father wants from you, listen to Me. If you want to know what pleases God the Father, obey My teachings. If you want to know what wondrous things God the Father has in store, believe in Me."

He Is the Savior.

As part of His work in revealing the plan of salvation that God originated, Jesus fulfilled the necessary requirements for the plan to be executed. To be more specific:

➤ He came to earth as a human.

➤ He lived a sinless life.

➤ He taught the truths of the kingdom of God to Jews and Gentiles.

➤ He allowed Himself to be arrested, tortured, and executed.

➤ He rose from the dead after three days.

➤ He ascended to heaven.

➤ He gave the gift of the Holy Spirit to take His place in the lives of believers.

➤ He promised to return in glory.

Because of Jesus' sacrifice and His victory over sin and death, the human race can now be reconciled with God and spend eternity with Him—just like He planned.

The Unsung Member of the Trinity

Like God the Father and Jesus, the Holy Spirit possesses the perfections of deity described in chapter 3. He is . . .

➤ holy

➤ just

➤ sovereign

➤ eternal

➤ omnipotent

➤ omniscient

➤ omnipresent

➤ unchanging

He is also intimately involved in every aspect of our daily Christian walk.

NOTABLE QUOTABLE

Praise God from whom all blessings flow;
Praise Him, all creatures here below;
Praise Him above, ye heavenly host;
Praise Father, Son, and Holy Ghost.

—THOMAS KEN

Five Works of the Spirit

Like God the Father and Jesus, the Holy Spirit has distinct responsibilities and ministries within the Trinity. We're going to take a look at five of them.

1. The Holy Spirit Dwells in Us.

John 14:15–27 suggests that the Holy Spirit is Jesus' going-away present for His followers. As gifts go, the Holy Spirit is about as personal as you can get.

When a person receives the gift of salvation from God, the Holy Spirit enters his or her life—for good.

Second Corinthians 1:22 puts it this way: "[God] set his seal of ownership on us, and put his Spirit in our hearts as a deposit, guaranteeing what is to come." Like everything else about God, His seal is permanent. Nothing can break it. Therefore, nothing can remove the Holy Spirit from the life of a believer.

That's good news, because the Holy Spirit's presence in a person's life is the litmus test for Christians. Romans 8:9 tells us that if you have the Holy Spirit in your life, you belong to Christ and are guaranteed salvation. If you don't have the Holy Spirit in your life, you will be subject to God's eternal judgment.

2. The Holy Spirit Convicts Us of Sin.

In John 16:8 Jesus offers this promise regarding the Holy Spirit: "When he comes, he will convict the world of guilt in regard to sin and righteousness and judgment." If that sounds like a conscience to you, you're on the right track in understanding this work of the Holy Spirit.

The fact is, we *need* Someone to tell us when we've sinned against God. Our human consciences are easily dulled. Given time and motive, we can justify practically any wrongdoing. Without the convicting work of the Spirit, most of us would have no idea of the damaging effect our sin has on our relationship with God. Not only does the Holy Spirit make us aware of that sin, but He urges us to confess and ask forgiveness for it, thereby restoring our relationship with God.

ON A PERSONAL NOTE

If you're like most Christians, you probably know far less about the Holy Spirit than you do about the other two members of the Trinity. Why not commit yourself to remedying that situation? Plan a week-long (or, better yet, a month-long) Bible study that focuses specifically on the Holy Spirit and His work in our lives. Here are some passages to get you started:

➤ John 14:15–31 (Jesus' promise of the Holy Spirit)
➤ Acts 2:4 (the arrival of the Holy Spirit at Pentecost)
➤ Luke 1:35 (the Holy Spirit's role in the conception of Jesus)
➤ 2 Peter 1:20–21 (the Holy Spirit's work in the recording of the Bible)

JUST WONDERING

If the Trinity isn't mentioned in the Bible, how did the doctrine get started?

First of all, though the word **Trinity** does not appear in the Bible, the concept of a triune God is certainly taught in Scripture. The doctrine of one God in three persons was explicitly spelled out in A.D. 325 by the Council of Nicaea, the first general council in Christian church history. Organized by the Roman emperor Constantine, it was made up of over two hundred of the leading Bible scholars of the day. The scholars debated the exact wording necessary for expressing God's triune nature. The result was the Nicene Creed, which affirms the deity of God, Jesus, and the Holy Spirit, as well as the oneness of God—and which is still recited by churches today.

3. The Holy Spirit Assists Us in Prayer.

The Bible is rather sketchy with the details, but passages such as Romans 8:26–27 indicate that the Holy Spirit "intercedes for us" when we pray. He doesn't just deliver our prayer messages to heaven; He acts as a "psychic translator" between us and our heavenly Father. That is, when we pray, the Holy Spirit searches our hearts and minds for the praise, confession, thanksgiving, and requests that we are unable to adequately express.

Then He communicates those elements to God the Father in a way that honors Him and receives His blessing.

4. The Holy Spirit Gives Us Our Spiritual Gifts.

Bible passages such as Romans 12, 1 Corinthians 12, and Ephesians 4 tell us that the Holy Spirit distributes to believers "spiritual gifts"—skills, abilities, and personal attributes designed to benefit the church. These gifts include:

➤ evangelism	➤ exhortation
➤ pastoring	➤ mercy
➤ serving	➤ giving
➤ teaching	➤ administration
➤ faith	➤ wisdom and knowledge

The Holy Spirit determines which gift (or gifts) each believer receives, based on what's best for the body of Christ.

5. The Holy Spirit Empowers Us to Accomplish God's Will.

In the Bible, God makes a point of using unlikely people to accomplish His work. Among the many Bible characters who fit into this category are:

> ➤ Moses, who was so unsure of himself that he brought his brother along to confront Pharaoh

> ➤ Gideon, who was a nobody from the tiny Israelite tribe of Manasseh

> ➤ Rahab, who was a prostitute

> ➤ Peter, who was an impetuous, occasionally unreliable, fisherman

God's reason for making such unusual personnel choices is simple. He wants to make sure that no one but He receives the credit and glory for what He accomplishes. God wants witnesses to His work to say, "I know that guy couldn't have done that on his own. He must have had divine help."

ON A PERSONAL NOTE

Have you ever felt empowered by God to accomplish His work? Perhaps a surge of confidence regarding a future task or challenge? If so, make a note of it in your journal. Include as many details as possible, including the situation, your initial attitude toward it, the catalyst that changed your mind, and the end result. Later you can use your journal for inspiration and encouragement by reading back over it when you feel discouraged.

Of course, those whom God chooses, He also equips. And that's where the Holy Spirit comes in. Judges 6:34 offers a glimpse into the role the Holy Spirit plays in equipping God's people for His service: "The Spirit of the LORD came upon Gideon, and he blew a trumpet, summoning the Abiezrites to follow him."

When the time comes to respond to God's call, the Holy Spirit—who dwells in us—makes His presence known in a very real way and gives us the power, confidence, and ability to accomplish God's will.

Thanks to Three . . . Praise for One

We may not be able to fully comprehend God's triune nature, but we can celebrate the fact that all three persons of the Godhead minister to us in unique and life-altering ways. We can thank God the Father for His originating work, Jesus for His revealing of God, and the Holy Spirit for His work in our daily lives.

We can also praise God for His unity and for the fact that we don't have to deal with or try to please three separate deities.

Know What You Believe

How much do you know about God's triune nature? Here's a quiz to test your knowledge.

1. Which of the following is not a fundamental truth of the Trinity?
   a. God is one.
   b. Jesus is not God or the Holy Spirit.
   c. God created the Holy Spirit to minister to His people after Jesus' ascension.
   d. The Holy Spirit is deity.

2. At what event does Matthew record God the Father, Jesus, and the Holy Spirit all being present in the same place, at the same time, in three different forms?
   a. Jesus' temptation by Satan
   b. Jesus' baptism
   c. Jesus' high school graduation
   d. Jesus' first miracle

3. Which of the following is not true of Jesus?
   a. He is fully God.
   b. He is fully human.
   c. He set aside His godly perfections when He came to earth as a human.
   d. He has existed almost as long as God has.

4. What gift did Jesus promise His followers in John 14?
   a. The Holy Spirit
   b. God the Father
   c. A stone from His burial tomb
   d. An opportunity to escape martyrdom

5. Which of the following is not a responsibility or ministry of the Holy Spirit?
   a. Praying on our behalf so that we don't have to
   b. Empowering us to accomplish God's will
   c. Convicting us of sin
   d. Distributing spiritual gifts

Answers: (1) c, (2) b, (3) d, (4) a, (5) a

The "Thou Shalts"

UNDERSTANDING GOD'S LAWS

<u>SNAPSHOT</u>

"Do you ever wish that God were a little more lenient?" Nick asked.

"What do you mean?" Brian asked.

"You know," Nick insisted. "Christians aren't allowed to drink or smoke or swear or party or anything like that. Wouldn't you like it if maybe He weren't so strict or judgmental?"

"You mean, do I ever wish He would just let some things slide?" Brian asked.

"Well, not *completely*," Nick said. "But maybe He could just shake His head and roll His eyes when things get a little out of hand, instead of coming down on us with guilt and judgment and all that."

"What kinds of things should He let slide?" Brian asked.

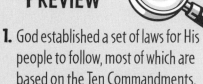

SNEAK PREVIEW

1. God established a set of laws for His people to follow, most of which are based on the Ten Commandments.
2. God's purpose in laying down His laws is not to spoil our fun but to protect us and to ensure order in society.
3. The only way for us to demonstrate a genuine understanding of God's laws is to obey them.

"You know, drinking, partying—" Nick began.

"Armed robbery, murder," Brian continued.

"No, I'm not talking about anarchy or chaos or anything like that," Nick objected. "I'm just talking about having a little more fun, that's all."

"Okay," Brian said, "but who's going to draw the line? Who's going to determine what should and shouldn't be allowed?"

"Oh, come on," Nick said. "It's pretty obvious what things are *really* bad and what things are just kind of . . . socially unacceptable."

"And it's the socially unacceptable stuff that you want God to pretend not to notice," Brian said.

"Exactly."

"Like shoplifting?" Brian asked.

Nick thought for a moment. "Yeah, I think shoplifting should be okay," he said. "When you think about it, those big corporations have been stealing from us all these years by charging higher prices than they need to."

"So would price gouging be okay in your dream world?" Brian asked.

"No way."

"I see," Brian said. "So it should be okay for people to take advantage of businesses, but not for businesses to take advantage of people."

"Uh . . . yeah," Nick said slowly.

"What about burglary, home invasion, that kind of stuff?" Brian asked.

"No, because then you're talking about personal stuff, and that should be off-limits," Nick said.

"Yeah, but when people shoplift, they're stealing the personal property of the store owner," Brian pointed out.

"Yeah, but if they're rich enough to own a business, they can afford to lose a little merchandise here and there," Nick reasoned.

"So it's all based on wealth," Brian observed. "Does that mean it should be okay to break into *rich* people's houses and take *their* stuff?"

"Well, I guess—" Nick began.

"What would you say is the minimum income that qualifies a person to be robbed without God taking any action?" Brian asked. "A million? A half million?"

"You're really making this complicated," Nick said. "You know that?"

"I know," Brian replied with a grin. "Suddenly 'Thou shalt not steal' is sounding pretty good, isn't it?"

* * * * * * * * * * * * * * *

Take a look at the following passage and see if you notice anything odd about it.

> *Oh, how I love your law!*
> *I meditate on it all day long.*
> *Your commands make me wiser than my enemies,*
> *for they are ever with me.*
> *I have more insight than all my teachers,*
> *for I meditate on your statutes.*
> *I have more understanding than the elders,*
> *for I obey your precepts.*
> *I have kept my feet from every evil path*
> *so that I might obey your word.*
> *I have not departed from your laws,*
> *for you yourself have taught me.*
> *How sweet are your words to my taste,*
> *sweeter than honey to my mouth!*
> *I gain understanding from your precepts;*
> *therefore I hate every wrong path.* (Psalm 119:97–104)

At first glance, this would appear to be just another psalm of David—a wonderful piece of writing, to be sure, but not terribly different in its pattern and rhythm than countless other psalms in the Bible. David's grand themes and exuberant praise are familiar characteristics of his writing. You can find similar expressions in almost any psalm he wrote.

What sets this passage in Psalm 119 apart is not its style but its subject matter. Take a closer look at what it is that has David so fired up:

➤ "I love your *law*" (verse 97, emphasis added)

➤ "I meditate on your *statutes*" (verse 99, emphasis added)

➤ "I obey your *precepts*" (verse 100, emphasis added).

This passage would be a lot easier to digest if David were cheering God's grace, faithfulness, love, or protection.

But His *law*? Talk about an unlikely source of joy and happiness!

Was David simply mindlessly excited about everything concerning God? Was he just doing a little "apple polishing" in front of the Almighty? Or is it possible that David understood something about God's laws—and about God Himself—that we need to pick up on?

In order to answer that question, we need to look at the individual laws of God to see if we can find some clues about Him. And if we're looking for information on the individual laws of God, there's only one place to begin.

Next stop: Exodus 20, Mount Sinai.

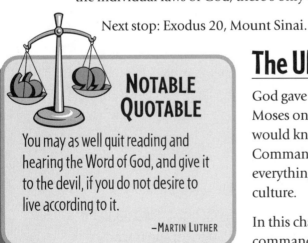

NOTABLE QUOTABLE

You may as well quit reading and hearing the Word of God, and give it to the devil, if you do not desire to live according to it.

—MARTIN LUTHER

The Ultimate Top Ten List

God gave the original Ten Commandments to Moses on Mount Sinai so that the people of Israel would know how to live. Since that time, those Ten Commandments have been incorporated into everything from our legal system to our pop culture.

In this chapter, we're going to examine each commandment, supplement it with related New

Testament passages and teachings, and then draw some conclusions about God based on it.

The One and Only

> *"I am the* LORD *your God, who brought you out of Egypt, out of the land of slavery. You shall have no other gods before me."*
> (Exodus 20:2–3)

The first sentence ("I am the LORD your God") serves as a preamble to the entire set of commandments that follow. In a sense, the first sentence answers the question, "Says who?" God declares His sovereign right to establish a set of rules for His people, based on His benevolent works on their behalf.

God demands that His people acknowledge His singularity and uniqueness. Even the most commandment-phobic among us can see the logic in this rule. A quick glance at God's résumé reveals that He . . .

➤ spoke the universe into existence,

➤ formed the human race from the dust of the earth,

➤ took the initiative in revealing Himself to His human creation,

➤ gave us opportunity to have a personal relationship with Him, and

➤ provides guidance, direction, comfort, and assistance when we need it most.

The first commandment—"You shall have no other gods before me"—is designed to ensure that the credit, as well as the accompanying praise and

ON A PERSONAL NOTE

Here are some questions you can use to supplement your study of God's laws and get you thinking about them from a different perspective:

➤ How strict were your parents when it came to rules?

➤ What specific rules did they expect you to follow?

➤ How did you respond to their rules, for the most part?

➤ Which rules were most difficult for you to follow?

➤ How long did it take you to understand that your parents' rules were for your own good?

After you've answered these questions, think about what conclusions you can draw about God based on the rules He's set down for His people.

worship, for that work goes where it is due, instead of to some imaginary deity.

Jesus expanded this commandment from a mere prohibition (don't give false gods priority) to an active pursuit in Matthew 22:37–38, when He told His followers: "'Love the Lord your God with all your heart and with all your soul and with all your mind.' This is the first and greatest commandment."

The point is that if we take a purposeful approach to praising and worshiping God—if we make Him the priority He deserves to be in our lives—we will never be guilty of placing another God before Him.

Idol Talk

"You shall not make for yourself an idol in the form of anything in heaven above or on the earth beneath or in the waters below. You shall not bow down to them or worship them; for I, the LORD your God, am a jealous God, punishing the children for the sin of the fathers to the third and fourth generation of those who hate me, but showing love to a thousand generations of those who love me and keep my commandments." (Exodus 20:4–6)

NOTABLE QUOTABLE

Ye call me master, and obey me not;
Ye call me light, and seek me not;
Ye call me way, and walk me not;
Ye call me wise, and follow me not;
Ye call me rich, and ask me not;
Ye call me eternal, and seek me not;
Ye call me gracious, and trust me not;
Ye call me noble, and serve me not;
Ye call me mighty, and honor me not;
Ye call me just, and fear me not;
If I condemn you, blame me not.

—IN THE CATHEDRAL AT LÜBECK, GERMANY

These commandments were originally given to Moses during a period of history when idol worship was rampant in and around the Promised Land. Every country, culture, and group of people had its own set of gods and goddesses, represented in various forms as statues and idols.

The Lord forbade His people from participating in idolatrous worship—even with idols representing *Him*—because it detracted from His glory. Remember, the Lord is perfect in every way, right down to His form. First Timothy 1:17 tells us that His form is invisible. John 4:24 tells us that God is spirit. To portray Him as flesh and blood, with all of the restrictions that entails—or as any physical object—is not only insulting; it's downright blasphemous.

This commandment also reveals the "jealous" nature of God alluded to in the previous section. He does not share His glory with anyone or anything, real or imaginary. And though few believers today may ever be tempted to bow down to an actual statue representing a false deity, that doesn't mean God's second commandment has no bearing on our lives.

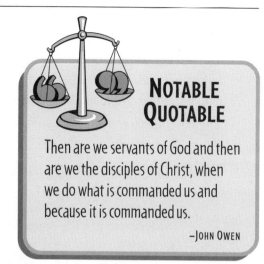

NOTABLE QUOTABLE

Then are we servants of God and then are we the disciples of Christ, when we do what is commanded us and because it is commanded us.

–JOHN OWEN

It's not much of a stretch to say that *anything* that disrupts our faithfulness to God, or that interferes with our responsibility to bring praise and glory to Him, could be considered an "idol." In light of such a possibility, the apostle Paul's words in Ephesians 5:15–17 become especially relevant: "Be very careful, then, how you live—not as unwise but as wise, making the most of every opportunity, because the days are evil. Therefore do not be foolish, but understand what the Lord's will is."

What's in a Name?

"You shall not misuse the name of the LORD your God, for the LORD will not hold anyone guiltless who misuses his name." (Exodus 20:7)

The idea here in the third commandment was that the Israelites were not to swear falsely in God's name. That is, they were forbidden from using His name in oaths that they had no intention of keeping. The Lord wanted to make sure that when people heard His name, they did not associate it in any way with untruths or unreliability. The closest modern equivalent would probably be the phrase "so help me, God," used in the swearing in of witnesses in many American courtrooms. The unspoken sentiment seems to be that using God's name should hold us to a higher standard of conduct.

The third commandment is not simply a matter of legalities and semantics, though. It's also a matter of respect—the "fear of the Lord," if you will. Our reverence for God should extend to His name. Because nothing about the Lord is idle, insincere, or frivolous, we must not use His name in an idle, insincere, or frivolous manner.

One Fine Day

"Remember the Sabbath day by keeping it holy. Six days you shall labor and do all your work, but the seventh day is a Sabbath to the LORD your God. On it you shall not do any work, neither you, nor your son or daughter, nor your manservant or maidservant, nor your animals, nor the alien within your gates. For in six days the LORD made the heavens and the earth, the sea, and all that is in them, but he rested on the seventh day. Therefore the LORD blessed the Sabbath day and made it holy." (Exodus 20:8–11)

The Sabbath (which was and is still observed among Jews on Saturday) was intended as a day of solemn worship in the ancient Hebrew tradition. Keeping it "holy"—that is, separate and special—was a way for God's people to demonstrate their devotion to Him.

ON A PERSONAL NOTE

The use of the Lord's name (or any variation thereof) as an exclamation of frustration, irritation, or surprise would certainly qualify as frivolous. If such exclamations are part of your vocabulary, try breaking yourself of the habit by substituting other terms such as "Wow" or "Yikes."

The fact that the Israelites were not to work on the Sabbath did not mean that they sat around doing nothing. Genuine observers of the Sabbath were very busy, in fact. Their efforts, though, were directed toward praising and worshiping God instead of getting their chores done.

For Christians, the day of worship has been changed from Saturday to Sunday, most likely because Sunday was the day of Jesus' resurrection. And though few of us have manservants or maidservants or aliens within our gates to worry about, the spirit of God's fourth commandment is still in effect for us.

We, as His people, still have a responsibility to set aside the first day of every week to focus specifically on Him. Considering all that He has done for us, it's the very least we can do.

Family Affair

"Honor your father and your mother, so that you may live long in the land the LORD your God is giving you." (Exodus 20:12)

Honoring parents, in the context of this verse, means to . . .

➤ obey them,

➤ submit to their authority,

➤ think highly of them,

➤ treat them with significance, and

➤ provide care for them.

God's commandments here and in Ephesians 6:1–4 reflect the importance of a well-functioning family. In Ephesians 6:4, the Scripture assigns responsibility to parents as well: "Fathers, do not exasperate your children; instead, bring them up in the training and instruction of the Lord."

A Matter of Life and Death

"You shall not murder." (Exodus 20:13)

JUST WONDERING

What if my parents aren't honorable people? Do I still have a responsibility to them? Exodus 20:12 doesn't set guidelines as to which parents are deserving of honor and which parents aren't. It just tells us to honor them. That doesn't mean we have to agree with their lifestyle or pretend not to notice their character flaws. And it certainly doesn't mean that we should endure abuse from them. It does mean, however, that we must find ways to treat them with significance and provide care for them, regardless of what they're like.

For those of us not given to fits of psychotic rage, the sixth commandment seems obvious to the point of being unnecessary. *Don't murder.* That's like being reminded not to rob a bank on the way home from work. What could be easier to obey? Every time we go to bed without having committed a premeditated homicide, we can claim complete obedience to God's sixth commandment for that day. Or not.

You see, in Matthew 5:21–22, Jesus extended the coverage of the sixth commandment quite dramatically: "You have heard that it was said to the people long ago, 'Do not murder, and anyone who murders will be subject to judgment.' But I tell you

JUST WONDERING

Does the command not to murder include situations such as war and the death penalty? Not in the context of Exodus 20, it doesn't. Elsewhere in God's law, He includes provisions for capital punishment (Exodus 21:15-17, 23) and warfare (Exodus 17:8-16). God's sixth commandment refers to a premeditated and deliberate act on the part of an individual against another individual (or other individuals).

that anyone who is angry with his brother will be subject to judgment. Again, anyone who says to his brother, 'Raca,' is answerable to the Sanhedrin. But anyone who says, 'You fool!' will be in danger of the fire of hell."

God judges us not only according to our actions but according to our thoughts. In other words, any ill wishes or short-tempered attitudes toward other people could be considered a violation of God's Sixth Commandment.

True Love

"You shall not commit adultery." (Exodus 20:14)

Marriage is a sacred institution in the eyes of God. In fact, He uses the faithful relationship between a husband and wife to describe the relationship between Christ and His church.

Neither husband nor wife may do anything to destroy the faithfulness of that relationship. Jesus' warning in Matthew 19:6 comes into play here: "Therefore what God has joined together, let man not separate." Marriage before God is a *union*, the process by which two people become one. To commit adultery is to tear that union apart.

According to Jesus, adultery can be committed without sexual contact. Look at His words in Matthew 5:27-28: "You have heard that it was said, 'Do not commit adultery.' But I tell you that anyone who looks at a woman lustfully has already committed adultery with her in his heart." The idea here is a willful stare, a desire to become sexually aroused by another person.

As was the case with the sixth commandment, God's people are expected to honor Him in their thoughts as well as their actions.

Personal Property

"You shall not steal." (Exodus 20:15)

In the eighth commandment, God recognizes the sanctity of personal property—not because He encourages materialism, but because He understands its importance in a community. After all, if every day were open season on other people's possessions, the result would be chaos and complete distrust.

NOTABLE QUOTABLE

Fifteen million laws have been passed to try to enforce the Golden Rule and the Ten Commandments.

–AUTHOR UNKNOWN

In addition to showing respect to other people's property and possessions, Christians have a responsibility to be free and selfless with our own things. Jesus summed up that responsibility tidily in Matthew 5:42: "Give to the one who asks you, and do not turn away from the one who wants to borrow from you."

The Whole Truth and Nothing but the Truth

"You shall not give false testimony against your neighbor." (Exodus 20:16)

This is another commandment tied to social order and the health of the community. For one thing, it protects people from slander, which is necessary for any kind of significant social interaction. People need to know that their neighbors aren't free to spread outrageous lies about them whenever they feel the urge to do so.

The prohibition against false testimony also lays the groundwork for an effective judicial system based on the testimony of witnesses. It establishes accountability on the part of those witnesses and encourages truthful testimony.

The ninth commandment is also one of the many rules and instructions in Scripture that deal with the tongue. The New Testament writer James compares the tongue to . . .

➤ a bit in the mouth of a large horse (James 3:3),

➤ a rudder on a ship (James 3:4), and

➤ a small spark that causes a great forest fire (James 3:5).

In other words, though the tongue is small, it is capable of influencing every part of us—for better or worse. That's why God's Word contains so many commandments regarding the use of our tongues. Here's just a sampling:

➤ "Do not lie" (Leviticus 19:11).

➤ "Do not deceive one another" (Leviticus 19:11).

➤ "Do not swear falsely by [God's] name" (Leviticus 19:12).

➤ "Each of you must put off falsehood and speak truthfully to his neighbor" (Ephesians 4:25).

➤ "Do not let any unwholesome talk come out of your mouths, but only what is helpful for building others up according to their needs" (Ephesians 4:29).

➤ "Nor should there be obscenity, foolish talk or coarse joking, which are out of place, but rather thanksgiving" (Ephesians 5:4).

James 3:8 makes it clear that "taming" the tongue is a difficult, never-ending task. However, God makes it clear throughout His Word that a genuine commitment to Him is marked by a genuine commitment to control the tongue.

NOTABLE QUOTABLE

The tiniest fragment of obedience, and heaven opens up and the profoundest truths of God are yours straightaway. God will never reveal more truth about Himself till you obey what you know already.

—Oswald Chambers

Satisfaction

"You shall not covet your neighbor's house. You shall not covet your neighbor's wife, or his manservant or maidservant, his ox or donkey, or anything that belongs to your neighbor." (Exodus 20:17)

Coveting in this context refers to an uncontrollable, selfish desire. It's dangerous and potentially destructive to God's people because it indicates a dissatisfaction and discontentment with what God has given us. The tenth commandment warns against this desire.

Beyond Justice

There's no getting around the fact that God expects His people to follow a tightly defined lifestyle, which involves more than a few rules. But if we concentrate solely on the rules themselves, we'll miss two important truths about God Himself.

1. He Isn't a Cosmic Killjoy.

God does not take pleasure in our misery. He doesn't look for people who are enjoying themselves and then issue a commandment to put an end to it. Don't forget that God is the One who created us with the capacity for joy in the first place. If it weren't for Him, we wouldn't know what fun is.

Jesus gave us a clue as to the perspective we should take toward God's rules in John 10:10, when He told His disciples, "I have come that they may have life, and that they have it to the full." In other words, life can only be lived to the fullest when the Lord is at the center of it.

God's rules are intended to maximize our pleasure and fulfillment, not spoil them. God, in His infinite wisdom, knows how we can avoid the . . .

➤ guilt,

➤ shame,

➤ regret,

➤ damaged self-respect, and

➤ negative consequences

. . . that go hand in hand with ungodly living. Any temporary thrill or advantage that is gained by breaking God's laws is far outweighed by the rewards of faithfully keeping them.

If that's not enough to tip the balance in favor of obedience, there's always the practical matter of God's perfection. Remember, everything about God— including His commands—is perfect. Any law He establishes is perfect because it comes from Him, whether we understand it or not.

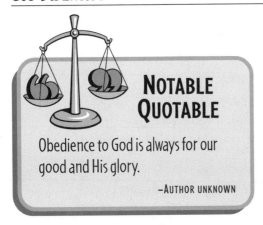

2. It Wouldn't Matter if He Were a Killjoy.

The fact that God's commandments actually benefit *us* is just icing on the cake, as far as we're concerned. Even if God's primary purpose in establishing His laws was to make us miserable all the time, we would have no choice but to obey or face the consequences.

Obedience is the only currency God accepts. Anyone who seeks to have a relationship with Him must do what He commands. Period.

From that standpoint, then, it doesn't really matter *why* God establishes His laws, or whether they're for our own good or not. All we need to know is that God has commandments for us to obey. It's really a three-step process:

1. See commandment.

2. Obey commandment.

3. Repeat as often as necessary.

Knowing—and Obeying—God's Laws

Ignorance is no defense when it comes to God's laws. When we stand before His judgment seat to answer for the things that we've done or haven't done in this life, He will not accept the fact that we were unfamiliar with His commandments as a legitimate excuse for not obeying them.

That's why it's important for us to search Scripture for God's instructions and then commit them to memory—and obey them—when we find them.

Know What You Believe

How much do you know about God's laws and commandments? Here's a quiz to test your knowledge.

1. Which of the following phrases is not part of David's prayer to God in Psalm 119:97–100?
   a. "I love your law!"
   b. "I contemplate your restrictions."
   c. "I meditate on your statutes."
   d. "I obey your precepts."

2. How did God introduce Himself before laying down the Ten Commandments?
   a. "I am the LORD your God, who brought you out of Egypt, out of the land of slavery."
   b. "I am the God of Shadrach, Meshach, and Abednego."
   c. "I am the cloud you will follow by day and the pillar of fire you will follow by night."
   d. "I am He who brings plagues on the land."

3. Why does God forbid His people from bowing down to idols, even if those idols are meant to represent Him?
   a. He didn't want the Israelites' idols to fall into enemy hands during battle, because then He would have been obligated to help those who possessed the idols.
   b. His original request, to be portrayed as a lynx, was not honored because the idol makers didn't know what a lynx was.
   c. God lives in a perfect form, as an invisible spirit; to try to put Him into an imperfect physical form is to dishonor Him.
   d. Idols in Old Testament times were usually built by amateurs—and it showed.

4. Which of the following is not true of God's commandment concerning the Sabbath?
   a. Saturday was the holy day for the Israelites; Sunday is the holy day for Christians.
   b. It extends to sons, daughters, servants, and even animals.
   c. It is a way of commemorating God's day of rest after the six days of creation.
   d. God expects us to do absolutely nothing on the Sabbath.

5. Which of the following is not one of the comparisons James used in describing the tongue?
   a. A rudder
   b. A serpent
   c. A spark
   d. A bit for a horse

Answers: (1) b, (2) a, (3) c, (4) d, (5) b

"THE WORLD'S EASIEST GUIDE"

PART TWO

God's Work

CHAPTER 7

Yes, That's the Book For Me

UNDERSTANDING GOD'S WORD

SNAPSHOT

"I'm not knocking the Bible," Rebecca said as she set her coffee cup on the table. "I'm just saying that we approach it from two different perspectives."

"And I'm just saying that I don't understand why you approach it at all," Ann replied between bites of a bagel smothered in cream cheese.

"What are you talking about?" Rebecca asked. "You're the one who thinks it's so life-changing!"

"Right," Ann said, "but only if you approach it as God's Word."

"Oh, no," Rebecca moaned. "Here we go with this again."

"If the Bible isn't God's Word, then what is it?" Ann asked.

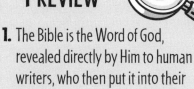

SNEAK PREVIEW

1. The Bible is the Word of God, revealed directly by Him to human writers, who then put it into their own words.

2. The Bible is inerrant, which means it can be fully trusted as the truth; it is understandable to those who genuinely desire to know it; it is necessary for a knowledge of the gospel; and it is sufficient–it contains everything we need to know about God and the Christian faith.

3. Because the Bible is the primary source of truth about God, His will, and His plans for the world, understanding God's Word must be a top priority in the life of every believer.

"Well, for one thing, it's one of the most valuable historical records ever written," Rebecca said. "Without it, our knowledge of Middle Eastern history wouldn't be nearly as complete. On top of that, it's a fascinating compilation—"

"Wah-wa wah; wa wah-wa wah."

"What are you doing?" Rebecca asked.

"I'm making the sound Charlie Brown's teachers used to make in those old cartoons," Ann explained.

"Why?"

"To snap you out of your grad student mode," Ann explained. "How about talking like a normal person?"

"What do you want me to say?" Rebecca asked.

"Tell me what the Bible means to you personally."

"Okay," Rebecca said as she picked at her cinnamon-and-raisin bagel. "I think there are some parts in it that may very well have come from a Higher Source. And I believe the world would be a better place if more people lived their lives according to certain biblical principles."

"Wow, that's some quality vagueness," Ann marveled. "It sounded like an answer a Miss America contestant would give."

"Did anyone ever tell you that you're hard to please?" Rebecca asked.

"Did anyone ever tell you that you have a fear of commitment?" Ann replied.

"*Commitment*?" Rebecca said. "See, that's what happens whenever we talk about this. You always go overboard. Even if I acknowledge that the Bible is God's Word, why would I want to *commit* myself to it?"

"What other response would make sense?" Ann asked. "Let me put it this way. Think about what would happen if someone discovered a book left by an advanced alien culture thousands of years ago."

"Suddenly I'm debating Rod Serling in the Twilight Zone," Rebecca muttered.

Ann ignored her and continued. "And let's say this book contained wisdom far greater than our own. What do you think the public response would be?"

Rebecca shrugged. "Okay, I'll play along. If it could be conclusively proven that it came from an extraterrestrial source, I'm sure it would be considered one of the greatest discoveries in human history."

"Exactly," Ann said. "And we'd have people working around the clock trying to figure out how to apply alien wisdom to everything from medicine to business to personal health."

"And colleges would start offering majors in extraterrestrial literature," Rebecca added.

Ann nodded and continued. "Yet here we have the Bible, which comes not only from an extraterrestrial source but from *Deity*, and it's treated as nothing more than a glorified book of quotations."

"Or a hotel room accessory," Rebecca added.

* * * * * * * * * * * * * * *

The Bible is the Word of God. Let's agree on that. If it's not the Word of God, you can stop reading this book right now. After all, in these pages you'll find such audacious claims as . . .

> ➤ God created the entire universe in six days.

> ➤ God loves us despite the fact that we are helpless sinners.

> ➤ Jesus rose from the dead.

> ➤ Anyone who repents and believes in Jesus is guaranteed eternal life in heaven.

The only reason we're able to include such claims and expect them to be accepted as fact is that the Bible declares them to be true. If we don't have God's *Word* on these matters, we have no reason to believe them.

Stripping the Bible of its divine origin creates a "domino effect" that ultimately results in spiritual chaos. Here's how the dominoes fall:

➤ If the Bible is not the Word of God, its origin is human.

➤ If the Bible is of human origin, it's fallible, because humans are fallible.

➤ If the Bible is fallible, it's not completely trustworthy.

➤ If the Bible is not completely trustworthy, it's left to us to decide which parts of it to accept and believe in.

➤ If it's left to us to decide which parts of the Bible to accept and believe in, we will naturally opt for the ones that require the least amount of effort on our part.

The last domino to fall is the one that represents any spiritual responsibility at all on the part of individuals. The result would be spiritual anarchy, a landscape in which all views of God, salvation, and the hereafter are equally valid—and equally ludicrous—in the absence of absolute truth.

Fortunately for us, the domino scenario is hypothetical.

NOTABLE QUOTABLE

The Bible is the light of my understanding, the joy of my heart, the fullness of my hope, the clarifier of my affections, the mirror of my thoughts, the consoler of my sorrows, the guide of my soul through this gloomy labyrinth of time, the telescope sent from heaven to reveal to the eye of man the amazing glories of the far distant world.

–SIR WILLIAM JONES

Dusting for God's Fingerprints

The fact that the Bible is God's Word isn't something we have to accept on blind faith. In fact, we have compelling evidence to back up claims that Scripture comes directly from God Himself.

The Bible claims to be God's Word.

Scripture itself repeatedly testifies to the origin of its message. To make the case for God's direct involvement, we call four witnesses to the stand:

➤ David—shepherd, psalmist, and king of Israel—who said, "The Spirit of the LORD spoke through me; his word was on my tongue" (2 Samuel 23:2);

➤ the Old Testament prophet Jeremiah, who wrote, "Then the LORD reached out his hand

and touched my mouth and said to me, 'Now, I have put my words in your mouth'" (Jeremiah 1:9)—and who uses the phrase, "the word of the LORD came to Jeremiah," over thirty times in his book;

➤ the apostle Paul, who wrote, "All Scripture is God-breathed" (2 Timothy 3:16), and "This is what we speak, not in words taught us by human wisdom but in words taught by the Spirit, expressing spiritual truths in spiritual words" (1 Corinthians 2:13); and

➤ the apostle Peter, who wrote, "For prophecy never had its origin in the will of man, but men spoke from God as they were carried along by the Holy Spirit" (2 Peter 1:21).

If the Bible isn't God's Word, then these passages, and many others like them, must be dismissed as exaggerations or delusions of grandeur on the part of the actual authors—or as bald-faced lies. Either way, the result is that the credibility of the entire book is tainted to the point of rendering it unreliable.

The circumstances of the Bible's creation can only be explained by divine involvement.

What do you think would happen if you put forty or so randomly selected strangers in a room together and instructed them to write a collection of sixty-six books on one topic—*God*, for example—with each person writing at least one book? Do you think they would be able to do it? If so, what kind of quality would you expect to see in their finished manuscripts? How much continuity would you expect to see among the books in the collection?

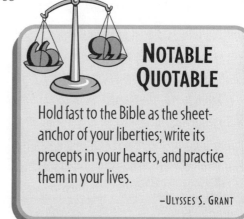

NOTABLE QUOTABLE

Hold fast to the Bible as the sheet-anchor of your liberties; write its precepts in your hearts, and practice them in your lives.

–ULYSSES S. GRANT

What if it turned out that the people in the room had very little in common—occupationally, economically, and socially speaking—that some of them were members of a royal family, while others were too poor even to buy clothes for themselves? Do you think they would be able to find much common ground in their writings?

What if it turned out that few, if any, of them had any previous writing experience? How would that affect your expectations?

What if, instead of being in the same room together, this diverse array of (non)writers was scattered about? What if they lived in different cities, different regions, or even different countries? What if some of them didn't even speak the same language? How do you think that would affect their assignment?

What if the writers were separated not only by distance, but by time as well? What difference, if any, do you think a decade would make in the way two authors approached their assignment? What difference do you think a century would make? How about a millennium?

What if the forty or so strangers chosen for the assignment wrote their books at various points over a sixteen-hundred-year period, in different countries and different cultures, with little or no knowledge of what the other writers had done, were doing, or would do? What do you think the end result would be?

Finally, what if it turned out that those forty-plus randomly selected strangers, with little common ground and even less writing experience among them, managed to create, over the course of sixteen hundred years, a collection of sixty-six books so unified and so complete that it could withstand the intense scrutiny and skepticism of scholars for almost a thousand years?

How could we even begin to describe such an occurrence? With a "B"—followed closely by "I-B-L-E."

ON A PERSONAL NOTE

Here's a question for you to think about: How would your life be different today if the Bible were not the Word of God, but merely another book conceived and written by humans? Think not just in terms of immediate, personal implications, but also in more universal terms. For example, if the Bible were not the Word of God, our notion of holidays would be radically altered. After all, why do we celebrate Christmas? Because the Bible tells us that Jesus was born under absolutely unique circumstances and for an absolutely essential purpose. Why do we celebrate Easter? Because the Bible tells us that Jesus emerged from His grave three days after being executed. Without the Word of God, our culture would be radically different.

The nature of the Bible's information can only be explained by divine involvement.

The Bible was indeed written over a period of 1,600 years. The earliest books of the Old Testament were written around 1500 B.C., and the final books of the New Testament were completed in the first century A.D. Forty or so writers, from widely diverse backgrounds, were involved in recording it. Few of the writers had access to the works of the others.

Yet somehow they managed to produce a work that is . . .

> unified,

> complementary,

> precise,

> accurate, and

> without a single contradiction or mistake.

NOTABLE QUOTABLE

I have found in the Bible words for my inmost thoughts, songs for my joy, utterance for my hidden griefs and pleadings for my shame and feebleness.

–SAMUEL TAYLOR COLERIDGE

What's more, the evidence of fulfilled prophecy fairly screams of God's involvement. Old Testament writers accurately predicted events, such as the coming of the Messiah, that would occur hundreds, even thousands, of years in the future—right down to specific details.

For example . . .

> Seven hundred years before Jesus' birth, Micah predicted that the Messiah would be born in Bethlehem (Micah 5:2). Luke 2:1–7 explains why Joseph and Mary were in Bethlehem when Jesus was born.

> Five hundred years before Judas betrayed Jesus, Zechariah predicted that the Messiah would be sold for thirty pieces of silver (Zechariah 11:13). Matthew 26:15 reveals that Judas was paid thirty silver coins for delivering Jesus into the hands of the Jewish and Roman authorities.

➤ Seven hundred years before Jesus was put on trial, Isaiah predicted that the Messiah would remain silent in the face of His accusers (Isaiah 53:7). Matthew 27:14 says that "Jesus made no reply" to the false charges brought against Him during His trial.

➤ One thousand years before Jesus was crucified, David predicted that the Messiah would suffer agonizing thirst (Psalm 22:15). John 19:28 tells us that one of Jesus' last statements on the cross was, "I am thirsty."

You can find dozens of other fulfilled prophecies like these scattered throughout Scripture.

There is no rational explanation for the Bible's creation and content that does not involve God's direction. Unless we're prepared to chalk it up to random chance or lucky guesses, we must acknowledge that the Bible *is* the Word of God.

NOTABLE QUOTABLE

It contains light to direct you, food to support you, and comfort to cheer you. It is the traveler's guide, the pilgrim's staff, the pilot's compass, the soldier's sword, the Christian's character.

—AUTHOR UNKNOWN

The evidence of changed lives points to the supernatural aspect of Scripture.

The Bible is *the* most influential book ever written. You could float that opinion to a hundred different people and probably not get much argument about it. It's safe to say that no other book in history has had even a fraction of the Bible's impact on the world. The words and principles of Scripture have played an integral role in the fields of medicine, law, philosophy, art, music, literature, and even pop culture.

Yet its influence in society pales in comparison to its influence in the lives of those who study it. Millions and millions of people have been *completely transformed* by the words of Scripture. They've found in the pages of the Bible . . .

➤ comfort,

➤ direction,

➤ peace,

➤ forgiveness, and

➤ self-worth

. . . that they couldn't find anywhere else.

The kind of changes that we're talking about can't be attributed to human wisdom. The effect that the Bible has on those who immerse themselves in it can only be described as *supernatural*. The involvement of a loving, all-knowing God is the only plausible explanation for it.

Of course, any discussion of lives that are changed by Scripture must include the accounts of the writers themselves. History tells us that six of the eight known New Testament writers were put to death because of their Christian beliefs. There's compelling evidence right there. After all, no one would die for something he knew to be the product of his own imagination! Obviously the writers of the New Testament—and the writers of the Old Testament, for that matter—believed that they had recorded the Word of God.

ON A PERSONAL NOTE

Take some time to think about this question: What impact has the Bible had on your life? If you keep a journal, write your answer in it. Be as specific as possible in responding to the question. Think about how your life would be different if you knew nothing about God, His will, or the principles in His Word. Later you can use the responses you come up with in a special prayer session in which you praise the Lord for His Word and thank Him for the impact it's had in your life.

Implications

The fact that the Bible is God's Word isn't something that can be casually acknowledged in passing and then forgotten. Think about it. What could be more intriguing or more thought-provoking than knowing we have direct access to the wisdom and instruction of the all-knowing, all-powerful, loving Creator?

The fact that the Bible is of divine origin—that it comes from a perfect source—presents us with a set of inescapable facts that we must consider. Let's take a look at four of them.

1. The Bible is trustworthy.

The fact that the Bible is God's Word means that it is as truthful and dependable as He is. That's good news for those of us who put our faith in Scripture, because God is the *standard* of truth and dependability. Titus 1:2 tells us that "God does not lie." Hebrews 6:18 takes the concept one step further by saying, "It is *impossible* for God to lie" (emphasis added).

NOTABLE QUOTABLE

Defend the Bible? I would as soon defend a lion! Unchain it and it will defend itself.

–C. H. Spurgeon

Psalm 12:6 tells us that the "the words of the LORD are flawless, like silver refined in a furnace of clay, purified seven times." Bible scholars refer to the "flawless" nature of Scripture as *inerrancy*. Defining inerrancy, however, is one of those nitpicky tasks that often raises more questions than it answers. For the purposes of this chapter, we'll simply suggest that the Bible always tells the truth concerning everything it talks about.

Skeptics are quick to seize on apparent irregularities, misquotes, or mistakes in Scripture as proof that it can't be trusted. For example . . .

➤ First Corinthians 10:8, referring to an infamous event in Israel's history, says that 23,000 people died in one day; Numbers 25:9, however, puts the death toll at 24,000.

➤ in 1 Corinthians 2:9, the apostle Paul quotes Isaiah 64:4 as "No eye has seen, no ear has heard, no mind has conceived what God has prepared for those who love him"; however, the actual verse in Isaiah reads, "Since ancient times no one has heard, no ear has perceived, no eye has seen any God besides you, who acts on behalf of those who wait for him."

➤ Matthew 20:29–34 describes how Jesus healed two blind men as He was leaving Jericho; Mark 10:46–52 and Luke 18:35–43, describing the same event, mention only one blind man (whom Mark identifies as Bartimaeus).

The question is, are these and other "problem passages" enough to make us reevaluate the Bible's inerrancy and trustworthiness? Before you answer, consider a few possibilities:

➤ First Corinthians 10:8 includes the phrase "in one day"; is it possible that another thousand people died the next day as a result of the plague?

➤ The Holy Spirit is ultimately the originator of both the Old Testament quote and the New Testament paraphrase; does He have the freedom to quote Himself as He wishes?

➤ Neither Mark nor Luke says that *only* one blind man was healed; is it possible that they chose to focus only on Bartimaeus?

Maybe these explanations satisfy you; maybe they don't. Maybe you can come up with better ones. That's not the point.

The point is that anyone who questions the inerrancy and trustworthiness of the Bible based on a few passages that *seem* contradictory or confusing is putting his or her own intelligence and reasoning skills above the perfect wisdom of God. In essence, it's a matter of saying, "If I can't reconcile this issue with what I know, it proves the Bible is untrustworthy."

Wrong. It proves human intelligence and reasoning is imperfect, incomplete, and occasionally unreliable. There's nothing wrong with questioning why certain passages don't jibe with what we know from other passages—as long as our questioning doesn't cause us to lose sight of the fact that the Bible and the truths it contains are ultimately and absolutely trustworthy.

2. The Bible is understandable.

Psalm 19:7b says, "The statutes of the LORD are trustworthy, making wise the simple." Psalm 119:130 says, "The unfolding of your words gives light; it gives understanding to the simple." Both of these passages offer noteworthy affirmation of the power of Scripture and helpful encouragement regarding the prospect of spiritual growth.

NOTABLE QUOTABLE

Men do not reject the Bible because it contradicts itself but because it contradicts them.

–AUTHOR UNKNOWN

Yet there's also an unspoken assumption in both passages that we shouldn't miss, and that is that the "simple" are able to understand God's Word.

Deuteronomy 6:6–7 takes the concept to the next level. "These commandments that I give you today are to be upon your hearts. Impress them on your children. Talk about them when you sit at home and when you walk along the road, when you lie down and when you get up." The point is, even *children* are able to understand Scripture, when it's presented properly.

That's not to say that the Bible is easy to understand. In fact, all indications are that the Bible was never intended to be a "piece of cake." Sure, passages such as John 3:16 and Romans 3:23 are pretty straightforward and easily grasped. Other passages, though, require a little more time and effort in order to be fully understood. Even the apostle Peter admitted as much. Check out what he said of the apostle Paul in 2 Peter 3:16: "His letters contain some things that are hard to understand."

The two keys to grasping Scripture are attitude and effort. First of all, we must approach Bible study with a genuine desire to understand God and His Word. David demonstrated the ideal attitude in Psalm 42:1: "As the deer pants for streams of water, so my soul pants for you, O God."

Second, we must be willing to put in the necessary work for understanding Scripture. That means actively seeking out God's truth—meditating on certain words and phrases; doing extra "legwork" in Bible dictionaries, concordances, and commentaries; sprinkling our study with liberal amounts of prayer—instead of passively waiting for it to dawn on us.

The Lord rewards diligent, genuine effort. That's why Jesus said, "Ask and it will be given to you; seek and you will find; knock and the door will be opened to you" (Matthew 7:7). If you really want to understand God's Word, and are willing to do

JUST WONDERING

What should I do if I have trouble understanding a passage of Scripture?

Don't forget that you have an "in house" Bible teacher in the Holy Spirit, who dwells within every believer. First Corinthians 2:9-11 suggests that the Holy Spirit assists believers in understanding the "deep things of God." That would certainly include Scripture. Before you read the Bible, spend some time in prayer, asking the Holy Spirit to help you understand what you'll be studying. You might also want to talk to a pastor, Sunday school teacher, or mature Christian about any problem passages you encounter.

the work involved, God will bless your efforts and "open the door" to comprehension.

3. The Bible is necessary.

Everything we know about the gospel message—including the pervasiveness of sin, the penalty for it, the love of God for sinners, the sacrificial death of His Son, the Resurrection, the promise of eternal life—comes from the Bible. The Bible is necessary first of all, then, because there is no possibility of saving faith apart from a knowledge of God's Word.

The Bible is also necessary for living a life that is pleasing to God. Jesus said, "Man does not live on bread alone, but on every word that comes from the mouth of God" (Matthew 4:4). First Peter 1:23–2:3 ties God's Word to spiritual maturity. Without the Bible, spiritual growth cannot occur.

> **NOTABLE QUOTABLE**
>
> God did not write a book and send it by messenger to be read at a distance by unaided minds. He spoke a Book and lives in His spoken words, constantly speaking His words and causing the power of them to persist across the years.
>
> —A. W. Tozer

4. The Bible is sufficient.

Everything that God intends us to know about Himself, His work and His will are contained in His Word. So are His plan of salvation and His plans for the future.

Second Timothy 3:16–17 offers this assurance: "All Scripture is God-breathed and is useful for teaching, rebuking, correcting and training in righteousness, so that the man of God may be thoroughly equipped for every good work." Talk about an all-purpose tool! All that's needed for a person of God to be *thoroughly equipped* is Scripture.

There are no sequels, addendums, or amendments to God's Word. What's more, no other book may be considered the *equal* of the Bible or even *essential* for understanding it. All we *need* is Scripture.

That's not to say we can't learn things about the Christian life or discover different perspectives on certain issues from other sources. Christian bookstores are full of helpful, highly recommended resources. But they are all supplements to the Bible. None of them is indispensable to our spiritual well-being or relationship with the Lord.

A Truly Inspired Piece of Writing

JUST WONDERING

I'm a Christian, but I've never really studied the Bible before. Where should I start?

Here are four potential starting places for you to consider:

1. The Gospel According to Matthew. This first book of the New Testament will get you acquainted with the life, teachings, and miracles of Jesus.

2. The book of Romans. This book offers a lot of great information about what it means to be a Christian.

3. The book of James. If you're looking for practical advice on improving your relationship with Christ, this is the book for you.

4. Hebrews 11. This passage, commonly known as the "Faith Hall of Fame," lists more than a dozen people in the Bible who were deemed especially faithful by God. Find out why.

Throughout this chapter (and this book), you'll find phrases such as "the apostle Paul said" or "the apostle Peter wrote" or "the author of Hebrews suggests," which would seem to contradict the notion of the Bible as *God's* Word. If it's His Word, one might ask, why did He let guys like Matthew, Mark, Luke, and John put their names on parts of it?

The answer can be found in the doctrine of *inspiration*. Second Peter 1:20–21 lays the groundwork: "Above all, you must understand that no prophecy of Scripture came about by the prophet's own interpretation. For prophecy never had its origin in the will of man, but men spoke from God as they were carried along by the Holy Spirit."

God is the creator of the Bible. He alone determined what would be included in it. However, He did not physically *write* it. For that task, He tapped forty or so of His human followers. God revealed His truth to them in very specific and very clear ways, and then allowed them to express that truth using their own individual styles of communication.

God did not, however, turn control of the project over to His writers. He monitored their work, making sure that they did not misrepresent Him or miscommunicate His truth. The fact that God is omniscient, or all-knowing, means that nothing in the original manuscripts could have slipped by Him without His knowing it. Therefore, we can have confidence in the fact that the information in the Bible is there because God wants it to be there.

Opening the Gift

Acknowledging that the Bible is God's Word—and His gift to us—is an empty gesture if we don't then commit ourselves to learning everything we can about it. A gift from God isn't like a gift from a distant cousin or a great aunt. It can't be dismissed or discarded simply because it doesn't seem "right" for us.

NOTABLE QUOTABLE

The greatest proof that the Bible is inspired is that it has stood so much bad preaching.

–A. T. ROBERTSON

God's Word can do nothing for us on a shelf. If we're serious about wanting to understand God, we must make the Bible a priority in our lives. Remember, it's all there in Scripture— every tantalizing truth and nugget of information that God wants us to know about Himself. And it's ours for the taking.

Know What You Believe

How much do you know about the Bible? Here's a quiz to test your knowledge.

1. Which of the following is not compelling evidence for the fact that the Bible is God's Word?
   a. Its internal claims
   b. The circumstances of its creation
   c. The number of churches with "Bible" in their name
   d. The lives that have been changed because of it

2. Which of the following is not true of the Bible?
   a. It was written over a period of sixteen hundred years.
   b. It was written by forty or so different people from widely diverse backgrounds.
   c. It contains dozens of prophecies that were fulfilled hundreds of years after they were made.

    d. It was originally supposed to be made up of sixty-*eight* books, but two of them had to be cut because they were too different from the others.

3. Which of the following terms does not apply to the nature of Scripture?
    a. Understandable
    b. Satirical
    c. Sufficient
    d. Necessary

4. Which of the following is not an actual prophecy fulfilled in the Bible?
    a. The Messiah would be recognized by His height and His unusual facial hair.
    b. The Messiah would be sold for thirty pieces of silver.
    c. The Messiah would remain silent in the face of His accusers.
    d. The Messiah would be born in Bethlehem.

5. How should we respond to seeming inconsistencies or discrepancies in the Bible?
    a. By acknowledging that God's perfect wisdom supersedes our human intelligence and understanding
    b. By carefully removing all offending passages with a pen knife
    c. By refusing to read the Bible until they are resolved
    d. By replacing certain words and phrases with others that make more sense to us

Answers: (1) c, (2) d, (3) b, (4) a, (5) a

In the Beginning

UNDERSTANDING GOD'S WORK IN CREATION

SNAPSHOT

"Admiring yourself?" Clara asked.

Lindsay closed the mirror on the car visor and loosened her seat belt so that she could turn to face Clara. "No, actually, I was just thinking about how incredible God's creation is."

"I see He blessed you with a pretty healthy ego." Clara laughed.

"No," Lindsay said. "I'm not saying *I'm* an incredible creation. I'm talking about the little details in creation, the things we take for granted."

"Like what?" Clara asked.

"Like our eyes, for instance," Lindsay replied. "Do you know how many different processes have to occur and how many different parts have to work together in order for us to see?"

SNEAK PREVIEW

1. Genesis 1–2 makes it clear that God created the world according to His specific design.
2. Science offers tantalizing evidence that the earth is much older than many creationists believe but cannot offer definitive proof of the nature of its origin.
3. Because of the lack of definitive proof, the theory of evolution requires just as much faith on the part of its supporters as creationism does.

"Three hundred and seventeen," Clara replied.

Lindsay stared at her but said nothing.

Clara shrugged. "Hey, it *could* be three hundred and seventeen—you don't know."

Lindsay sighed and rolled her eyes. "As I was *saying*, I don't understand how someone could believe that something as complicated as our eyes could have just randomly evolved out of nothing. The way our bodies work is just too incredible to be an accident."

"Zits," Clara said.

"What?"

"Zits are like that too," Clara repeated.

"What are you *talking* about?" Lindsay sputtered.

"The way zits instinctively know when you have a big date," Clara explained, "and then pop out all at the same time the night before. That's not something that happens by chance either."

"I should have known better than to mention this to you," Lindsay muttered.

"Come on, I'm joking!" Clara explained. "I agree with you. I don't know how people can say we come from fish or monkeys or whatever."

"I know!" Lindsay agreed. "I mean, I understand how they could say it about my brother and his friends, but not about people like us."

Clara laughed. "I've got to admit, though, there are some parts of creation that I don't understand," she said.

"Such as?" Lindsay asked.

"Well, for example, I don't know why God made it so that my esophagus empties directly into my hips," Clara explained. "Everything I eat goes straight there and stays there."

Lindsay laughed. "I know what you're talking about. Except, with me, it's an elbow problem."

"An elbow problem?" Clara asked.

"Yeah," Lindsay explained, "every time my elbow bends, my mouth opens."

* * * * * * * * * * * * * *

"In the beginning God created the heavens and the earth."

That's how the Lord chose to begin His Word. That's the first thing He wanted made clear when people opened the Bible. It's Roman numeral "I" in the outline of Scripture.

You'd be hard-pressed to find a more straightforward statement in either Testament. The construction of the sentence is as simple and clear as a statement like, "Last Thursday Joyce knitted a scarf." In just ten words, Genesis 1:1 manages to answer three of the five questions of basic journalism:

> ➤ Who? ("God")

> ➤ What? ("created the heavens and the earth")

> ➤ When? ("In the beginning")

Yet, for all of its simplicity, few sentences in the history of the recorded word have inspired as much controversy and debate as Genesis 1:1. The problem is not what the verse *says*, but what it *doesn't* say. The fourth basic journalism question, *where?* is irrelevant; however, the fifth one, *how?* is vital.

NOTABLE QUOTABLE

No philosophical theory which I have yet come across is a radical improvement on the words of Genesis, that "in the beginning God made heaven and earth."

–C. S. LEWIS

That's the question we're going to address in this chapter: "*How* did God create the universe?" We're going to explore the topic from a biblical perspective, a "scientific" perspective, and a perspective that combines the two, in order to better understand the *who*, the Creator of all.

In the Beginning God

Beyond Genesis 1:1, the Bible divides God's creative work into six days. On each day, He performed a specific act of creation. Let's take a look at God's schedule for the first week of recorded history in order to get a sense of what He did and when:

Day 1
God called forth light, separated light from darkness, and called the light "day" and the darkness "night."

Day 2
God created an "expanse"—the sky or firmament—in order to separate "the water under the expanse from the water above it."

Day 3
God gathered the waters on the earth in one place and called for dry land to appear. He called the dry ground "land" and the waters "seas." He called for the land to produce vegetation—plants and trees.

Day 4
God created the heavenly bodies, including "the greater light to govern the day" (the sun), "the lesser light to govern the night" (the moon), and the stars.

Day 5
God created birds and sea creatures and instructed them to populate the earth and the waters.

Day 6
God created land animals, from livestock to wildlife. He created man to rule over the earth and all of the creatures on it.

The division of days and even the very definition of a "day" will come into play later in the chapter. For the time being, though, let's consider four facts concerning God's six-day creative spree, as recorded in Genesis 1.

1. *Creation was a verbal act.* God didn't wave a magic wand or point His finger and let loose a mighty *zap* as He created the various elements of the universe. Instead, He simply *spoke* the world into existence. The description of each day

of creation begins with the phrase "God said." The power of God's words—and that power alone—is responsible for our existence and the existence of everything around us.

2. *The universe came into existence in obedience to God's command.* Genesis 1 records the phrase "And it was so" six times as the response to God's verbal act of creation. In other words, the physical universe had no choice but to obey God's commands. The earth, the sky, the oceans, the sun, the moon, the stars, plants, animals, and humans were all compelled to come forth exactly as God directed. His creation demonstrates His power over everything.

3. *Creation occurred* ex nihilo. *Ex nihilo* is a Latin phrase meaning "out of nothing." The idea is that before God created the universe, there was nothing. Nothing existed but God Himself. He had no raw materials to work with, no blueprint, no model to follow. He brought absolutely everything in the universe into existence.

4. *God was pleased with what He created.* According to Genesis 1, on six occasions during His work of creation, God looked at the results of His labor and "saw that it was good." Genesis 1:31 says, "God saw *all* that he had made, and it was very good" (italics added). The fact that God was satisfied with His labor suggests that the design and result were exactly as He intended.

The fact that God finds delight in His creation means that we should too. Despite the fact that the universe has been tainted by our sin and the results of it, we can still glorify God for His incredible work of creation.

ON A PERSONAL NOTE

Here's an exercise you might want to incorporate into your devotional or quiet time. Make a habit of listing in your journal ten things that are "good" about creation (echoing God's pronouncements in Genesis 1). Be as specific as possible in your praise. Here are some ideas to get you started:

➤ The way water tastes when you're really thirsty

➤ The way an apple tastes when you're really hungry

➤ The way "butterflies in the stomach" feel when you're in love

Make a conscious effort not to repeat yourself in your list. This will encourage you to continuously look for new and praiseworthy details in the world around you.

Traditional creationism promotes a literal interpretation of Genesis 1. That is, God accomplished the work of creation in six successive, twenty-four days.

You Say You Want an Evolution?

If creationism, the belief that God brought the universe into existence, lies at one end of the origin-theory spectrum, evolution lies at the other. Generally speaking, evolution is the belief that the universe came into existence through random chance over a period of indefinite time.

We're not going to go into a lot of detail regarding the various theories of evolution in this chapter. We will, however, address some of its main points for the sake of contrast and comparison with creationism.

The "big bang" theory suggests that the universe originated from a mass of rotating protons and neutrons that eventually compressed and exploded. This explosion, or "big bang," caused particles to expand away from the original mass at incredible speeds. Those particles eventually became the universe as we know it.

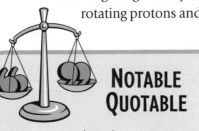

NOTABLE QUOTABLE

One must conclude that, contrary to the established and current wisdom, a scenario describing the genesis of life on earth by chance and natural causes which can be accepted on the basis of fact and not faith has not yet been written.

–Dr. Hubert P. Yockey

From there, evolutionists contend that on one of the billions of spheres hurtling through space in the aftermath of the "big bang," conditions—including sunlight, water, and air—became just right to sustain a living organism. Thus, completely by chance, a single cell appeared from nonliving matter.

That single cell, evolutionists theorize, developed—through gradual and complicated mutations and natural selection—into plants, animals, and people. In other words, the living world as we know it today evolved from that first single-celled organism.

Obviously, this is a simplification of a very complex theory, and scholars may disagree on certain specific points. However, it does give us an accurate representation of how other people explain the origin of the universe.

The problem with the traditional theory of evolution, as far as Christians are concerned, is obvious: It leaves no room for a Creator. "In the beginning God" becomes, "In the beginning a molecular mass."

Scripture is extremely consistent in its portrayal of the beginning of the universe. Passages such as the following leave little room for doubt as to where the credit for the universe is supposed to go:

➤ "By the word of the LORD were the heavens made, their starry host by the breath of his mouth. . . . For he spoke, and it came to be; he commanded and it stood firm" (Psalm 33:6, 9).

➤ "Through him all things were made; without him nothing was made that has been made" (John 1:3).

➤ "'Sovereign Lord,' they said, 'you made the heaven and the earth and the sea, and everything in them'" (Acts 4:24b).

➤ "For by him all things were created: things in heaven and on earth, visible and invisible, whether thrones or powers or rulers or authorities; all things were created by him and for him" (Colossians 1:16).

➤ "You are worthy, our Lord and God, to receive glory and honor and power, for you created all things, and by your will they were created and have their being" (Revelation 4:11).

Keep in mind too that God is not One to share His glory (Exodus 20:4–5). The universe is His creation; He deserves all glory and praise for it. To give credit anywhere else—even to a random mass of particles—is to rob God of His due. And that's never a good idea.

A Matter of Timing

Creationists generally believe that the earth was created between 6,000 and 20,000 years ago. They base that number on the genealogies and life spans recorded in Scripture. The Bible provides fairly detailed lists of who begat whom and when. By adding the ages of the people on the lists and creating a time line based on the known dates of certain other events—and by accounting for "gaps" in the genealogical record—many creationists put the age of the earth (in years) in the low five-digit range.

Evolutionists, on the other hand, suggest that the earth's age is about 4,500,000,000 years and the universe's age is about 15,000,000,000 years—that's 15 billion years. They base their estimates on evidence gathered from . . .

JUST WONDERING

What is theistic evolution?

Some Christians have attempted to combine the two theories regarding the origin of the universe by suggesting that the world came into existence through the process of evolution–with God's guidance. In other words, God stepped in at various points of the evolutionary process–specifically, at the creation of matter, the creation of the earliest life form, and the creation of man–to make sure that things progressed according to His will. Advocates of this position point out that it satisfies the demands of both camps. Detractors, however, point out that the description in Genesis 1 suggests a series of purposeful creative acts, instead of the passive randomness that is evolution.

➤ deep space observation, examining the origin and activity of stars and other astronomical phenomena. For example, the length of time required for the light of stars to reach the earth would seem to necessitate that the earth is at least millions and millions of years old.

➤ geological excavation, studying the arrangement of fossils in rock formations. For example, the time and pressure required to form certain metamorphic rocks that contain small fossils necessitate that they be buried twelve to eighteen miles under-ground before being brought to the surface—a process that would take millions and millions of years.

➤ radiometric testing, using state-of-the-art methods to determine the age of various materials. For example, though some scientists argue that radiometric dating techniques are skewed by the changes that occurred on the earth during the Flood, other scientists have found that tests on meteorites and rocks brought back from the moon—which wouldn't have been affected by the Flood—consistently point to an age close to 4.5 billion years.

Needless to say, there's quite a difference between the two estimates. (However, the first point of agreement between the two camps should be that the earth would do very well at one of those "guess your age" booths found at amusement parks and fairs.)

Aging the Earth

How do we account for such disparate estimates? If we reject the theory of evolution, how do we explain the scientific evidence that suggests that the earth is much, much older than creationists give it credit for?

Bible scholars have suggested several different possibilities. Let's take a look at three of the best-known "old earth" theories.

The Gap Theory

Advocates of this view suggest that there is a gap of millions of years between Genesis 1:1 ("In the beginning God created the heavens and the earth") and Genesis 1:2 ("now the earth was formless and empty, darkness was over the surface of the deep"). During that time, "gap" theorists contend, God's original creation—the one described in Genesis 1:1—was judged by Him, perhaps in relation to Satan's rebellion. As a result, the earth became formless and empty.

ON A PERSONAL NOTE

First Peter 3:15 instructs believers to "always be prepared to give an answer to everyone who asks you to give the reason for the hope that you have." Toward that end, you should familiarize yourself with the issues and arguments surrounding the creation-versus-evolution debate. If you can make an effective case for God's creative work, you may find yourself with an opportunity to talk about His saving work as well.

This theory satisfies the demands of creationism because it contends that Genesis 1:3–2:3 describes six literal, twenty-four-hour days of creation—though, in this case, it would be God's *second* creation. The theory also satisfies the evidence of the fossil record because the animals from the first creation would have been dead for millions of years before the second creation.

Arguing against the gap theory is the fact that no verse in Scripture specifically mentions two different acts of creation. In fact, passages such as Exodus 20:11 ("For in six days the LORD made the heavens and the earth, the sea, and all that is in them") seem to directly contradict the notion of a second creation.

The Day-Age Theory

Proponents of this theory believe that the word *day* in the creation account of Genesis 1 does not refer to a twenty-four-hour period, but to an entire *age*— possibly as long as millions of years. Instead of creation being completed over the course of 144 hours, day-age theorists suggest that it was completed over the course of millions and millions of years.

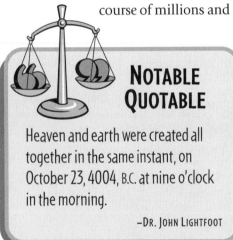

NOTABLE QUOTABLE

Heaven and earth were created all together in the same instant, on October 23, 4004, B.C. at nine o'clock in the morning.

–Dr. John Lightfoot

This theory satisfies the requirements of creationism because it maintains that God is responsible for the origin of the universe, as is described in Genesis 1. The theory also satisfies the old-age requirements suggested by scientific testing.

Problems with the day-age theory include the fact that the sequence of God's creative acts described in Genesis 1 doesn't correspond to the current scientific understanding of how life developed. For example, scientists believe that sea creatures predate plant life on earth by millions of years. However, in Genesis 1, plant life is created on Day 3 and sea creatures don't appear until Day 5.

More significant is the fact that, according to the sequence in Genesis 1, plant life on the earth appeared (on Day 3) before the creation of the sun and the moon (on Day 4). If we're talking about millions of years for each "day," how did the plants survive without the sun? What's more, how did the waters on the earth keeping from freezing without the sun's heat?

The Literary Framework Theory

Advocates of this theory suggest that the description of creation in Genesis 1 is not intended as a chronological account, but as a "literary framework" to illustrate God's creative work. According to theorists, the framework is designed so that the first, second, and third "days" correspond with the fifth, sixth, and seventh "days."

For example, on the first day, light is separated from darkness; on the fifth day, the sun and moon are created. On the second day, the waters are separated by the sky; on the sixth day, fish and birds appear. On the third day, land and water are separated. On the sixth day, land animals and man are created.

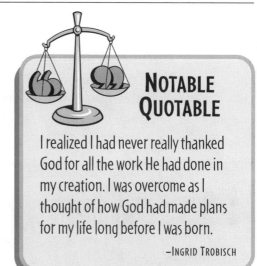

NOTABLE QUOTABLE

I realized I had never really thanked God for all the work He had done in my creation. I was overcome as I thought of how God had made plans for my life long before I was born.

—INGRID TROBISCH

The literary framework theory satisfies the basic requirement for creationism by acknowledging that God is responsible for creation. It avoids disagreement with scientific evidence by ignoring the issue of chronology altogether. The literary framework view offers no theories as to *when* the events of creation took place.

The primary argument against this theory is that the text of Genesis 1 doesn't seem to suggest a literary interpretation. The events of Genesis 1 make sense in a chronological way. In fact, the very act of numbering the days of creation sequentially seems to suggest that it should be interpreted chronologically.

What's more, in Exodus 20:8–11, God's people are commanded to follow His example of working six days and resting on the seventh. If God did not work six successive days during creation, that command doesn't make sense.

Younger Than It Looks

Many Christians would argue that the fact that the earth *appears* to be billions of years old does not mean that it is, in fact, billions of years old. In fact, they see no problem in putting the earth's age at 20,000 years or less, despite its aged appearance.

There are two primary theories used to support a "young earth" view. Let's take a look at each one.

Mature Creationism

Advocates of mature creationism suggest that God, in His original creative work, gave everything in the universe the appearance of age. They point to the fact that Adam and Eve were not formed as babies, but as mature adults. Likewise, in the Genesis 1 account of creation, animals, plants, and trees all have the appearance of age and maturity.

How much of a stretch is it, proponents ask, to believe that God created geological formations with the appearance of age too? Or that He created stars with their light beams to earth already in place? If that's the case, it could account for the disparity in ages suggested by the Bible and science. The earth seems old because God determined that it would seem old.

Opponents of this position point out that even if God did give His creation the appearance of age, He wouldn't have gone so far as to "plant" fossil evidence that animal life existed hundreds of thousands of years before it actually did. Such deception would be completely out of character for the "God of truth" (Psalm 31:5).

Supporters of mature creationism are left with the question, If the earth isn't really 4.5 billion years old, why does it appear that way? The two most credible answers are:

1. The current scientific methods for determining age are severely flawed.

2. Some cataclysmic event in the earth's history upset the natural order of things to the point that accurate interpretation through science isn't possible.

The first option certainly falls within the realm of possibility. Scientific thought is fluid, constantly updating, revising, and correcting itself. It's possible that what we accept as fact regarding radiometric testing today may be scoffed at fifty years from now. Where human thought is involved, error is always a possibility.

The second option leads us to the next "young earth" theory.

Flood Geology

This view suggests that the catastrophic forces unleashed during God's judgment of the earth in Genesis 6–8 significantly altered the face of the planet. Advocates of this view suggest that the tremendous pressure of the water that covered the earth was enough to speed up certain natural

NOTABLE QUOTABLE

No rain, no mushrooms. No God, no world.

—AFRICAN PROVERB

processes by as much as hundreds of millions of years. (Talk about getting old overnight!) What's more, they argue that the Flood left fossils buried in incredibly deep sediment. When the sediment hardened, the result was our current fossil record.

Proponents of flood geology contend that the result of such cataclysmic changes in the earth makes it impossible for scientists today to accurately gauge its age.

Origin-al Thinking

Regardless of which position makes the most sense to you, the issue of God's creative work in the world comes down to one word: *could*.

➤ *Could* God have created the world in six successive twenty-four-hour days?

➤ *Could* God have accomplished creation by waiting millions of years between each day of creation?

➤ *Could* God have brought the universe into existence over the course of six different ages that the Bible calls "days"?

➤ *Could* God have given the universe the appearance of age without being deceptive?

➤ *Could* God have altered the face of the earth with His flood to the point that we can no longer trust our scientific evaluation of it?

➤ *Could* our entire understanding of God's creation be flawed?

The answers, in no particular order, are: yes, yes, of course, yes, yes, and absolutely. The bottom line is that God created the universe. And if we never learn anything else about creation, that should be enough to satisfy us and provoke our praise for the rest of our lives.

JUST WONDERING

So what should we believe about God's creation?

The final word on the matter of the age of the earth and the manner in which it was created is … that there is no final word on the matter. It may very well be that God does not intend us to know the details of His creative work until we're done with this life. That's not to say that we shouldn't continue our pursuit of knowledge concerning creation. It is to say, however, that we should guard against intellectual arrogance, believing that our way of thinking is the only way of thinking for "true" Christians.

Evolution: A Matter of Faith

The ongoing debate between creationists and evolutionists is often characterized as a matter of faith versus reason, and dismissed with the notion that creation requires unsupported belief in a higher power while evolution can be proven by scientific evidence.

It's time to refute that characterization once and for all. The fact is, evolution requires every bit as much faith as creation does. No one has tangible, irrefutable proof of how the universe originated. Even the most dedicated creationists will admit that there are some aspects of creation they cannot fully explain. Even the staunchest evolutionists will admit that the odds of the universe and life on this planet being created according to their theories go beyond astronomical and into the realm of the unbelievable.

The issue isn't whether you must rely on faith or not; the issue is what you choose to place your faith in.

Know What You Believe

How much do you know about God's work of creation? Here's a quiz to test your knowledge.

1. Which of the five basic journalism questions is not answered in Genesis 1:1?
   a. Who?
   b. What?
   c. When?
   d. How?

2. What is the significance of the phrase *ex nihilo?*
   a. It describes how God created the universe out of nothing.
   b. It is the only Latin phrase spoken by God in the entire Bible.
   c. It's how someone who is a former "nihilo" refers to himself or herself.
   d. It was originally intended to be one word, but no one knows what the missing letter is between "x" and "n."

3. Which of the following statements is not true concerning the age of the earth?
   a. Many creationists estimate it to be 6,000–20,000 years.
   b. The Bible does not tell us how old the earth is.
   c. If you believe that God was involved in creation, you cannot date the earth as any older than 50,000 years.
   d. Many evolutionists estimate it to be 4,500,000,000 years.

4. Which of the following is not one of the "old age" theories used to explain why the earth could be 4.5 billion years old?
   a. The Face-Lift View
   b. The Day-Age View
   c. The Literary Framework View
   d. The Gap Theory

5. Which of the following statements does not support a "young earth" view?
   a. The tremendous pressure of the water that covered the earth during the Flood was enough to speed up certain natural processes by as much as hundreds of millions of years.

   b. God, in His original creative work, gave everything in the universe the
      appearance of age.
   c. The Flood left fossils buried in incredibly deep sediment that eventually
      hardened, creating our fossil record.
   d. Current scientific methods for determining the earth's age are beyond
      reproach.

Answers: (1) d, (2) a, (3) c, (4) a, (5) d

Undeserved and Unearned

UNDERSTANDING GOD'S WORK OF SALVATION

SNEAK PREVIEW

1. Our sin creates a chasm between us and God; as sinners, we are powerless to bridge that chasm, creating the need for salvation.

2. Jesus' sacrifice and His victory over sin and death makes Him the only means of salvation for the human race. Those who believe in Him are saved; those who don't are condemned.

3. God's plan of salvation involves election, a gospel call, regeneration, conversion, justification, adoption, sanctification, perseverance, death, and glorification.

SNAPSHOT

"I believe good people go to heaven and bad people go to hell," Jeff explained. "And I don't know why you and your church friends have to make it more complicated than that with your prayer and baptism and stuff."

"Good people go to heaven and bad people go to hell," David repeated. "Which category do you put yourself in?"

"The good one, of course," Jeff emphasized. "Why—what have you heard?"

David shrugged. "Let's just say I know you've done some things that are deserving of hell."

"Says who?" Jeff challenged.

"Paul."

"Paul? You mean that skinny guy who plays softball with us?" Jeff asked. "Look, if he told you about the time we . . ."

"No, no, no—not *that* Paul," David interrupted. "I'm talking about the *apostle* Paul, the guy who wrote most of the New Testament."

"And he talked about me?" Jeff asked with a confused look on his face.

"Actually, he talked about people *like* you," David corrected.

"People *like me?*" Jeff asked with a slight edge in his voice. "What's that supposed to mean?"

"Oh, you know, people who have done just enough to earn God's wrath," David explained.

"And you *know* that that includes me," Jeff challenged.

"Absolutely," David replied.

"What makes you such an expert on people who deserve hell?" Jeff asked.

"Because I'm one of them," David replied.

"You?!" Jeff roared. "What's the worst thing *you've* ever done—serve milk past its expiration date?"

"It doesn't really matter *what* I've done," David pointed out. "The thing is, I've sinned at least once in my life, and that makes me deserving of hell."

"*One* sin?" Jeff asked. "You've got to be kidding me!"

"No, I'm not," David assured him. "That's why Paul said *all* have sinned and fall short of God's glory."

"Well, you seem pretty religious and Christian-y for someone who's on his way to hell," Jeff commented.

"Oh, I'm not going to hell," David corrected.

"I thought you said you've done things to deserve hell," Jeff said.

"I *have*," David emphasized. "I *do* deserve to go to hell. . . . But I'm not going."

"How's that possible?" Jeff asked.

David smiled. "I'm glad you asked."

* * * * * * * * * * * * * * *

The doctrine of salvation is complex enough to warrant its own field of theological study—called *soteriology*, by the way, in case the question ever comes up on *Jeopardy!* Yet it's simple enough to be accurately summarized in two words ("Jesus saves") or less ("John 3:16") by any rainbow-wigged, sign-carrying sports fan with a knack for making his presence known to a TV audience.

Regardless of how thoroughly you choose to explore the topic, you should recognize that understanding God is impossible apart from a personal knowledge of His work of salvation.

Holy, Holy, Holy

First, there is God's holiness. That's where the need for salvation begins. The fact that God is holy is emphasized throughout Scripture:

> ➤ "He is a holy God; he is a jealous God" (Joshua 24:19).

> ➤ "There is no one holy like the LORD" (1 Samuel 2:2).

> ➤ "Holy, holy, holy is the LORD Almighty" (Isaiah 6:3).

As we mentioned in chapter 3, the fact that God is holy means He can have nothing to do with sin or anything sinful. Where God is, sin cannot be. In other words, God's holiness creates a "gulf" or "chasm" between God and anyone tainted by sin.

Three Strikes

That's bad news for . . . well, every member of the human race. We've not only been *tainted* by sin; we're thoroughly saturated by it. Every person born into this world (with the exception of Jesus) is affected by sin in three different ways:

1. Our Relation to Adam's Sin

Romans 5:12 introduces a concept that, at first glance, seems unfair: "Sin entered the world through one man, and death through sin, and in this way death came to all men, because all sinned." That "one man" is Adam, and his disobedience brought sin to all of us.

The theological term for this concept is *imputed* sin. To *impute* means to "ascribe" or "attribute." In other words, God attributed Adam's original sin to all of us. Because Adam was guilty of sin, all of us are guilty of sin.

Some people believe that God imputes Adam's sin to us because Adam was our representative. Just as a representative in Congress acts on behalf of his constituents, Adam acted on our behalf when he disobeyed God's command in the Garden of Eden. He represented the entire human race before God. That's why when he acted sinfully, God viewed it as the entire human race acting sinfully.

Other people believe that God imputes Adam's sin to us because Adam carried the biological seed of all of us. From an organic standpoint, then, we were all part of Adam when he sinned; therefore, we are guilty of his sin as well.

As for the relative "fairness" of our being held accountable for someone else's sin, you might want to reserve judgment for a few more pages. If you think this example of imputed sin is unfair, you ain't seen nothin' yet.

NOTABLE QUOTABLE

The very animals whose smell is most offensive to us have no idea that they are offensive, and are not offensive to one another. And man, fallen man, has just no idea what a vile thing sin is in the sight of God.

–J. C. Ryle

2. The Sin Nature We're Born With

Along with the color of our hair and eyes and the size and shape of our nose and ears, each of us inherited from our parents a sin nature. From our earliest days, we have a predilection for sin because we come from parents who have a predilection for sin.

Of course, we can't blame our parents for our predicament. After all, they got their sin nature from *their* parents, who inherited it from their parents, and so on, all the way back to Adam and Eve.

Ephesians 2:3 describes the situation this way: "All of us also lived among them at one time, gratifying the cravings of our sinful nature and following its desires and thoughts. Like the rest, we were by nature objects of wrath." There is no "us and them" where the sin nature is concerned. All of us are sinful.

When you combine our inherited sin with our imputed sin, the result is that, spiritually speaking, we are alienated from God from the day of our birth.

3. The Sins We Commit Because of Our Sin Nature

None of us can legitimately claim to be innocent victims of God's wrath. We can't blame our situation on Adam or on our sin-natured ancestors. The fact is, every person who's ever been born has done something personally to earn God's wrath.

The Bible identifies several specific sins that are all too familiar to most of us. Check out this list from Galatians 5:19–21:

➤ sexual immorality

➤ impurity

➤ debauchery

➤ idolatry

➤ witchcraft

➤ hatred

➤ discord

➤ jealousy

➤ fits of rage

➤ selfish ambition

➤ dissensions

➤ factions

➤ envy

➤ drunkenness

➤ orgies

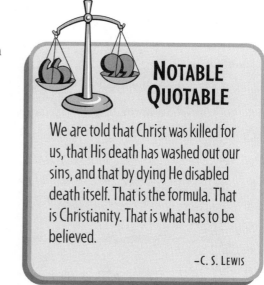

NOTABLE QUOTABLE

We are told that Christ was killed for us, that His death has washed out our sins, and that by dying He disabled death itself. That is the formula. That is Christianity. That is what has to be believed.

–C. S. LEWIS

It's safe to say that even this short list of offenses is enough to knock 99.9 percent of all humans from the sinless ranks.

As for the remaining fraction, Jesus established a standard certain to remove any doubt as to the possibility of complete sinlessness: "You have heard that it was said, 'Do not commit adultery.' But I tell you that anyone who looks at a woman lustfully has already committed adultery with her in his heart" (Matthew 5:27–28).

In other words, sinful thoughts are every bit as offensive to God as sinful actions.

Even without our imputed sin and inherited sin, each and every one of us would still be facing separation from God based on our own collection of personal sins. Romans 3:9–26 makes it clear that the bar for sinlessness (or righteousness) is set too high for the human race.

The Penalty

As disturbing as the thought of being separated from God is, that is not the only result of our sin. As we pointed out in chapter 3, God is not only holy, but He is also just. He requires perfect justice. In His justice, He demands a penalty for sin.

Romans 6:23 tells us that that penalty is death—not immediate physical death, although that will certainly come, but eternal spiritual death.

Revelation 20:2, 14–15 paints a stark picture of what will happen when final judgment is pronounced on those who remain separated from God:

> Then I saw a great white throne and him who was seated on it. Earth and sky fled from his presence, and there was no place for them. And I saw the dead, great and small, standing before the throne, and books were opened. Another book was opened, which is the book of life. The dead were judged according to what they had done as recorded in the books. . . . Then death and Hades were thrown into the lake of fire. The lake of fire is the second death. If anyone's name was not found written in the book of life, he was thrown into the lake of fire.

As Helpless As (Really Sinful) Babies

Compounding the fact that our sin separates us from God is the fact that we have no power whatever to change our position in God's eyes. The fact that we have sin in our lives automatically disqualifies us from saving ourselves.

Many people believe that if they can do enough good works, they may somehow be able to "cancel out" their sin. However, Isaiah 64:6 tells us that our good works—as a means for earning God's approval—"are like filthy rags" to God. They are meaningless. Our sin is so reprehensible to God that no amount of charity work or church service can ever make up for it.

Let's be clear about something here. Good works and a God-honoring lifestyle are vital elements of a growing Christian faith. However, as a means of salvation, they are worthless.

Behold the God-Man

The fact that we are unable to make ourselves righteous in God's eyes means that we need Someone to do the job for us. We need Someone to rescue us from God's justified wrath. We need a Savior.

Of course, not just any savior would do. In fact, only *one* Savior would do. Since all humans are in the same sin boat, the Savior could not be another person, no matter how brave or morally upstanding he may be. Our only hope was for God Himself to save us from His own wrath.

However, God's justice requires a payment of death for sin. And God is eternal; He cannot die. Therefore, God became human. He took on human flesh and lived among us as one of us.

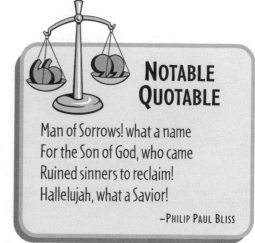

NOTABLE QUOTABLE

Man of Sorrows! what a name
For the Son of God, who came
Ruined sinners to reclaim!
Hallelujah, what a Savior!

—Philip Paul Bliss

Luke 1:26–38 tells us that Jesus was supernaturally conceived by the Holy Spirit in the womb of His mother Mary, who was a virgin. Because He was born of the Holy Spirit, Jesus was not subject to the imputed sin of Adam. Neither did He inherit a sin nature from His parents. In other words, He didn't come into the world with two strikes against Him, as far as God was concerned.

That left only the issue of His personal sins. The Bible makes it clear, though, that Jesus did not sin, even though He faced the same kinds of temptations that we all face. Jesus Himself asserted His sinlessness in several passages. For example, He said, "If you obey my commands, you will remain in my love, just as I have obeyed my Father's commands and remain in his love" (John 15:10). He challenged His enemies to show that He was a sinner, by asking, "Can any of you prove me guilty of sin?" (John 8:46). Needless to say, no one could.

The apostle Paul says that Jesus "had no sin" (2 Corinthians 5:21). The book of Hebrews describes Him as "holy, innocent, undefiled, separated from sinners" (Hebrews 7:26 NASB). By living a perfect life, Jesus defeated sin and provided hope for sinners everywhere.

Talk About the Passion

Anyone familiar with the Easter story knows that living a sinless life was only part of Jesus' saving work. God's plan for salvation also required Jesus to endure pain and suffering unimaginable to us. The question is . . . Why? Why did salvation have to involve such agony for Jesus? Wasn't there an easier way for God's plan to be accomplished? Interestingly, Jesus asked a question very similar to that one on the night before His crucifixion.

Matthew 26:39 tells us that, regarding His suffering and death, Jesus prayed, "My Father, if it is possible, may this cup be taken from me. Yet not as I will, but as you will." The fact that God did not change His plan to spare His Son tells us that there was no other way. Let's take a look at why that's so.

Remember the imputed sin that we discussed earlier, and how unfair it seemed to have Adam's sin attributed to us? Well, because Jesus offered Himself as a sacrifice for us, all of our sins were imputed to Him. In other words, Jesus—the only innocent person who ever lived—took the blame for every sin we ever committed.

God's wrath was aimed directly at us, but Jesus stepped in front of us and took the hit that we had coming.

The Gospels describe the passion of Jesus—that is, His sufferings between the night of the Last Supper with His disciples and His crucifixion—in excruciating detail. Here are just a few of the things Jesus endured because of our sins:

➤ He was betrayed by one of His own disciples.

➤ He was arrested on false charges.

➤ He was deserted and denied by His closest friends.

➤ He was blindfolded, insulted, spat upon, and beaten by Roman soldiers.

➤ He was made to wear a crown of thorns.

➤ He was flogged with a whip studded with pieces of metal and bone, designed to tear chunks of flesh with each lash.

On a Personal Note

Jesus' sacrifice isn't something that deserves attention only on Good Friday or Easter Sunday. Make a point of sincerely praising and thanking God for His sacrifice every time you pray.

➤ He was forced to carry the horizontal beam of His cross, a thick piece of wood approximately six feet long and weighing about thirty pounds, to the place of His execution.

➤ His hands and feet were nailed to the cross with spikes about seven inches long.

➤ He endured insatiable thirst, not to mention the pain from the nails and the raw wounds of His flogging.

➤ He was forsaken by His heavenly Father when the sins of the world were placed on Him.

➤ He was left to hang until the weight and position of His body suffocated Him.

As we explore the theological significance of Jesus' sacrificial death, there are four terms we need to examine: *substitution, redemption, reconciliation,* and *propitiation.* Let's take a look at each one.

Substitution

Jesus was our substitute in facing God's wrath. He—instead of us—paid the punishment for our sins. First Peter 3:18 says, "For Christ died for sins once for all, the righteous for the unrighteous, to bring you to God."

Redemption

To be *redeemed* is to be set free as a result of a payment. In the case of salvation, we are set free from our slavery to sin (remember our inherited sin nature) because of the price Jesus paid—with His blood and His life—on the cross.

The concept involves not only being redeemed from something (sin) and by something (Jesus' sacrifice); it also involves being redeemed to something—that is, a life of service to the Lord. Titus 2:14 tells us that Jesus "gave himself for us to redeem us from all wickedness and to purify for himself a people that are his very own, eager to do what is good."

Reconciliation

Reconciliation, as it relates to salvation, is more than just a "patching up" of our relationship with God; it is a complete transformation of the nature of that relationship—from hostility and separation to peace and intimacy. Romans 5:10 emphasizes that our sin makes us enemies of God. That same verse tells us that reconciliation is possible only because of Jesus' sacrifice.

That's not to say that complete reconciliation occurred for everyone in the universe the moment Christ died. The universal *possibility* for reconciliation occurred at that moment. However, Romans 4:24–25 makes it clear that we must believe in Christ in order to experience reconciliation with God.

Propitiation

Propitiation may be described as appeasing God or satisfying His wrath with an appropriate offering. As we mentioned earlier, the only acceptable offering to God for our sin was the sacrifice of Jesus. Jesus' death brought about "propitiation in His blood" (Romans 3:25 NASB). First John 4:10 (NASB) ties in Jesus' propitiation with God's love, pointing out that "God . . . loved us and sent His Son to be the propitiation for our sins."

Alive Again

The resurrection of Jesus has been called the central event in human history. In his first letter to the Corinthians, the apostle Paul shed some light on why Jesus' emergence from His tomb is so vital to the human race: "If Christ has not been raised, your faith is futile; you are still in your sins. Then those also who have fallen asleep in Christ are lost. If only for this life we have hope in Christ, we are to be pitied more than all men" (1 Corinthians 15:17–19).

The fact that Jesus lived a sinless life would have been meaningless to us if death had been His final stop. After all, what good is a dead Savior?

Remember, Romans 5:12 says that as a result of Adam's sin, sin and death entered the world. Sin *and* death. Jesus had to defeat two foes in order to provide salvation for men and women.

The Bible offers overwhelming evidence of Jesus' victory over death. First of all, there are the eyewitness accounts. Jesus appeared up close and personal to over five hundred people after His resurrection (1 Corinthians 15:6). From a legal perspective, the testimony of over five hundred eyewitnesses leaves little room for argument.

Second, there's the testimony of the apostles' changed lives. Mark 14:50 tells us that on the night of Jesus' arrest, His disciples deserted Him and went into hiding, afraid for their lives. Three days later, however, they were openly proclaiming Jesus' message. What could have changed them, apart from their encounter with the risen Jesus?

What's more, ten of the original twelve disciples were martyrs—that is, they were put to death because of their faith. (The only exceptions were Judas Iscariot, who committed suicide after betraying Jesus, and John, who died after being exiled to an island because of his faith.) People will die for what they know to be true but not for what they're unsure about. The fact that Jesus' disciples were so inspired is evidence of Jesus' postresurrection appearances to them.

In his sermon at Pentecost shortly after Jesus' ascension back to heaven, the apostle Peter made it clear that Jesus' resurrection validated His claim to be Lord and Savior (Acts 2:36). In Romans 1:4, the apostle Paul tells us that Jesus' resurrection proves that He's the Son of God.

The Order of Salvation

We've looked at the facts of salvation; now let's look at the process. At one level, salvation is a very simple process. The apostle Paul summarized it for his Philippian jailer by saying, "Believe in the Lord Jesus, and you will be saved" (Acts 16:31). At another level, though, the process can be divided into at least ten different elements. Let's take a look at each one.

1. Election

The first element of salvation is perhaps the most controversial. *Election* refers to the work of God that took place before creation in which He *chose* people to be saved. Evidence of God's election can be found throughout Scripture. For example, Revelation 13:8 refers to people "whose names have not been written in the book of life . . . from the creation of the world." That would suggest that other people *have* had their names in the Book of Life "from the creation of the world."

Luke addressed the matter more directly in his description of the results of Paul and Barnabas's ministry in Antioch: "When the Gentiles heard this, they were glad and honored the word of the Lord; and all who were appointed for eternal life believed" (Acts 13:48).

In his letter to the believers in Ephesus, the apostle Paul wrote, "For he chose us in him before the creation of the world to be holy and blameless in his sight. In love he predestined us to be adopted as his sons through Jesus Christ, in accordance with his pleasure and will—to the praise of his glorious grace, which he has freely given us in the One he loves" (Ephesians 1:4–6).

Lest we begin to think of God as being less than fair in His selection of those who will be saved, we need to remember who it is we're talking about. God is not simply a loving deity; He *is* love—that is, He is the standard against which our idea of love must be based. He cannot do anything that is unloving.

What's more, God is omniscient, which means He knows full well all of the alternative possibilities involved in His choices. He is sovereign, which means He was not persuaded or forced to make the choices He made. He is just, which means that there is nothing "unfair" about His work of election, regardless of how it may seem to our finite minds.

Finally, we need to understand that being elected is not the Christian equivalent of winning the lottery. Those who are chosen by God to receive His gift of salvation can't sit back and bask in their spiritual "wealth."

Passages such as John 15:16 ("I chose you and appointed you to go and bear fruit") and Ephesians 2:10 ("we are . . . created . . . to do good works, which God prepared in advance for us to do") makes it clear that our election is for the purpose of serving God and performing His good works. As its placement in the "order of salvation" would suggest, it is not the finish line, but the starting line for our spiritual journey.

2. The Gospel Call

The apostle Paul refers to *the gospel call* in Romans 8:30: "Those he predestined, he also called; those he called, he also justified; those he justified, he also glorified." The idea is that at some point, everyone who is predestined, or elected, receives a specific "summons" from God Himself to accept and believe the truth about His Son.

JUST WONDERING

Does the fact that God chooses who will be saved mean that we have no choice in the matter?

Not necessarily. Yes, it's true that everyone whom God elects will accept Christ and that no one whom God intends to save will be lost. Within that truth, however, there is room for the concept of personal choice. That is why Jesus said, "Come to me . . . and I will give you rest," and "Whoever comes to me I will never drive away" (Matthew 11:28; John 6:37).

Look closely at the previous verse, and you'll see that God's call cannot be resisted. The apostle Paul makes it clear that those who are "called" are also "justified." The call of God provokes a response in our hearts. That response is a saving faith in Jesus Christ.

The gospel call includes three elements:

1. *An explanation of why salvation is necessary.* To put it simply, everyone has sinned (Romans 3:23), God's punishment for sin is death (Romans 6:23), and Jesus paid the penalty for our sin with His life (Romans 5:8).

2. *An invitation to respond to Christ personally.* This involves asking for forgiveness for sin; repenting—that is, turning away from sin and to the

life Christ calls you to; and putting your faith and trust in Jesus to save you from your sin.

3. *A guarantee of eternal life.* Everyone who responds to the gospel call with repentance and belief will live forever in the presence of God (John 3:16).

3. Regeneration

Regeneration is the theological term for being "born again." It's also the act in which God creates in us a new spirit. How He accomplishes that work is something of a mystery. Jesus said in John 3:8, "The wind blows wherever it pleases. You hear its sound, but you cannot tell where it comes from or where it is going. So it is with everyone born of the Spirit."

What we do know is that God works in the lives of people who are spiritually dead (Ephesians 2:1) and makes them a "new creation" (2 Corinthians 5:17). Scriptural evidence suggests that regeneration is an instantaneous event. One moment we're spiritual corpses; the next moment we're spiritually alive.

Some people can point with assurance to the moment they experienced regeneration. For other people, particularly those who have grown up in the church, pinpointing their moment of spiritual awakening is more difficult.

The results of regeneration are obvious, though. They include:

➤ a genuine faith in Christ

➤ a desire to understand God's Word

➤ increased communication with God through prayer

➤ an interest in spending time with other Christians

➤ a hunger for spiritual knowledge

➤ a sense of responsibility to share the gospel of Christ with others

The apostle Paul lists several other results of regeneration under the heading "fruit of the Spirit" in Galatians 5:22–23: "love, joy, peace, patience, kindness, goodness, faithfulness, gentleness and self-control." Those aren't characteristics, qualities, and tendencies we spontaneously develop on our own. They are the products of God's regeneration.

4. Conversion

Hearing the gospel call isn't enough. Understanding why Christ died for our sins isn't enough. Developing a genuine interest in spiritual things isn't enough. At some point, we have to *respond* to the gospel call. We must specifically and genuinely repent of our sins and place our full trust in Jesus for salvation. That's *conversion*.

Romans 1:32 underscores the difference between a head knowledge of salvation and a heartfelt conversion: "Although they know God's righteous

NOTABLE QUOTABLE

God is none other than the Savior of our wretchedness. So we can only know God well by knowing our iniquities. . . . Those who have known God without knowing their wretchedness have not glorified Him, but have glorified themselves.

—BLAISE PASCAL

decree that those who do such things deserve death, they not only continue to do these very things but also approve of those who practice them." Such people know God's decrees but don't like them. As a result, they remain unconverted.

Conversion is an intensely personal act. It's not a matter of acknowledging that Jesus died to save sinners; it's a matter of saying, "Jesus died for *my* sins." The first element of conversion is *faith*. That is, we must believe in the saving power of Jesus to the exclusion of all other possibilities. Practically speaking, conversion means putting all of your spiritual eggs in one basket and living your life in a way that demonstrates your trust.

Contrary to popular opinion, we're not talking about blind faith either. Evidence of Jesus' trustworthiness is found throughout the New Testament. Romans 10:17 says, "Faith comes from hearing the message, and the message is heard through the word of Christ." That means the more time we spend getting to know Jesus through Scripture, the stronger our faith becomes.

The second element of conversion is *repentance*. Repentance is more than a simple apology for sin. Repentance involves genuine sorrow and a determination to turn from disobedience to Christ to obedience.

Isaiah 55:6–7 describes how faith and repentance go hand in hand: "Seek the LORD while he may be found; call on him while he is near. Let the wicked forsake his way and the evil man his thoughts."

Conversion is a one-time experience. When we place our genuine faith in Christ and sincerely repent of our sins, we are "converted," once and for all. At the same time, though, continual faith and repentance are traits of a growing Christian faith; they should mark our daily Christian journeys.

5. Justification

Justification, as it relates to salvation, is the act of sinners being declared righteous by God. The word has an obvious root connection to the word *justice,* and the legal image is apt. After all . . .

➤ God is the sovereign Judge of all; there is no higher authority or court to appeal to.

➤ God's Word is the law; it cannot be revised, updated, or ignored without dire consequence.

➤ God's judgment is final; His sentence is eternal.

When you consider God's perfect holiness and justice, you're left with the same question Job asked thousands of years before Jesus came to earth: "How can a mortal be righteous before God?" (Job 9:2).

The answer, according to Romans 3:21–26, is to be made righteous by God. That's not to say that God simply snapped His fingers and said, "From now on, everyone is righteous." No, we are made righteous through Christ's righteousness. Romans 3:22 tells us that righteousness comes "through faith in Jesus Christ." That is, we must put our trust in the fact that Jesus can make us righteous.

When we do that, we are placed in Christ. You might think of it as being "wrapped" in Christ's righteousness, so that when God looks at us He doesn't see the desperately sinful people we used to be; He sees the righteousness of Christ.

That, then, is what He bases His verdict on. He justifies us—that is, He declares us to be righteous—because of Christ's righteousness. To use a term that's familiar by now, God *imputes* Jesus' righteousness to us. He considers it ours. We don't deserve it; we didn't do anything to earn it. But He gives it to us anyway. That's why the apostle Paul calls it the "gift of righteousness" in Romans 5:17.

The result of our justification, our being declared righteous in God's eyes, is a commuting of our death sentence for our sins. The apostle Paul describes it this way: "Therefore, there is now no condemnation for those who are in Christ Jesus" (Romans 8:1).

6. Adoption

One of the chief benefits of being declared righteous by God is that it opens the door to an intimate relationship with Him. The image used in Scripture to describe this relationship is *adoption,* the act in which God makes us part of His family. John 1:12–13 puts it this way: "Yet to all who received him, to those who believed in his name, he gave the right to become children of God—children born not of natural descent, nor of human decision or a husband's will, but born of God."

Becoming a child of God isn't something that happens naturally. We're not born into His family. In fact, it is only by His grace that we can call ourselves children of God. It is God's choice and His initiative to make us His children in response to our trusting Christ (Galatians 3:23–27).

The immediate benefits of adoption include:

➤ an intimate relationship with God—that is, the right to approach and communicate with Him as a child would approach a good and loving father (Matthew 6:9)

➤ the care of a loving Father—that is, a God who understands and supplies what we need (Matthew 6:32)

➤ the inheritance of heaven—the knowledge that our eternal future will be spent with our heavenly Father (1 Peter 1:3–5)

➤ the privilege of forgiveness—knowing that every day we can ask for forgiveness of sins that interfere with our Father-child relationship and have things made right again (1 John 1:9)

➤ the leadership of the Holy Spirit—that is, guidance in our daily lives and wisdom regarding how to live in a God-honoring way (Romans 8:14)

➤ fellowship—that is, a familial relationship with every other adoptee of God (1 Timothy 5:1–2)

However, there is another element of adoption that won't be experienced until Christ returns and we receive our resurrection bodies. Romans 8:23 tells us that "we ourselves, who have the firstfruits of the Spirit, groan inwardly as we wait eagerly for our adoption as sons, the redemption of our bodies."

7. Sanctification

Sanctification is the process of becoming more and more Christlike in our daily lives. Unlike regeneration, justification, and adoption, which are all specific, one-time-only events, sanctification is a progressive aspect of salvation that continues throughout our lives.

Sanctification begins at regeneration. First John 3:9 describes the situation this way: "No one who is born of God will continue to sin, because God's seed remains in him; he cannot go on sinning, because he has been born of God."

NOTABLE QUOTABLE

Justification is the criminal pardoned; sanctification, the patient healed. The union of both constitutes present salvation.

–JOEL BEEKE

The new life God creates in us includes an obvious, definitive change in our moral outlook. Our priorities are rearranged. Our sense of right and wrong is sharpened. Our ability to withstand temptation is bolstered. Our desire to please God is increased.

The fact that God sets us free from slavery to sin means that we no longer have an excuse for choosing to indulge in sinful activities or attitudes. The apostle Paul instructs us to consider ourselves "dead to sin" (Romans 6:11).

Instead, we have a responsibility to pursue righteousness and God's will, following the example Jesus set. Sanctification is the work that springs from that new responsibility.

That's not to say that we can accomplish sanctification in our spiritual lives. In 1 Thessalonians 5:23, the apostle Paul wrote, "May God himself, the God of peace, sanctify you through and through." Hebrews 13:20–21 says, "May the God of peace . . . equip you with everything good for doing his will, and may he work in us what is pleasing to him." The clear indication in these and many other passages is that sanctification is primarily the work of God. He initiates the changes in us that result in a more Christlike life.

Second Corinthians 3:18 says that we "are being transformed into his likeness with ever-increasing glory, which comes from the Lord." The idea is that the work of sanctification continues throughout our lives. We don't plateau at a certain level of spirituality and then stay there for the rest of our lives. Instead, we become a little more like Christ every day, through the work of God, as well as the decisions we make and the actions we take.

Death marks the completion of sanctification in our lives, at least where our souls are concerned. Passages such as 1 John 1:8 ("If we claim to be without sin, we deceive ourselves") make it clear that we will never completely eliminate sin from our lives. However, when our souls leave our bodies at death, they will be made perfect, thus completing the work of sanctification in them. Revelation 21:27 tells us that "nothing impure will ever enter" the presence of God. Therefore, the transformation of our souls will occur before they reach heaven.

8. Perseverance

The element of *perseverance* introduces two ramifications to salvation:

1. Those who are truly born again will, by God's power, maintain their "saved" status until the end of their lives.

2. Only those who persevere to the end are truly saved.

John 10:27–29 presents a vivid support of the first aspect of perseverance, the idea of "once saved, always saved." Jesus said, "My sheep listen to my voice; I know them, and they follow me. I give them eternal life, and they shall never perish; no one can snatch them out of my hand. My Father, who has given them to me, is greater than all; no one can snatch them out of my Father's hand."

ON A PERSONAL NOTE

If you have questions about whether you are truly born again, identify the issues that cause you to doubt the genuineness of your salvation. Here are some questions to ask yourself:

1. Do you still trust Christ for salvation?

2. Do you see evidence of regeneration –a change in attitude toward sin– in your life?

3. Do you see a consistent pattern of spiritual growth in your life?

Once you've identified a problem area, you can ask the Lord to help you overcome it. For example, if you struggle with faithfulness in studying God's Word, you might ask the Holy Spirit to increase your hunger for spiritual "food" or to help you eliminate some of the distractions and obstacles that prevent you from spending time in God's Word.

That assurance should fill all true believers with unshakable confidence. Christ will not allow us to be separated from Him.

Neither will the Holy Spirit. Ephesians 1:13 offers further evidence of the eternal security of believers. The apostle Paul wrote, "And you also were included in Christ when you heard the word of truth, the gospel of your salvation. Having believed, you were marked in him with a seal, the promised Holy Spirit." God's seal, His Holy Spirit, is His guarantee that we will receive the salvation He promised us.

The second aspect of perseverance serves as a sobering warning to people who have fallen away or are considering falling away from their faith in Christ. Look at these words of Jesus: "If you hold to my teaching, you are really my disciples" (John 8:31). "He who stands firm to the end will be saved" (Matthew 10:22).

The apostle John wrote of people who had left the fellowship of the church: "They went out from us, but they did not really belong to us. For if they had belonged to us, they would have remained with us; but their going showed that none of them belonged to us" (1 John 2:19).

The warning in these passages (and dozens more like them) is not that the people in question will lose their salvation, but that they were never saved in the first place. Scripture makes it clear that genuine Christian faith is marked by a desire to learn and obey God's Word, to remain ultimately faithful in the face of persecution and doubt, and to participate in fellowship with other believers.

9. Death

As we mentioned earlier, *death,* the end of life, completes the work of sanctification in the soul. The Bible also makes it clear that the believer's sanctified soul goes immediately into the presence of God when he or she dies. This truth can be found in Jesus' promise to the thief on the cross: "Today you will be with me in paradise" (Luke 23:43). In 2 Corinthians 5:8, the apostle Paul indicates that to be "away from the body" is to be "at home with the Lord."

In terms of salvation, then, the end of life on earth is the beginning of eternal life with God.

10. Glorification

In Romans 8:30, the apostle Paul wrote that "those [God] predestined, he also called; those he called, he also justified; those he justified, he also glorified." *Glorification,* the final element of salvation, has three aspects:

➤ the resurrection of believers' bodies

➤ the reunion of those bodies with the believers' souls

➤ the transformation of those bodies into perfect resurrection bodies, like that of Jesus

JUST WONDERING

What effect does sin have in a Christian's life?
Primarily, it causes a loss of fellowship. A believer does not get tossed out of the family of God for committing a sin, but he may lose some privileges within the family. When the person confesses his sin and receives forgiveness, he is restored to fellowship.

First Corinthians 15:51–52 describes it this way: "We will not all sleep, but we will all be changed— in a flash, in the twinkling of an eye, at the last trumpet. For the trumpet will sound, the dead will be raised imperishable, and we will be changed."

The Bible doesn't go into a lot of detail regarding the features of our resurrection bodies. However, it does provide some useful clues. Based on passages such as 1 Corinthians 15, we can conclude that our glorified bodies will . . .

➤ not be susceptible to age, sickness, disease, injury, or disability;

➤ reflect God's original design in our creation;

➤ be unimaginably beautiful; and

➤ have a brightness and radiance to them.

Our new bodies will come in handy—in fact, they will be a necessity—when we inhabit the new heavens and new earth that God will create. (For more details, check out chapter 15.)

Why God Offered to Rescue Us

It's one thing to understand that God has a plan of salvation for us; it's quite another thing to understand why. Why would God choose to save people who disobeyed Him and rejected His plan for their lives? (Hint: It has nothing to do with our sparkling personalities or witty repartee.)

The Bible offers at least three reasons as to why God offers salvation to sinful humans.

1. *As a demonstration of His love.* John 3:16 makes it clear that love is one of the motivating factors for God's salvation: "For God so loved the world that he gave his one and only Son, that whoever believes in him shall not perish but have eternal life." (See also Romans 5:8.)

2. *As an eternal display of His grace.* Ephesians 2:6–7 suggests that God uses saved people as evidence of His grace. He can point to a saved individual and say, in effect, "See that guy over there? He was headed straight for hell until I gave him an opportunity to be saved."

3. *As an example of the kind of love He wants from us.* In John 15:12–13, Jesus offers these instructions to His followers: "Love each other as I have loved you. Greater love has no one than this, that he lay down his life for his friends." That's not to say that God expects us to die for someone else, as Jesus did. But God does expect us to follow Jesus' model of sacrificial love as we interact with the people He has put in our lives.

Know What You Believe

How much do you know about the doctrine of salvation? Here's a quiz to test your knowledge.

1. Which of the following is not true of God's plan of salvation?
   a. God's holiness and our sin create the need for it.
   b. Without it, every person who ever lived would be condemned to hell.
   c. It involves substitution, redemption, reconciliation, and propitiation.
   d. Jesus' role in it is often overstated.

2. Which of the following is an example of imputation?
   a. Abraham daring to "bargain" with God over the number of righteous people in Sodom
   b. Jesus commanding His followers to cut off their hands if those hands cause them to sin
   c. God attributing Adam's sin to every person
   d. Peter denying Jesus three times on the night before the Crucifixion

3. Which of the following is not true of Jesus?
   a. Hours before His crucifixion, He asked His heavenly Father to remove the responsibility from Him, if at all possible.
   b. He was not born with a sin nature.
   c. He never made any claims about being sinless.
   d. He was arrested on false charges.

4. Which of the following is not an element in the order of salvation?
   a. Election
   b. Diversion
   c. Gospel call
   d. Regeneration

5. Which of the following is not a biblical explanation for why God chooses to offer us salvation?
   a. It's a way of making Satan really mad.
   b. It's a way of demonstrating God's love.
   c. It's a way of demonstrating the kind of love He wants from us.
   d. It's a way of demonstrating His grace for eternity.

Answers: (1) d, (2) c, (3) c, (4) b, (5) a

CHAPTER 10

Still Busy After All These Years

UNDERSTANDING GOD'S WORK IN THE WORLD

SNAPSHOT

"At what point did we stop enjoying the scenery and start becoming hopelessly lost?" Kristin asked as she looked around the rough forest terrain. Their day trip seemed suddenly rocky.

"About the time we started listening to Mr. I-Think-the-View's-Better-Off-the-Beaten-Path over there," Karen replied with a quick nod toward Kurt.

"What should we do?" Kristin asked.

"I think it might be a good idea to say a quick prayer," Karen offered.

"I was just going to suggest that," Doug said as he took a swig from his water bottle. "Shall I do the honors?"

"Please," Karen urged.

Kurt watched while Doug, Kristin, and Karen bowed

SNEAK PREVIEW

1. God's work in the world today includes communicating through prayer, governing and judging the human race, opposing Satan, and intervening when He deems it necessary.

2. God is as active in the world today as He was during biblical times; the fact that His work may not be as apparent to us as it was to people in the Bible says more about our powers of observation and our understanding of His Word than it does about His activity level.

3. The only logical response to God's work in the world is praise and worship.

their heads. "Heavenly Father," Doug prayed, "we ask for Your protection and guidance now as we face the situation before us. Please keep our heads clear, our spirits positive, and our eyes focused on You. In Jesus' name. Amen."

"Why didn't you ask Him to just transport us back to the van?" Kurt asked in a tone that was not quite joking and not quite serious.

"You mean, 'Beam me up, Scotty' kind of stuff?" Doug said with a laugh.

"Yeah, why not?" Kurt asked. "Didn't God used to do that kind of stuff in the Bible?"

"There is the story of Philip," Karen pointed out.

"Yeah, Philip!" Kurt said. "Who's Philip?"

"He was one of the leaders of the first-century church," Karen explained. "There's a story in the book of Acts in which he's supernaturally transported from one place to another to help a traveler who's having trouble understanding Scripture."

"Yeah, that's what we need," Kurt chuckled. "Why don't you all pray again and ask for the 'Philip treatment'?"

"That's not the way it works," Doug explained.

"You'll never know until you try," Kurt said with a half-joking smile.

"Do you know what Jesus said when Satan tempted Him to jump off a high place and let God's angels catch Him?" Karen asked.

"Get behind me, Satan?" Kurt guessed.

"Don't put the Lord to the test," Karen replied.

"Are you comparing me to Satan?" Kurt asked with mock indignity.

"Hey, if the cloven-footed shoe fits, wear it," Doug replied.

"I see a road!" Kristin called out.

"Where?" the rest of the group replied simultaneously.

Kristin pointed to a clearing on the left. "Over there, on the other side of the dam."

"You're right," Karen said. "We've got a way out!"

"Thank You, Lord, for such a quick answer to prayer," Doug prayed aloud as he picked up his backpack and slung it over his shoulder. "We give You all the praise and glory—"

"Whoa, whoa, whoa! Wait a minute," Kurt interrupted. "That's not an answer to prayer. We could have found that road on our own. Besides, that's got to be a four-mile walk around the dam. That seems more like a punishment than a blessing."

"So what's *your* idea of an answered prayer?" Doug asked.

"Personally, I'd like to see a little 'parting of the Red Sea' action," Kurt replied. "Maybe have God clear a straight path through the trees and water so that we can get to the road as fast as possible. But apparently God doesn't do stuff like that anymore."

"Do me a favor, will you?" Karen asked. "Walk about ten feet behind us for the rest of the way."

"Why?" Kurt asked.

"So that *we* don't get hit by the lightning that's coming down from heaven for you at any moment."

* * * * * * * * * * * * * *

We have a good idea of what God did during Old Testament times—how, among countless other things, He . . .

> ➤ created the universe,

> ➤ parted the Red Sea,

> ➤ made covenants with His people,

> ➤ anointed kings,

> ➤ bestowed supernatural wisdom, and

> ➤ revealed the future to His prophets.

We also have a good idea of what God did during New Testament times—
how He . . .

> ➤ sent His Son to save the world,

> ➤ sent angels to make announcements and provide comfort,

> ➤ sent His Spirit to dwell in the hearts of believers,

> ➤ fulfilled prophecies that were hundreds of years old, and

> ➤ revealed His truths to the New Testament writers.

But how much do we know about what God does today?

Think about it. Creation's done. The Bible's finished. The plan of salvation is in
place. Satan's defeat is guaranteed. The future is set. So what's a deity to do now?

Technically speaking, we can't ask how God spends His days, because He exists
outside the realm of time. We can, however, ask how He spends *our* days—what
He does in the universe and why. The Bible identifies four ongoing works of God
that deserve our attention: *communication, judgment, opposition,* and
intervention.

NOTABLE QUOTABLE

He that seeks God in everything is
sure to find God in everything. When
we thus live wholly unto God, God is
wholly ours, and we are then happy in
all the happiness of God; for by uniting
with Him in heart and will and spirit,
we are united to all that He is and has
in Himself.

—WILLIAM LAW

Each of these tasks reveals something essential
about God's nature and His relationship with the
created world. In order to understand Him as fully
as possible, we need to discover why these tasks are
necessary and how He accomplishes them.

One-on-One with God

The image presented in Scripture of God's work in
response to the prayers of His people is not one of
an overworked telephone operator trying to field
millions of calls at once. Nor is it one of an
overbooked therapist professionally indulging one
patient after another.

Instead, the biblical image of God's work in prayer is that of a patient, loving Father, anxious to hear as much as possible about His children's lives, and ready to give them everything He knows they need. Jesus emphasized that point by starting the Lord's Prayer with the words, "Our *Father* in heaven" (Matthew 6:9, italics added).

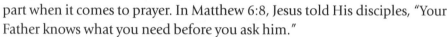

NOTABLE QUOTABLE

There is no other method of living piously and justly than that of depending upon God.

–John Calvin

When it comes to communication with God, recall that God is omniscient (all-knowing). So it's safe to say that there is no discovery process on God's part when it comes to prayer. In Matthew 6:8, Jesus told His disciples, "Your Father knows what you need before you ask him."

The question we're faced with, then, is *why*. Why does God want us to pray when our requests and needs are foregone conclusions to Him? Here are three reasons you'll need to consider if you're serious about understanding God.

1. Prayer Demonstrates Our Trust in God.

Passages such as Matthew 7:7–11 and James 5:13–16 encourage believers to pray with faith—that is, with trust in God and dependence on Him. Prayer, then, is a tool for us to acknowledge God's wisdom, power, and love in a personal way. It's one thing to be able to recite a list of God's attributes; it's quite another thing to actively seek those attributes and request them to be put to use in our lives.

Veteran pray-ers attest to the fact that one of the benefits of a committed, God-honoring prayer life is a strengthening of one's faith. In other words, the more we place our trust in God through our prayers, the more trust He gives us to place in Him.

The result of such compounded faith and trust can be seen in Jesus' words to His disciples in Matthew 17:20: "I tell you the truth, if you have faith as small as a mustard seed, you can say to this mountain, 'Move from here to there' and it will move. Nothing will be impossible for you."

2. Prayer Demonstrates Our Love for God.

Genuine prayer brings believers into deeper fellowship with God. The more we

JUST WONDERING

What is the best way to approach God in prayer?

The acronym ACTS is useful in remembering our priorities when we pray. ACTS stands for **A**doration, **C**onfession, **T**hanksgiving, and **S**upplication. Adoration is a matter of praising God for who He is, what He's done in the past, and what He continues to do. Confession is admitting guilt for sin and asking for God's forgiveness in order to restore fellowship with Him. Thanksgiving is a matter of recognizing how truly blessed we are and giving God credit for each one of the blessings in our lives. Supplication is the process of bringing requests on behalf of ourselves and others to God's attention. By placing adoration, confession, and thanksgiving before supplication, we guard against treating prayer as a "wish list"–that is, bringing our requests to God and then signing off. Prayer is, first and foremost, an opportunity for us to respond to who God is in a one-on-one setting.

turn to Him with our praise, thanksgiving, and requests, the closer our bond with Him becomes.

One of the many things that make a relationship with God unique is His perfection. Because God is perfect, for example, we never have to worry about uncovering an incident in His past that will color our opinion of Him or growing tired of an annoying character trait of His. Therefore, it's safe to say that the more time we spend with God, the more we will come to love Him.

The mind-blowing flip side of this equation is that the Lord actually *delights* in our love for Him. He takes pleasure in the fellowship that occurs through prayer. That should be reason enough for us to pursue a genuine prayer life with everything we've got.

3. Prayer Allows Us to Participate in God's Plan.

Prayer is more than a personal conversation with God; it is a tool for accomplishing God's work in the world. When we pray according to God's will— that is, in agreement with His Word—we are taking an active role in furthering His kingdom.

That's not to suggest that God is dependent on us to accomplish His will, or that His power is somehow diminished without our participation. The fact that God involves us in His work at all is a testament not to His neediness, but to His kindness and mercy. After all, He's giving us an opportunity to be involved in something of eternal significance.

James 5:16 says, "The prayer of a righteous man is

powerful and effective." With power comes responsibility, though. As participants in God's work, we have a duty to make the most of our prayers—to learn to pray as powerfully and effectively as we possibly can.

Benchwork

In addition to responding to the prayers of His people, God also fulfills His role as the Supreme Judge of all. From His throne, He listens to continuous "prosecution" and "defense" arguments regarding His human creation.

The case for prosecution is made by Satan, the adversary of all things related to God, including His plan and His people. His accusatory tactics are spelled out in Scripture. For example, in Job 1:6–11, when Satan saw that God was taking delight in His servant Job, Satan accused God of stacking the deck in Job's favor. He argued that Job had no reason *not* to be faithful, because God had blessed him with everything he would ever need. Satan then challenged God to devastate Job's life by removing His blessings.

That's Satan the accuser at work. Scripture suggests that he's tireless in his pursuit of prosecution when it comes to God's people:

> ➤ "Then he showed me Joshua the high priest standing before the angel of the LORD, and Satan standing at his right side to accuse him" (Zechariah 3:1).

> ➤ "Then I heard a loud voice in heaven say: 'Now have come the salvation and the power and the kingdom of our God, and the authority of his Christ. For the accuser of our brothers, who accuses them before our God day and night, has been hurled down'" (Revelation 12:10).

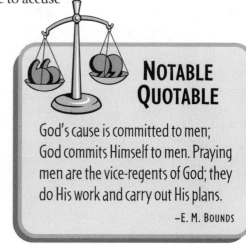

NOTABLE QUOTABLE

God's cause is committed to men; God commits Himself to men. Praying men are the vice-regents of God; they do His work and carry out His plans.

–E. M. BOUNDS

With such a relentless accuser working against us, we need a persuasive voice representing us before God. The Bible makes it clear that we have one in Christ.

JUST WONDERING

Doesn't Satan live in hell?

Contrary to popular media portrayals, Satan isn't laughingly stoking the flames of hell while the damned suffer in abject misery. In fact, Satan wants nothing to do with the place. Though Satan will spend eternity in hell (Revelation 20:10), he's not there now. The Bible suggests that he is a wandering spirit who splits his time between the earth and God's throne.

➤ "Who will bring any charge against those whom God has chosen? It is God who justifies. Who is he that condemns? Christ Jesus, who died—more than that, who was raised to life—is at the right hand of God and is also interceding for us" (Romans 8:33–34).

➤ "My dear children, I write this to you so that you will not sin. But if anybody does sin, we have one who speaks to the Father in our defense—Jesus Christ, the Righteous One. He is the atoning sacrifice for our sins, and not only for ours but also for the sins of the whole world" (1 John 2:1–2).

Although the Bible doesn't offer many details as to how the "courtroom" proceedings before God's throne work, it's not hard to picture Satan watching our every move, ready to pounce on any wrongdoing he spots as evidence of our unworthiness of God's saving work. ("Did you see what that guy just did? How can you consider him righteous?")

Jesus' defense on our behalf is as simple as it is effective. In essence, He says, "I gave My life as a sacrifice for that person's sins. He claims Me as Savior and Lord. He is covered by My blood." God then weighs Satan's charges against Christ's defense . . . and rules in favor of the accused.

NOTABLE QUOTABLE

Satan looks back and sees the believer's sin. God looks back and sees the cross.

—AUTHOR UNKNOWN

The fact that Satan has never won a case against a believer in God's court doesn't discourage him. His accusing work continues, as does Christ's work in defending us and God's work in judging us.

The Ultimate Authority

Biblical titles such as "the god of this age" (2 Corinthians 4:4) or "the ruler of the kingdom of the air" (Ephesians 2:2) would seem to apply to our heavenly Father or Christ. The fact is, though, they refer to the devil.

The Bible makes it clear that Satan is the ruler of this world. As citizens of the earth, we live under his regime. The point we must hasten to make, though, is that Satan reigns over the earth *only* because God allows him to as part of His (God's) sovereign plan. In other words, the devil wields authority over the universe only because God gives him permission to.

The story of Job sheds some light on the unusual arrangement between God and Satan. In Job 1:12, God gives Satan permission to do as he pleases with anything in Job's life but forbids him from harming Job himself. Without God's permission, Satan would have been helpless to do anything to Job. Notice also that God gives Satan leeway to tempt and afflict His (God's) people—up to a certain point. Beyond that, Satan is prevented from causing harm.

God's work in the world, then, includes overseeing Satan's reign (as oxymoronic as that may seem). Satan has the freedom to try to disrupt God's plans, tempt His people, and wreak havoc on their efforts to live for Christ. Ultimately, though, God holds Satan's leash and prevents him from overstepping his boundaries.When it comes to the opposition we face, remember God is on our side, and He has the final word.

ON A PERSONAL NOTE

Here are some questions to get you thinking about God's work of intervention in the world today:

➤ How would you define the word **miracle?**

➤ Based on that definition, have you ever witnessed a miracle? If so, what was it?

➤ If you believe you've witnessed a miracle, describe your initial reaction to it and feelings about it.

➤ Have you ever shared your experience with anyone else? If so, how did you explain it? What responses did you get?

➤ How often do you think genuine miracles occur?

➤ What events or occurrences should be considered miracles, as far as you're concerned?

Write your responses in your journal and plan a special time of prayer to glorify God for His miraculous work.

Intervention

In the Bible,

➤ God rained bread from the sky every day for almost forty years so that His people would have something to eat in the wilderness (Exodus 16).

➤ God held the sun still in the sky so that the Israelites would have enough daylight to finish their battle against the Amorites (Joshua 10:1–15).

➤ God sent ravens carrying bread and meat to feed His prophet Elijah (1 Kings 17:1–6).

➤ God protected three of His servants from being so much as singed while they were standing inside a burning furnace (Daniel 3).

Feel free to add any other miraculous events from Scripture to this list. If you're a stickler for comprehensiveness, chances are you'll be writing for a while. God makes Himself known in many, many astonishing ways throughout Scripture.

The usual immediate result of such momentous biblical events was that people who didn't believe in God already began to believe in Him, and people who already believed in Him found themselves strengthened in their faith.

Jesus acknowledged the impact of such obvious displays of God's power and presence on a person's ability to believe when He told His disciples, "Because you have seen me, you have believed; blessed are those who have not seen and yet have believed" (John 20:29).

The fact is, we live in an age of faith. God has no need to demonstrate His power on a grand scale anymore. We have the Bible and the Holy Spirit, and that's all we need in order to get to know Him. He doesn't need to use miraculous means to reveal Himself to us.

The fact that we live in the age of faith, however, doesn't mean that God doesn't still intervene in universal and personal affairs in powerful ways. To put it another way, miracles still happen.

Some acts of God in the world are more obvious than others. Some are known only to people who were directly affected by them. Some are the direct result of prayer. Some come as complete surprises. Some are mistaken for dumb luck, good fortune, or coincidence.

The bottom line is that God is as active in the world today as He was during biblical times; the fact that His work may not be as apparent to us as it was to people in the Bible says more about our powers of observation and understanding of His Word than it does about God's activity level.

Beyond Comprehension

As we wrap up this chapter, we need to emphasize that God has not reduced His workload to four simple tasks. The truth is, there's not enough room in this book—or in our brains, for that matter—to identify and explain *every* work of God in the world.

David seemed to recognize the futility of trying to attain an all-encompassing view of God's work in the universe when he wrote: "Such knowledge is too wonderful for me, too lofty for me to attain" (Psalm 139:6). That didn't stop David from trying to learn more about God, however, and it shouldn't stop us either.

JUST WONDERING

Wouldn't more people become Christians if they could see evidence of God's work with their own eyes?

You'd think so, wouldn't you? However, the Bible makes it clear that that's not the case at all. Check out Jesus' story of the rich man and Lazarus in Luke 16:19–31. After the rich man died, he found himself in hell, the place of extreme torment. After Lazarus, a beggar, died, he found himself in paradise. In the story, the rich man sees Lazarus and requests that Lazarus be sent back to earth to warn the rich man's family not to make the same mistake he (the rich man) made. The response he gets is chilling, but telling: "If they do not listen to Moses and the Prophets [the Bible], they will not be convinced even if someone rises from the dead."

Know What You Believe

How much do you know about God's work in the world? Here's a quiz to test your knowledge.

1. Which of the following was not an act of God in the New Testament?
   a. Fulfilling prophecies that were made hundreds of years earlier
   b. Changing the "thees," "thous," and other arcane terms in the Old Testament to something more reader friendly
   c. Sending angels to make announcements and provide comfort
   d. Sending His Spirit to dwell in the hearts of believers

2. Which of the following statements is not true regarding God's work in responding to the prayers of His people?
   a. The biblical image of His response to prayer is that of a patient, loving Father, anxious to hear as much as possible about His children's lives.
   b. He will not respond to prayers that don't begin with "Dear heavenly Father" and end with "In Jesus' name—Amen."
   c. God knows what we need before we ask Him.
   d. God gives us an opportunity to participate in His work through our prayers.

3. Which of the following terms is not used in Scripture to refer to Satan?
   a. "The accuser of our brothers"
   b. "The god of this age"
   c. "The master of all he surveys"
   d. "The ruler of the kingdom of the air"

4. Which of the following statements is accurate regarding God's miraculous work in the Bible?
   a. God held the Amorite army still so that the Israelites wouldn't have to chase them when the sun went down.
   b. The beasts of the field kept the prophet Elijah fed by bringing him ravens and other birds to eat.
   c. God rained bread from the sky every day for almost forty weeks so that the Israelites would have something to eat in Egypt.
   d. God protected Shadrach, Meshach, and Abdenego from harm after they were thrown inside a burning furnace.

5. Which of the following statements does not explain why God chooses not to use dramatic, obvious miracles today as He did during biblical times?
   a. We have the Bible.
   b. We have the Holy Spirit.
   c. We live in an age of faith.
   d. We have advanced scientific research that could prove His works to be not so miraculous.

Answers: (1) b, (2) b, (3) c, (4) d, (5) d

CHAPTER 11

Getting Personal

UNDERSTANDING GOD'S WORK IN OUR LIVES

SNAPSHOT

"What are you reading?" Scott asked.

"It's a workbook from our adult Bible fellowship," James explained. "We're studying the heroes of the faith."

"Sounds interesting," Scott said. "Did you spot any Bible character you'd like to be?"

"Sure," James replied. "Any of the good guys— Abraham, Joseph, David. I just think it would be cool to see God at work up close and personal."

"Hey, don't you think God works in people's lives today?"

"That's not what I'm saying," James protested. "I'm talking about miracles and things like that—real obvious stuff."

SNEAK PREVIEW

1. Because He is a personal God, the Lord works directly in the lives of His people to accomplish His purposes.
2. The Bible is full of examples of God's work of calling, equipping, providing, protecting, disciplining, forgiving, restoring, and arranging.
3. We have a responsibility to recognize, yield to, and offer praise and thanksgiving for God's work in our lives.

"Divine intervention," Scott added.

"Exactly," James said.

"Let me ask you a question," Scott said. "Do you carry a picture of your family with you?"

"My family?" James asked as he pulled out his wallet. "Sure, I've got a picture. Why?" He pulled out a photo and handed it to Scott.

Scott pointed to the picture. "Look at your wife," he said.

"What about her?" James asked slowly.

"I think most people would agree that she's a beautiful woman, right?" Scott said.

"Oh, yeah," James said with a grin.

Scott held up the photo. "Now look at that gargoyle sitting next to her," he said.

"Hey!" James objected. "I admit it's not the best picture I've ever had taken, but—"

"Oh, come on," Scott interrupted. "Let's call a spade a spade. I've seen better looking faces on a head of cabbage."

"What's your point?" James asked.

Scott pointed to the picture again. "My point is that *this woman* married *you*. Talk about miracles! As far as I'm concerned, the only possible explanation for your marriage is divine intervention."

* * * * * * * * * * * * * * *

When it comes to God's work in the lives of His people, everyone has a story to tell—whether we realize it or not. Some Christians are eager to broadcast their experiences of the Lord's work in their lives—anywhere, at any time, and to as many people as possible. Other Christians prefer a more laid-back approach, choosing to share their experiences only with a close circle of friends or a Bible study group. And some Christians fail to even *recognize* God's work for what it is.

If we're serious about understanding God, it is essential that we develop a working knowledge of what He does in our lives, why He does it, and how He accomplishes it. In this chapter, we've divided His "personal" work into eight categories:

➤ calling   ➤ disciplining

➤ equipping   ➤ forgiving

➤ providing   ➤ restoring

➤ protecting   ➤ arranging

You may refer to them by different names, but chances are you've experienced each of these works of God in your life. Let's take a closer look at each one.

God Calls

God has a specific plan for every one of His people. One of the ways He works in our lives, then, is by making His plans known. The way He *accomplishes* that work differs from person to person, but the work itself is a constant in the lives of all believers.

God's work of calling people to His service can be seen in the lives of numerous Bible characters—from Moses, who received a visit from the Lord in the form of a burning bush and was told to lead the Israelites out of Egypt (Exodus 3:1–4:17), to the disciples, who were instructed point-blank by Jesus Himself to follow Him (Matthew 4:18–22).

A lesser-known but equally revealing call is found in the story of the Old Testament prophet Samuel. First Samuel 3 tells us that when Samuel was a boy, he lived and worked at the temple, assisting the priest Eli. One night, while Samuel was lying in his bed, he heard a voice calling his name. Thinking that it was Eli, Samuel ran to the priest, only to discover that Eli hadn't called him.

When Samuel returned to his bed, he heard the voice again calling his name. Again Samuel ran to Eli, only to discover that the priest hadn't called him. Samuel went back to bed and heard the voice again. This time, though, when the boy ran to Eli, the old priest figured out that it was the Lord Himself who was calling Samuel.

Eli instructed Samuel to return to his bed, wait for the voice again, and then respond by saying, "Speak, LORD, for your servant is listening" (verse 9). Samuel did as he was instructed. In return, the Lord revealed to the boy His plans regarding Eli and his wicked family.

Samuel responded faithfully to God's call, relating the details of God's plan to Eli. For his faithfulness, Samuel was given a position of authority, respect, and responsibility in Israel. In fact, it was Samuel who revealed to a young shepherd named David that one day he would be king.

If you're wondering why Samuel didn't recognize God's call from the start, the answer may be found in 1 Samuel 3:1: "In those days the word of the LORD was rare; there were not many visions."

The same might be said of the era in which we live. We don't go to bed expecting to be awakened by the voice of God. Few of us have ever experienced Deity in the form of smoldering shrubbery. We've never seen the Son of God in person, let alone been verbally invited to follow Him.

Yet God calls us, just the same.

His *methods* may have changed, but His *work* has not. Jeremiah 1:5 reveals that God has specific plans for individuals even before conception. Romans 8:30 affirms, "those he predestined, he also *called*" (italics added). One way or another, God makes His desires and plans known to us.

First, there are the instructions—or *calls*—contained in His Word. For example, in Matthew 28:19, Jesus instructs His followers to "go and make disciples of all nations." That's a call. When a follower encounters an unbeliever, he doesn't have to wonder what God wants him to do. The Christian already knows—he's

JUST WONDERING

How can I be sure whether something is God's call or not?
Keep in mind that God's call never contradicts His Word. If you're confronted with an opportunity that requires you to compromise biblical principles—whether by lying, taking advantage of someone else, restructuring your priorities, or something else—you can be sure that it's not God's call. Don't forget too that if a call seems vague or unclear to you, you can always ask God for wisdom or a sense of peace to let you know that you're doing the right thing.

received God's call. God wants the believer to communicate the gospel message as effectively as possible and work to "make a disciple" of the person.

Second, God calls us through the work of His Holy Spirit. John 14:17 emphasizes that the Holy Spirit dwells inside every believer. First Corinthians 2:9–11 indicates that the Holy Spirit assists believers in understanding "the deep things of God"—which would certainly include His call for our lives. The fact that the Holy Spirit works *in* us means that we shouldn't necessarily expect dramatic circumstances or "signs" in our call from the Lord.

NOTABLE QUOTABLE

If God sends us on stony paths, He will provide us with strong shoes.

—ALEXANDER MACLAREN

God can communicate His plans just as effectively through an inner sense of purpose, peace, or direction as He can with the blinding light from heaven that Paul experienced (Acts 9:1–30) or the giant fish that set Jonah back on the right track (Jonah 1:1–2:10).

God Equips

The idea of being "called" by God is a daunting proposition for mere humans. It's only natural that we—as fallible, imperfect people—feel a little overwhelmed by and underprepared for God's assignments. Fortunately for us, the Lord isn't One to issue a call and then expect us to muster the resources to perform the task. He also specifically equips and prepares us—physically, mentally, emotionally, and spiritually—to accomplish His work, no matter how difficult or intimidating the tasks may seem.

"For we are God's workmanship, created in Christ Jesus to do good works, which God prepared in advance for us to do," Paul explained in Ephesians 2:10. The fact that we are *created* to do God's works means that we have the physical, mental, emotional, and spiritual "hardware" to get the job done that He has planned for us. In other words, we're "built" to do His will.

Second Timothy 3:16–17 identifies the primary tool God uses to prepare us for His work: "All Scripture is God-breathed and is useful for teaching, rebuking, correcting and training in righteousness, so that the man of God may be thoroughly equipped for every good work." Studying God's Word is a way of opening a line of communication with Him and allowing Him to give us the vital information we need regarding His plans for us.

As we mentioned earlier in the chapter, God's *call* in Moses' life was for him to return to Egypt (where Moses faced a murder charge) and demand from the ruler Pharaoh the release of millions of Israelites from slavery. Like almost anyone else in his position, Moses first felt a sense of inadequacy. His reply to the Lord went something like this: "Why would Pharaoh listen to me? I can't even talk clearly! I think You should send someone else to do it."

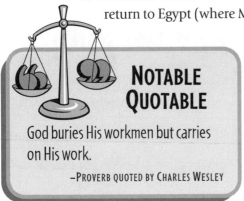

NOTABLE QUOTABLE

God buries His workmen but carries on His work.

—PROVERB QUOTED BY CHARLES WESLEY

In response, God told Moses to throw down his shepherd's staff. When Moses did, his staff turned into a snake. When he reached down to pick it up, it turned back into a staff again. Though Moses may not have fully comprehended it at the time, God was preparing him for the task ahead. God *equipped* Moses for his rendezvous with Pharaoh by providing tangible evidence of His awesome power—in the form of a shape-shifting staff—not only to gain Pharaoh's attention but to reassure Moses.

The apostle Thomas experienced God's equipping in a locked room shortly after Jesus' resurrection. John 20:19–24 tells us that Thomas was absent the first time Jesus appeared to His disciples. When the other disciples told Thomas that they had seen the risen Lord, he replied, "Unless I see the nail marks in his hands and put my finger where the nails were, and put my hand into his side, I will not believe it" (John 20:25).

John 20:26–28 completes the story. A week later, the risen Jesus appeared to His disciples again. This time Thomas was present. Jesus said to him, "Put your finger here; see my hands. Reach out your hand and put it into my side. Stop doubting and believe."

The only response Thomas could muster in the face of such overwhelming physical evidence was, "My Lord and my God!"

Notice how God responded to Thomas's doubt in this passage. He didn't revoke Thomas's membership in the disciples. He didn't strike Thomas dead for his less-than-reverent words about Jesus' wounds. Instead, God gave Thomas what he needed.

Thomas's faith was weak, so God equipped him with the visual assurance he asked for. Like the other remaining apostles, Thomas had an important task ahead of him, that of spreading the news of Jesus to the world. It was a task that would eventually result in Thomas's execution. God made sure that Thomas had the mental certainty he needed to carry out his task.

God continues His work of equipping, preparing, and strengthening today. That's not to say that He will supply us with a supernatural stick to demonstrate His power as He did for Moses, or that Jesus will appear physically to us as He did to Thomas. As Jesus mentions in John 20:29, believers today live in a time of *faith*, not sight.

In order to understand God's work of equipping, we first have to understand His strategy in assigning tasks to believers. First Corinthians 1:26–29 sums it up this way:

> *Brothers, think of what you were when you were called. Not many of you were wise by human standards; not many were influential; not many were of noble birth. But God chose the foolish things of the world to shame the wise; God chose the weak things of the world to shame the strong. He chose the lowly things of this world and the despised things—and the things that are not—to nullify the things that are, so that no one may boast before him.*

In other words, it is in God's best interest to choose people with glaring weaknesses to accomplish His work. That way, no one will be tempted to give credit to the person doing the work. Instead, they will say, "Obviously that person had a lot of help in accomplishing that task, because there's no way she could have done it on her own."

Depending on the circumstances and the believer, God's equipping may involve . . .

➤ helping us overcome a fear or phobia,

➤ giving us the right words to say at the right time,

NOTABLE QUOTABLE

NOTABLE QUOTABLE

What a wonderful experience mine has been during these thirty-nine years! What inexhaustible supplies have been vouchsafed to the work in my hands. How amazing to mere unaided human reason have been the answers to prayer, even when faith has almost failed and our timidity has begotten distrust instead of love and hope! And God has not failed us once!

—THOMAS BARNARDO

➤ helping us understand a relevant Bible passage,

➤ bringing people into our lives who have had similar experiences, or

➤ providing training or knowledge that ultimately proves useful.

Whatever God chooses to do in and through us, our attitude should match that of the psalmist who wrote, "It is God who arms me with strength and makes my way perfect" (Psalm 18:32).

God Provides

At the end of his letter to the Christians in Philippi, the apostle Paul offered a remarkable guarantee to his readers: "My God will meet all your needs according to his glorious riches in Christ Jesus" (Philippians 4:19). That offer still applies for believers today. Whatever we need, God will supply.

In certain situations, God's provision involves sustenance—food, drink, shelter—the basic elements of life. An example of this kind of provision is found in the story of Hagar and Ishmael in Genesis 21:8–20. When Abraham sent Hagar and Ishmael away from his dwelling and into the desert, Hagar resigned herself to the fact that she and her son were going to die. When the heat became unbearable, she placed her son under a bush to protect him from the sun. She couldn't bear to watch him suffer, so she moved to a spot several feet away from him and began to sob.

God heard her cries and told her not to be afraid. He told her that He had plans for her son—plans to make a great nation from his offspring. Genesis 21:19 says that God then "opened her eyes and she saw a well of water." Hagar's greatest need at that point in her life was something to drink for her and her son, and God met that need.

The Israelites also experienced God's sustenance. Exodus 16 describes how, after a month or two in the wilderness on their way to the Promised Land, the people of Israel began to fear that they would starve to death in such a desolate location.

In response, the Lord "rained" bread from heaven called *manna*. Every morning when the Israelites woke up, they found the ground covered with manna. All they had to do was gather what they needed. Exodus 16:35 reveals that God's provision of manna to the Israelites lasted forty years. The Israelites' greatest need was food, and God met that need.

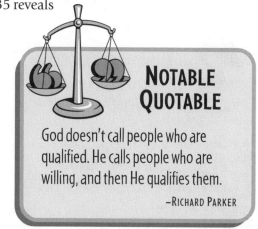

NOTABLE QUOTABLE

God doesn't call people who are qualified. He calls people who are willing, and then He qualifies them.

–RICHARD PARKER

Other Bible characters experienced God's provision in the form of physical healing. The New Testament records over two dozen accounts of Jesus' healing work. He caused blind people to see, deaf people to hear, and crippled people to walk. He removed sickness and lifelong disabilities from people's bodies. He even raised people from the dead. Physical wholeness was the need Jesus saw, and He met that need.

Elsewhere, David describes God as a "father to the fatherless" and a "defender of widows," and One who "sets the lonely in families" (Psalm 68:5–6). In other words, He is what we need Him to be.

God still provides for His people today, though we may not always experience His provision as dramatically as Bible characters did. Jesus explains what difference God's provision should make in our lives in Luke 12:22–24: "Therefore I tell you, do not worry about your life, what you will eat; or about your body, what you will wear. Life is more than food, and the body more than clothes. Consider the ravens: They do not sow or reap, they have no storeroom or barn; yet God feeds them. And how much more valuable you are than birds!"

The operative word in God's work of provision is *needs*. God doesn't cater to our every whim or satisfy our every desire. He provides for our every need.

The Lord is not a cosmic Santa Claus who gives us every gift we ask for. He's the omniscient Creator who knows far better than we do what is actually *necessary* in our lives. In Matthew 6:8, Jesus affirms, "Your Father knows what you need before you ask him."

God Protects

JUST WONDERING

Does the fact that God protects us give us the freedom to live recklessly and take risks in the way we live?

Jesus answers this question in His response to Satan's second temptation (Matthew 4: 5–7). Satan took Jesus to the top of the temple in Jerusalem and challenged Him to jump off, noting that God would protect Him. Jesus responded to the temptation by paraphrasing Deuteronomy 6:16: "Do not put the Lord your God to the test." Taking the Lord's protection for granted is never advisable.

Even in the midst of the worst that the earth and its inhabitants can throw at us, God protects His people. The psalmist declares that "we [need] not fear, though the earth give way and the mountains fall into the heart of the sea" (see Psalm 46:1–3).

For vivid proof of this, we need look no further than the Old Testament book of Daniel and a test by fire of God's protection.

Shadrach, Meshach, and Abednego, three young Israelite men living in captivity in Babylon, were given honored positions by King Nebuchadnezzar of Babylon. Eventually, though, the king commissioned a ninety-foot-high idol to be erected in the province; all his subjects were ordered to bow before the completed idol. This presented a problem for Shadrach, Meshach, and Abednego, whose faithfulness to God prohibited them from bowing down to an idol.

When the appointed time came, everyone in the kingdom bowed down to the king's idol—except Shadrach, Meshach, and Abednego. The punishment was to be thrown into a blazing furnace, and a surprised Nebuchadnezzar gave them one more chance to bow down to the statue.

Here's the response he received: "O Nebuchadnezzar, we do not need to defend ourselves before you in this matter. If we are thrown into the blazing furnace, the

God we serve is able to save us from it, and he will rescue us from your hand, O king. But even if he does not, we want you to know, O king, that we will not serve your gods or worship the image of gold you have set up" (Daniel 3:16–18).

This enraged the king, and he ordered the furnace stoked seven times hotter than usual. The fire became so intense that it consumed the soldiers who threw Shadrach, Meshach, and Abednego into the furnace.

Nebuchadnezzar expected the same fate to befall his three administrators. However, when he looked into the furnace, he was shocked to see Shadrach, Meshach, and Abednego walking around unharmed and unsinged in the middle of the fire. What's more, he saw a fourth figure walking with them—One who looked, according to the pagan king, "like a son of the gods" (3:25).

Shadrach, Meshach, and Abednego remained faithful to the Lord; in return, He protected them in a miraculous way. Nebuchadnezzar was so impressed by the display of protection he witnessed that he called Shadrach, Meshach, and Abednego out of the furnace and issued a decree making it illegal for anyone to say anything against the God of Israel.

You can find other examples of God's work of protection scattered throughout the Bible, including His keeping Noah and his family alive during the Flood, keeping the Old Testament prophet Daniel safe all night in a den of starving lions, and allowing the apostle Paul to survive a shipwreck and a deadly snakebite.

Before we wrap up this section, there's one more point about God's protection that we need to make. Look back at the bold reply of Shadrach, Meshach, and Abednego when King Nebuchadnezzar threatened to have them thrown into the fiery furnace. Their response takes on a whole new resonance when you consider the five words tucked right in the middle of it: "even if he does not."

The three faithful Israelites knew that God was *capable* of protecting them from the flames. However, they didn't know whether it was His *will* to protect them or not. For all they knew, God's plan was for them to become martyrs—and they were okay with that.

As difficult as it may be to accept, sometimes God's will for our lives involves tragedy, suffering, and loss. That doesn't mean His protection falters; it means His work is being accomplished in ways we may not be able to comprehend.

God's protective hand is still at work today, though not always in miraculous, or even apparent, ways. Who knows how many close calls we experience every day? Who knows how many catastrophes God has quietly prevented in our lives? Who knows what would happen if God ever removed His protection from our lives?

God Disciplines

Hebrews 12:6 is quite clear on the matter: "The Lord disciplines those he loves, and he punishes everyone he accepts as a son." Job 5:17 adds, "Blessed is the man whom God corrects; so do not despise the discipline of the Almighty."

If we have trouble equating discipline with love and correction with blessing, it's likely due to a misunderstanding of the nature and purpose of God's discipline. The reality is that God loves us too much to stand by and watch us mess up our lives with sin. Therefore, He will take whatever steps He deems necessary to get our attention, help us recognize the seriousness of our situation, and turn us in the right direction.

Occasionally, God's discipline is painful—sometimes extremely so. King David would certainly attest to that. Second Samuel 11 tells the story of how David committed adultery with Bathsheba and then plotted to have her husband killed so that David could marry her and cover up his sexual sin. God disciplined the king in the wake of his sin by (among other things) allowing David's newborn son—who was conceived during the illicit affair—to die, despite the king's desperate pleas.

Moses also experienced the business end of God's painful discipline. You'll recall that Moses was chosen by God to lead millions of Israelites from captivity in Egypt to their new home in the Promised Land. Along the way, though, the Lord became fed up with the people's lack of faith, complaining spirit, and general insubordination. He sentenced the Israelites to wander in the desert wilderness of the Middle East for forty years, or until the adult generation died out.

You can probably imagine what forty years in the desert with a bunch of whining travel companions did to Moses' attitude and outlook over time. One day, at a place called Meribah, Moses' frustration and impatience got the better of him. Numbers 20:1–13 picks up the story from there. When the Israelites started complaining about being thirsty, God told Moses to *speak* to a rock, and He (God) would cause water to flow from it.

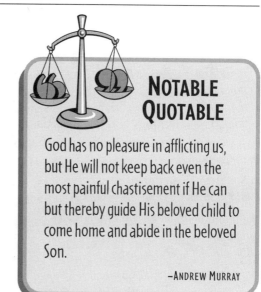

NOTABLE QUOTABLE

God has no pleasure in afflicting us, but He will not keep back even the most painful chastisement if He can but thereby guide His beloved child to come home and abide in the beloved Son.

—Andrew Murray

In a fit of rage, Moses *struck* the rock with his staff instead. Water gushed out, but the Lord was not pleased. His rebuke of Moses was swift and devastating. Because Moses had failed to follow God's instructions completely, he was prohibited from ever entering the Promised Land.

The goal that Moses had worked so long to achieve, the reward that had motivated him to keep going through the long days and nights in the desert, was taken away from him because of one ill-considered act. Moses lived out the final days of his life camped on a hill overlooking the Promised Land—so close, yet so far away—as the result of God's discipline.

Lest we be tempted to throw around words like "unfair" or "unjust" in relation to God's judgment, we must remind ourselves who we're talking about. God is not simply *just*; He's the perfect standard of justice. That means His discipline is never cruel, pointless, or more than people can handle.

In fact, in many cases, God's discipline simply involves allowing people to suffer the consequences of their actions. For example, a person who . . .

> ➤ is prone to lying may develop a reputation for being untrustworthy.

> ➤ cannot control the urge to gossip may be confronted by the subject of one of her rumors.

> ➤ seeks only her own good may find herself without any true friends.

> ➤ commits adultery may lose the love and respect of his spouse.

> ➤ gives in to greed may end up bankrupt.

You can probably think of dozens of other examples of "chickens coming home to roost." The point is, part of God's discipline involves letting people learn the hard way why His rules are in place.

Psalm 89:30–33 provides a fitting summary to God's work of discipline. Though the passage refers specifically to the descendants of David, its words apply to every one of God's children: "If his sons forsake my law and do not follow my statutes, if they violate my decrees and fail to keep my commands, I will punish their sin with the rod, their iniquity with flogging; but I will not take my love from him, nor will I ever betray my faithfulness."

God Forgives

The forgiveness principle is prevalent throughout Scripture, but it is perhaps most clearly stated in 1 John 1:9: "If we confess our sins, he is faithful and just and will forgive us our sins and purify us from all unrighteousness."

True repentance on our part results in complete forgiveness on God's part. The Lord doesn't hold grudges. He doesn't throw past transgressions in our faces. In fact, Psalm 103:12 tells us that God removes our sin from us "as far as the east is from the west."

The Old Testament Israelites serve as a testament to the Lord's work of forgiveness. Israel's relationship with the Lord in Scripture is a continuous cycle of wickedness-repentance-forgiveness. In certain portions of Scripture, the Israelites' penchant for idolatry and rebellion is staggering. Yet each time they recognized the error

ON A PERSONAL NOTE

Think of a time when God allowed you to experience the consequences of your sin. Answer these questions:

➤ What consequences did you suffer?

➤ How did those consequences affect your life?

➤ How did you react to those consequences?

➤ What effect do you think God intended the experience to have on your life?

➤ What effect did it actually have?

➤ How do you view the experience now?

If you haven't prayed about the experience, this would be a great time to do it. Thank the Lord for caring enough about you to discipline you and teach you a lesson.

of their ways and returned to God, He forgave them and took them back.

That same consideration is offered to all believers and unbelievers alike. If we approach God with genuine repentance—by turning away from sin and toward Him—He will wipe our slate clean and give us a fresh start.

God Restores

Not only does God "forgive and forget," but He also makes sure that those who repent of their sin are restored to their rightful place in His work and will. The apostle Peter is one of the best-known beneficiaries of God's restorative work.

When Jesus announced at the Last Supper that He was about to be arrested and killed, Peter was quick to flash His typical bravado: "Lord, I am ready to go with you to prison and to death" (Luke 22:33).

Jesus' reply must have mystified Peter: "I tell you, Peter, before the rooster crows today, you will deny three times that you know me." No doubt Peter thought of himself as one of Jesus' most loyal and trusted followers. The idea of ever *denying* Jesus probably never crossed his mind.

Peter seemed to prove Jesus' prediction wrong when the priests and soldiers came to arrest Jesus. Peter's first response was to draw his sword and attack in order to defend the Lord. (Although it should be pointed out that the person Peter chose to slice was not one of the armed soldiers but a defenseless servant of the high priest.)

Luke 22:54–62 picks up the story from there. Peter secretly followed Jesus after His arrest to the courtyard of the high priest's house. While Jesus was put on trial for His life inside, Peter waited outside. A passing servant girl recognized Peter as a follower of Jesus and announced to the assembled crowd: "This man was with him."

Peter's reply was emphatic and immediate: "Woman, I don't know him."

A little while later, Peter was recognized again as one of the disciples. "Man, I am not!" was his swift reply. An hour or so later, he was recognized again, this time because of his Galilean accent. Matthew 26:74 says that Peter "began to call down curses on himself," swearing that he had no idea who Jesus was.

About that time, a rooster crowed, and the reality of what he had just done hit Peter. Luke 22:62 says that the disciple "went outside and wept bitterly."

Three times Peter had an opportunity to promote the truth about Christ. Three times he had an opportunity to vouch for Jesus' authority. Three times he had an opportunity to align himself with the true Messiah. Three times Peter failed miserably.

The law of "just deserts" would dictate that Peter die a broken and shamed man, banished for life from service in Christ's kingdom. Of course, if God trafficked in "just deserts," we would have nothing to look forward to but a future in hell.

NOTABLE QUOTABLE

Would you like me to tell you what supported me through all the years of exile among a people whose language I could not understand, and whose attitude to me was always uncertain and often hostile? It was this, "Lo, I am with you alway, even unto the end of the world." On these words I staked everything, and they never failed.

–DAVID LIVINGSTONE

Fortunately for Peter—and for us—God not only forgives our sins and shortcomings; He makes us useful to Himself again. He *restores* us.

Peter's restoration occurred shortly after Jesus' resurrection. John 21:1–19 tells us that the risen Christ appeared to Peter and the other disciples on the Tiberian seashore. Three times Jesus asked Peter if he loved Him. Three times Peter replied, "You know that I love you." And three times Jesus responded with an instruction to feed and take care of His "sheep."

With that exchange, the Lord restored Peter to service. In essence, He told Peter to get over his failure and concentrate on what lay ahead. For Peter, that included spreading the news of Jesus far and wide, establishing the first-century church, writing two books of the New Testament, and (according to tradition) being crucified upside down because of his faith. Because of God's restorative work, Peter's legacy is not one of failure, but one of vital importance in Christian history.

David recognized God's restorative power. That's why, even after his egregious sin with Bathsheba, he felt confident enough to pray, "Restore to me the joy of your salvation and grant me a willing spirit, to sustain me" (Psalm 51:12).

That same restorative power is available to us today. God doesn't discard us when we fail Him. He doesn't write us off as a bad risk. He doesn't disqualify us from His service. Instead, He works through our genuine repentance to make changes in our attitude and lifestyle, changes that reenergize us for service to Him. He restores us to positions of value in His work.

God Arranges

The fact that God is omniscient (as we discussed in chapter 3) means that He knows every possible outcome of every circumstance, every situation, and every decision that we encounter. The fact that He is sovereign and omnipotent means that He can manipulate any circumstance, situation, or decision to achieve a desired goal.

Take the story of Joseph and his brothers, for example. Genesis 37 describes how Joseph's brothers, jealous of Joseph's favored status with their father, sold Joseph as a slave to a caravan of Midianite merchants. The brothers then told their father that Joseph had been killed; then they proceeded to get on with their lives.

Joseph's life, on the other hand, took twists and turns that no one could have anticipated. No one except God, that is. Genesis 39–50 relates the long and complicated tale. Joseph was sold again to an Egyptian official named Potiphar. Potiphar was so impressed with Joseph's character that he put the young man in charge of his entire household.

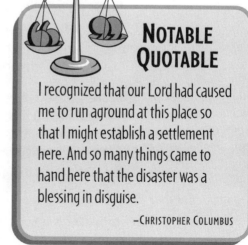

NOTABLE QUOTABLE

I recognized that our Lord had caused me to run aground at this place so that I might establish a settlement here. And so many things came to hand here that the disaster was a blessing in disguise.

–Christopher Columbus

Unfortunately, Joseph also attracted the attention of Potiphar's wife. When Joseph refused her sexual advances, Potiphar's wife accused him of attempted rape and had him thrown in prison. There Joseph met the king's cupbearer and baker, both of whom had also been arrested and both of whom were having mysterious dreams. Using his God-given ability, Joseph interpreted the two men's dreams. He told the cupbearer that he would be

NOTABLE QUOTABLE

It is not what I do that matters, but what a sovereign God chooses to do through me. God does not want worldly successes; He wants me. He wants my heart in submission to Him. Life is not just a few years to spend on self-indulgence and career advancement. It is a privilege, a responsibility, a stewardship to be lived according to a much higher calling, God's calling. This alone gives true meaning to life.

–Elizabeth Dole

released in three days and restored to his old position. He told the baker that he would be executed in three days. Both of Joseph's interpretations came true.

Two years later, Pharaoh, the king of Egypt, began having a dream of his own, which none of his advisors could interpret. The cupbearer remembered Joseph in prison and recommended him to Pharaoh. Joseph was brought before the king. Pharaoh described his dream of seven fat cows being eaten by seven scrawny cows and seven heads of grain being swallowed by seven withered heads of grain. Joseph told Pharaoh that his dream represented seven years of abundance for Egypt, followed by seven years of famine. Joseph recommended that Pharaoh appoint an official to oversee the storage of grain during the seven years of abundance so that the people would have food to eat during the seven years of famine.

Pharaoh was so impressed by Joseph's wisdom that he put Joseph in charge of storing food in preparation for the famine—and made him the second most powerful man in Egypt in the process. Joseph fulfilled his responsibilities admirably. When the famine struck, people from all countries were able to come to Egypt to buy grain, thanks to Joseph's vision.

Among the people who came to Joseph to ask for food were his brothers, who did not recognize their long-lost sibling. After testing his brothers to make sure that they had changed, Joseph revealed himself to them and then sent them back to their home to retrieve their father, as well as their wives and children. Joseph moved his entire family to Egypt and kept them alive and fed, despite the famine that ravaged the land.

Using circumstances no one could have imagined, God *arranged* to have Joseph in a position of power in Egypt when his family needed him most.

God continues His arranging work today, though it often goes unrecognized. If we don't look for His "fingerprints" on the events, circumstances, situations, and interactions that affect our lives and the lives of others, we may mistake God's arranging work for mere coincidence or simply "being in the right place at the right time."

David gives lie to that last notion in Psalm 23:3, when he says of God: "He guides me in paths of righteousness for his name's sake." If you're serious about understanding God and His work in your life, you must recognize that your "paths of righteousness" intersect with the paths of countless other people also being led by God. Those intersections represent your daily encounters and interactions with other people— friends, family members, coworkers, teammates, casual acquaintances, and complete strangers included.

If we recognize those individual encounters and interactions as being part of God's arranging work, we will be more likely to give them the attention they deserve. In other words, questions such as "Why has God brought this person into my life?" or "What is God's purpose for me in this situation?" should never be far from our thoughts.

ON A PERSONAL NOTE

Think of a time when you or someone you know seemed to be in the right place at the right time. Ask yourself these questions:

➤ Looking back on the situation now, can you see God's hand in it?

➤ If so, what "arrangements" did He make in order to make sure that you were in the right place at the right time?

➤ What do you think His purpose was?

➤ What do you think of your handling of the situation, in light of the fact that it was likely God-ordained?

After you've answered the questions, think about what, if anything, you will do differently the next time you find yourself in the right place at the right time.

Responding the Right Way

As the recipients and beneficiaries of God's work, we must diligently guard against ever taking His work for granted. We must keep in mind that none of us has ever done anything to deserve the attention that God lavishes on us. Therefore, we have a responsibility to respond to God's work in our lives in a way that honors Him.

The first thing we need to do is *recognize* His work. In order to do that, we must diligently search for it. We must learn not to . . .

➤ take "little things" for granted,

➤ mistake our God-given blessings for luck, or

➤ confuse God's perfectly executed plans for coincidence.

The second thing we need to do is *yield to* His work. Isaiah 64:8 compares the relationship between God and His people to that of a potter and his clay. God is the Artist, the Creator, the Worker; we are the raw material with which He works. Our responsibility, then, is to be the best "clay" we can be, completely malleable and responsive to His shaping.

The third thing we need to do is *show our thankfulness* for His work. One obvious way of accomplishing that is through prayer, expressing our gratefulness in a one-on-one setting with God. In order to make your prayer time as effective as possible, you might want to keep a list of the evidence of God's work you spot in your life. (You don't want to forget anything.)

Another way to show your thankfulness is to spread God's fame and bolster His reputation among the people you encounter. Don't be shy about sharing your experiences. Let others know what kind of God you serve. Give them a reason to desire His work in *their* lives.

Know What You Believe

How much do you know about the work of God in people's lives? Here's a quiz to test your knowledge.

1. Which of the following is not a work of God in our lives?
   a. Disciplining
   b. Protecting
   c. Bullying
   d. Forgiving

2. How did God equip Thomas for service?
   a. He sent him to rabbinical school for three years.
   b. He gave him physical evidence of Christ's resurrection.
   c. He gave him Moses' old shape-shifting staff.
   d. He taught him vital horse-riding and sword-fighting skills.

3. Which of the following is not true of God's provision?
   a. Post-Pentecost Christians have no reason to expect it in their lives.
   b. The Israelites experienced it in the form of manna.
   c. Hagar and Ishmael experienced it in the form of a desert well.
   d. The apostle Paul promised it to the believers in Philippi.

4. What does the Bible tell us about God's discipline?
   a. He disciplines those He loves.
   b. His discipline causes Him more pain than it does the person being disciplined.
   c. No one will experience His discipline until the final judgment.
   d. God withholds His discipline because no human would ever be able to survive it.

5. Which of the following is not true of God's work of "arranging"?
   a. It's a logical extension of His omniscience, sovereignty, and omnipotence.
   b. It's demonstrated in the biblical story of Joseph and his family.
   c. It's often mistaken for coincidence or being in the right place at the right time.
   d. It's nothing for busy Christians to concern themselves with.

Answers: (1) c, (2) b, (3) a, (4) a, (5) d

"THE WORLD'S EASIEST GUIDE"

PART THREE

God's Plans

CHAPTER 12

Model Behavior

UNDERSTANDING GOD'S EXPECTATIONS FOR HIS PEOPLE

SNAPSHOT

"What in the world are you doing now, roomie?" Kevin asked as he walked into the apartment.

Mike peeked out from behind a pile of gauze and elastic on the table. "I'm rolling bandages," he replied.

"Why?" Kevin asked.

"It's for one of our ministries at church," Mike explained. "Our medical missionaries to Cameroon are leaving in two weeks, and we're trying to get some supplies ready for them to take back with them."

Kevin shook his head. "He's got you on a pretty short leash, doesn't He?"

"Who?" Mike asked.

SNEAK PREVIEW

1. The privilege of claiming Jesus as Savior and Lord carries with it the responsibility of living according to His instructions.
2. The Bible identifies several different actions and attitudes that should characterize the life of a Christian.
3. Before eternity, all Christians will be judged by God and rewarded for their faithfulness in obeying His commands.

"God."

"What do you mean?"

"If you're not wrapping bandages, then you're serving food at a soup kitchen or shoveling snow for the old guy across the street or sending get-well cards to people you barely know," Kevin pointed out.

"And you see that as one big, miserable existence?" Mike asked.

"I'm not saying you're *miserable*," Kevin said. "I know you have fun. It's just that— well, I don't think you think about yourself enough."

Mike rolled his eyes and continued working.

Kevin motioned toward the wrapped bandages on the table. "So does all this stuff you do have to do with your religion?"

"Not *religion*," Mike corrected. "It has to do with the fact that I'm a Christian."

"Same difference."

"No, it's really not," Mike said. "Religion is about doing things to show how good you are. Christianity is about doing things because Christ did them."

"I don't understand," Kevin admitted.

"The fact that I call myself a Christian means that I want to be like Christ," Mike explained. "That's what *Christian* means—'like Christ.'"

"So if you thought about *yourself* more or did the things that *you* want to do, that would make you a Mike-ian," Kevin said.

"I guess so." Mike chuckled. "And that's no good. That's why Jesus is my model. The way He lived His life is the way I want to live my life. The attitude He had is the attitude I want to have. The priorities He lived by are the priorities I want to live by."

Kevin nodded slowly but said nothing.

"Think of it this way," Mike said. "If I were an *Elvis-ian*, I'd wear my hair in a pompadour, grow my sideburns, and eat fried-peanut-butter-and-banana sandwiches."

"Yeah, I see what you're saying," Kevin acknowledged.

"And if I were a *Kevin-ian*, I'd . . . learn to snore . . . do my laundry no more than twice a year . . . leave take-out Chinese food in the refrigerator for months at a time . . . and raid my roommate's closet whenever I had a big date."

"Hey, you take that back!" Kevin growled with mock ferocity. "I don't . . . snore."

* * * * * * * * * * * * * * *

If it's true that membership has its privileges, as American Express contends, it's also true that membership has its responsibilities. Any club, organization, association, affiliation, union, or group worth its salt has its own set of rules, regulations, requirements, prohibitions, and expectations for its members.

The Boy Scouts, for example, are expected to be trustworthy, loyal, helpful, friendly, courteous, kind, obedient, cheerful, thrifty, brave, clean, and reverent. Doctors are expected to honor the terms of their Hippocratic oath ("I will apply, for the benefit of the sick, all measures which are required. . . . I will not be ashamed to say 'I know not.' . . . I will respect the privacy of my patients"). Attorneys have rules of professional conduct that govern their actions. (Insert your own lawyer joke here.)

Even Western heroes have their own "Ten Cowboy Commandments," courtesy of screen legend Gene Autry. (In case you're wondering, the code by which "real cowboys" live includes not taking unfair advantage of an enemy, always telling the truth, and refraining from alcohol and tobacco.)

Country clubs require members to meet certain standards and fulfill certain obligations. Professional sports teams have rules for behavior, both on and off the field (or court), that players must abide by.

NOTABLE QUOTABLE

Of a Christian believer . . . it may be said that every act of his life is or can be as truly sacred as prayer or baptism or the Lord's Supper. To say this is not to bring all acts down to one dead level; it is rather to lift every act up into a living kingdom and turn the whole life into a sacrament.

–A. W. Tozer

Some groups prefer to keep their requirements and expectations private; others find their identity in the public behavior or appearance of their members.

Lights...Action!

The church would certainly fall into the latter category. God wants the affiliation of His people to be screamingly obvious. He wants us to leave no doubt in the minds of the people we encounter as to whom we belong to and whose example we follow.

Look at Jesus' words to His followers in Matthew 5:14–16: "You are the light of the world. A city on a hill cannot be hidden. Neither do people light a lamp and put it under a bowl. Instead they put it on its stand, and it gives light to everyone in the house. In the same way, let your light shine before men, that they may see your good deeds and praise your Father in heaven."

To put it another way, we as believers are lightbulbs. When we repent and believe in Jesus, we begin to "shine," spiritually speaking. Jesus' point in Matthew 5 is that if we're going to shine, we should do it as brightly as possible. Instead of trying to dim our lights and fade into the crowd in our daily existence, we should crank up the wattage to spotlight proportions in order to get people's attention and demonstrate the changes that God can effect in a person's life.

The Bible makes it clear that our "lights" are made visible through the *actions, attitudes,* and *priorities* that we demonstrate to others. We have a responsibility to reflect Jesus in the way we live—to speak and act in a manner that is recognizably Christian.

The bottom line is that people should notice something "different" in us, something that sets us apart from unbelievers. The difference should be so noticeable, in fact, that people can't help asking about it.

When people express interest in, or curiosity about, our uniqueness, it presents us with an opportunity to explain why we follow the example of Christ in our lives and why our uniqueness is only possible through God and His work.

He's Number One! He's Number One!

Any discussion of the responsibility of believers must begin with Matthew 22:36–40. In this passage, Jesus is asked point-blank: "Which is the greatest commandment in the Law?" In other words, of all the instructions in the Bible, which one is the most important for a believer to follow?

Jesus didn't have to think twice about His answer: "'Love the Lord your God with all your heart and with all your soul and with all your mind.' This is the first and greatest commandment" (Matthew 22:37–38).

Demonstrating one's love for God is a full-body workout. Everything we *do*—from the way we spend our free time to the way we spend our money—should reflect our love for God. Everything we *say*—from the way we joke with our friends to the way we respond to rude salespeople—should be evidence of our commitment to the Lord. Everything we *feel*—from the way we process anger to the way we respond to tragedy—should be colored by our abiding love for our heavenly Father. Everything we

NOTABLE QUOTABLE

Lord, we don't mind who is second as long as Thou art first.

—W. E. Sangster

think—from our opinions of world events to our views on controversial issues—should mirror the truth found in God's Word.

The love that Jesus calls for in Matthew 22 demands that God be the number one priority of our lives—in word and in deed. We can't claim to love God with all of our heart, soul, and mind if we . . .

➤ pursue our own desires at the expense of His will,

➤ ignore the instructions in His Word, or

➤ place the opinions of others above our desire to please Him.

In other words, we must not "talk the talk" of loving God if we're not prepared to "walk the walk."

Won't You Be My Neighbor?

Not only did Jesus reveal the greatest commandment in Matthew 22, He also revealed the runner-up. "And the second is like it: 'Love your neighbor as yourself'" (Matthew 22:39).

A *neighbor*, in the context of this passage, may be anyone from the person who lives next door to the person standing in line in front of you at Starbucks. The point of this passage is not *who* the Lord is talking about; it's what He expects from His followers.

You'll notice that Jesus didn't say, "*Feel* love for your neighbor." This isn't a greeting card sentiment we're talking about. *Love,* in this case, is an action verb. The instruction to Jesus' followers in this passage is to *demonstrate* a loving attitude to the people around us in the way we act and the things we say— whether we "feel" like it or not.

If that seems hypocritical, consider that God's Holy Spirit dwells within every believer. From His vantage point, He can work to change our heart attitudes and help us begin to feel the love that we demonstrate. The key, though, is obedience— doing what God commands regardless of our personal feelings about it.

NOTABLE QUOTABLE

The nearer we draw to God in our love for Him, the more we are united together by love for our neighbor; and the greater our union with our neighbor, the greater our union with God.

–DOROTHEUS OF GAZA

The last two words of Matthew 22:39, "as yourself," up the ante further. Practically speaking, we have a responsibility to be as concerned about the welfare of others as we are about our own welfare.

The bad news is that the kind of selfless attitude that God expects from His people isn't developed overnight. The good news is that we have a foolproof blueprint for obeying the command. All we have to do is ask ourselves, "What would I do for *myself* in this situation?" or "What would I want from someone else here?" and then do it. That's the way we love our neighbors as ourselves.

Family Matters

In addition to loving our neighbors, Christians also have a responsibility to demonstrate love to one another. Look at the apostle Paul's instructions to the first-century church in Rome: "Love must be sincere. Hate what is evil; cling to what is good. Be devoted to one another in brotherly love. Honor one another above yourselves. Never be lacking in zeal, but keep your spiritual fervor, serving the Lord. Be joyful in hope, patient in affliction, faithful in prayer. Share with God's people who are in need. Practice hospitality" (Romans 12:9–13).

Galatians 6:10 takes the concept to the next level: "Therefore, as we have opportunity, let us do good to all people, especially to those who belong to the family of believers." Our relationship with fellow members of the body of Christ *must* be a priority in our lives.

As the adoptive children of God, all Christians are members of the same family. And, like it or not, people will judge the family by the way we get along with one another and the love we show to each other.

> **NOTABLE QUOTABLE**
>
> The love of God and the God of love constrain you to love one another that it may be said of Christians as it was at first, "Behold how they love one another."
>
> —RALPH VENNING

We'll explore this responsibility further in the discussion of fellowship in chapter 14. For now, we need to point out that the responsibility to love fellow believers means we must not allow . . .

➤ personality clashes,

➤ minor annoyances,

➤ territorial ministry issues,

➤ differing opinions, or

➤ long-standing grudges

. . . to interfere with our relationships in the church. As brothers and sisters in Christ, we may not always agree—all families have squabbles, after all—but we must resolve to work out our disagreements in a spirit of love.

Enemy Territory

In educational terms, loving God would be considered an "introductory" course for Christians. It's a concept even "freshmen" believers can grasp. After all, who is more deserving of our love than our heavenly Father? Loving our neighbors and our fellow believers, on the other hand, would probably be considered "intermediate" courses—not as easy as loving God but still relatively comprehensible.

Matthew 5:44, however, presents us with a doctorate-level concept: "Love your enemies and pray for those who persecute you." Though Jesus doesn't define the word *enemies* in this passages, we can operate under the assumption that He's referring to:

➤ backstabbers

➤ people who cut you off in traffic

➤ gossips

➤ drunken louts

➤ bullies

➤ telemarketers

➤ cutthroat coworkers

➤ anyone who makes your life miserable

This passage effectively eliminates our option of treating unpleasant people . . .

➤ in a way that we think they deserve to be treated,

➤ in a way that satisfies our immediate need for retribution or satisfaction,

➤ in a way that other people would treat them under similar circumstances,

➤ in a way that other people would like us to treat them, or

➤ in the way they treat us.

As far as God is concerned, these people don't deserve our wrath—or even our passive indifference. They deserve our love—not a feelings-based kind of benevolence, but an action-oriented desire for the best in that person's life.

There are two compelling reasons for us to treat our enemies with genuine love, concern, and care. The first reason is that if we don't, we're guilty of infringing on God's authority. When we treat an enemy badly, it's because we've judged that person to be worthy of such treatment. However, passages such as James 4:12 make it clear that God alone is worthy to judge.

The second reason is that demonstrating love toward enemies sets Christians apart from practically everyone else in the world. This is the point Jesus makes in Matthew 5:46–47: "If you love those who love you, what reward will you get? Are not even the tax collectors doing that? And if you greet only your brothers, what are you doing more than others? Do not even pagans do that?"

There's nothing remarkable or outstanding about showing love to family members and friends. Even the worst people in society do that. God wants *His* people to stand out in the world. That's why He expects Christians to take the notion of loving others to its logical extreme and apply it to their enemies.

Have Mercy!

If you knew that Jesus was . . .

➤ suffering the effects of hunger and thirst,

➤ lonely,

➤ in need of clothing,

➤ extremely ill, or

➤ locked up in prison

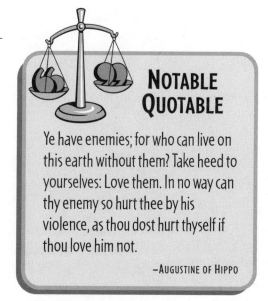

NOTABLE QUOTABLE

Ye have enemies; for who can live on this earth without them? Take heed to yourselves: Love them. In no way can thy enemy so hurt thee by his violence, as thou dost hurt thyself if thou love him not.

—Augustine of Hippo

. . . how far would you go to meet His needs? (Be warned: The answer you give will have tremendous implications for your life.)

That's the scenario Jesus posed to His disciples in Matthew 25:35–36: "For I was hungry and you gave me something to eat, I was thirsty and you gave me something to drink, I was a stranger and you invited me in, I needed clothes and you clothed me, I was sick and you looked after me, I was in prison and you came to visit me."

Apparently, this came as news to the disciples, none of whom could remember providing any of those ministries to Jesus. As was their habit when faced with a teaching they couldn't grasp, the disciples asked Jesus to explain what He was talking about.

That's when Jesus hit them with the truth that still impacts every believer to this day. Showing mercy to people in need is the same as showing mercy to Jesus Himself. Therefore, we can conclude that the way we treat a person in need is an accurate barometer of our feelings about Jesus.

The gospel writers suggest that many of the people Jesus came into contact with during His earthly ministry were drawn to Him *first* by His mercy—His willingness to respond in a profound and personal way to those in need—and not necessarily by His message.

Look at the cries of the people who encountered Jesus during His travels:

➤ "Lord, if you are willing, you can make me clean" (Matthew 8:2).

➤ "Have mercy on us, Son of David!" (Matthew 9:27).

➤ "Lord, Son of David, have mercy on me!" (Matthew 15:22).

➤ "Lord, help me!" (Matthew 15:25).

Conversely, you won't find many accounts in Scripture of people clamoring for Jesus to tell them a parable or preach a sermon. Jesus used His healing power as an instrument of mercy in order to prepare the hearts of His audience for His message.

That same "mercy first" principle should serve as a lesson to us, His followers. The fact is, all of the preaching, witnessing, warning, and teaching in the world won't have as much impact on another person's life as one act of mercy or kindness.

If we're serious about ministering to Jesus in a "Matthew 25" way—that is, by ministering to the needy—we must first open ourselves up to recognizing the needs around us. Unfortunately, many of us have spiritual "blinders" that prevent us from seeing and acknowledging the hurts of all but a small circle of loved ones. Removing those blinders is the first step in responding to people's needs in a way that satisfies Jesus.

The first thing we'll recognize upon removing our blinders is that there is no shortage of potential recipients of our mercy. We live in a hurting world. In fact, there are so many hurting people around us that we may become discouraged or overwhelmed by our responsibility.

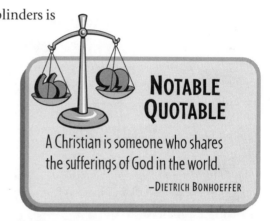

NOTABLE QUOTABLE

A Christian is someone who shares the sufferings of God in the world.

–DIETRICH BONHOEFFER

To prevent that from happening, we need to keep in mind that mercy is not always shown through grand gestures. In fact, mercy is often most effectively demonstrated in small, but meaningful, ways:

➤ We may not be able to ease the pain of a grieving widow or widower, but we can express our sentiments in a card or note.

➤ We may not be able to do much about a cancerous growth on the lungs of an elderly church member, but we can visit him in the hospital and keep him company during his difficult times.

➤ We may not be able to put a down payment on an apartment for a homeless mother and her kids, but we can volunteer at the shelter where she stays.

➤ We may not be able to cure the loneliness of a wife who's been left by her husband, but we can meet regularly with her to pray about her situation.

Hebrews 4:16 tells us that God provides "grace to help us in our time of need." What we need to recognize, though, is that in addition to being the *recipients* of God's grace, we are also occasionally the *instruments* of His grace. In other words, God often shows His mercy through our actions.

Above and Beyond

When it comes to God's expectations for His people, there's no such thing as going "above and beyond" the call of duty. In fact, our duty, as outlined in Matthew 5:38–42, *is* to go above and beyond in everything we do.

"You have heard that it was said, 'Eye for eye, and tooth for tooth.' But I tell you, Do not resist an evil person. If someone strikes you on the right cheek, turn to him the other also. And if someone wants to sue you and take your tunic, let him have your cloak as well. If someone forces you to go one mile, go with him two miles. Give to the one who asks you, and do not turn away from the one who wants to borrow from you."

JUST WONDERING

What happened to the old system of "an eye for an eye and a tooth for a tooth"? I liked that way better.

Jesus' words in Matthew 5:38–42 served to correct a popular misunderstanding about the Old Testament "law of retaliation." The law was intended to ensure that the penalty for any given crime did not exceed the crime itself. It was not a license for vigilante justice, but a means of protecting the accused. There is no evidence in Scripture that an actual eye or tooth was ever required of a person convicted of a crime.

Our personal conduct must reflect our commitment to Christ. That means doing what is expected of us—and then some. In our vengeance-minded, lawsuit-happy, self-centered world, the actions and attitudes described by Jesus in this passage are bound to set believers apart and make our lights visible.

Jesus gave His followers a model for the ages in turning the other cheek on the night of His arrest. Mark 15:16–20 tells us that before His crucifixion, Jesus was mocked and beaten by Roman guards. Over and over again, they struck Him. Yet Jesus remained silent and did nothing.

This is especially significant in light of Jesus' words to Peter in Matthew 26:53: "Do you think I cannot call on my Father, and he will at once put at my disposal more than twelve legions of angels?" At any point during His beating, Jesus could have called down tens of thousands of angels to tap-dance on the heads of His tormentors.

The fact is, though, He didn't. He refused to take revenge. He left that task to His heavenly Father, as instructed in Romans 12:19 ("'It is mine to avenge; I will repay,' says the Lord").

Jesus understood that refusing the opportunity for justified payback creates a memorable impression in the lives of those who witness it. If we're serious about letting our lights shine, we need to learn that same principle.

Though the *application* of Jesus' words in Matthew 5:38–42 may differ from person to person and from situation to situation, the *principle* remains constant. God calls us to be actively generous not only with our material possessions but also with our time, energy, effort, and encouragement—and not only with those who "deserve" it (in our judgment) but with those who don't.

Contrary to a notion that was popular before the events of September 11, 2001, the world is full of "good Samaritans," people willing to help—sometimes in extraordinary ways—in times of need. And we should be thankful for that. However, people who are willing to go the *extra mile*—to provide assistance, concern, and care when it is completely unwarranted—are rare. And rare people are memorable people to those who encounter them. That's why God expects us to go above and beyond the call of duty in helping others.

ON A PERSONAL NOTE

The principle of turning the other cheek should never be construed as a command to endure abuse. Jesus does not expect His followers to be human punching bags. His point is that Christians should not take revenge on those who hurt us. Anyone in an abusive situation should seek safety immediately and take all necessary legal steps to prevent the abuse from ever happening again.

Disciple Quest

"Therefore go and make disciples of all nations, baptizing them in the name of the Father and of the Son and of the Holy Spirit, and teaching them to obey everything I have commanded you." That was Jesus' final instruction to His followers in Matthew 28:19–20.

Whether you call it witnessing, spreading the gospel, or doing freelance publicity work on behalf of the Messiah, the fact remains that each of us who love God and the Son He sent has a responsibility to tell other people what we know about Jesus.

The word "go" in Jesus' instructions negates the possibility of "passive evangelism"—that is, waiting for people to notice our shining lights and come to us with all manner of questions regarding Jesus. Evangelism is an active process. It involves the following:

➤ seeking out unbelievers

➤ establishing relationships with them

➤ praying for the Holy Spirit's direction in determining the right time to share with them

➤ communicating the truth about Jesus in a way that they can personally relate to

➤ preparing ourselves to answer questions they may have

➤ encouraging them to make a decision for Christ

➤ leading them in a prayer of repentance

JUST WONDERING

Practically speaking, our service to others could take up every minute of our schedule and every penny of our bank account, if we allow it to. At what point can we say we've done enough for someone?

This is an area in which the wisdom and leading of the Holy Spirit is an absolute necessity. Ask Him to guide your service and to give you a sense of completion and a sense of peace about when it's time to move on.

Second Corinthians 5:19–20 tells us that God "has committed to us the message of reconciliation. We are therefore Christ's ambassadors, as though God were making his appeal through us." There's no higher honor—or greater responsibility—in the Christian life.

Judgment Day

The fact that God instructs His people to follow certain codes of conduct and attitude is reason enough for us to comply to the best of our ability. Yet God, in His infinite goodness, sweetens the pot with the promise of rewards for faithfulness when believers die.

Second Corinthians 5:10 says, "For we must all appear before the judgment seat of Christ, that each one may receive what is due him for the things done while in the body, whether good or bad." The purpose of this judgment is not to determine our eternal destiny, but to determine which rewards we believers are due.

The Bible identifies various potential rewards as "crowns"; they include the "crown of righteousness" (2 Timothy 4:8), the "crown of life" (James 1:12), and the "crown of glory" (1 Peter 5:4). The Bible doesn't list the rules of eligibility for each reward or even tell us how many crowns are available. God's Word does, however, make it clear that the heavenly rewards that await those who are faithful in obeying God's commands are much more significant and valuable than we can ever understand in this lifetime.

Trying to Be Perfect

If you think God sets the bar high in His expectations for His people, you're right. In Matthew 5:48, Jesus goes so far as to say, "Be perfect, therefore, as your heavenly Father is

ON A PERSONAL NOTE

Take the advice of the apostle Peter to heart: "Always be prepared to give an answer to everyone who asks you to give the reason for the hope that you have" (1 Peter 3:15). Anticipate the type of questions you might receive from unbelievers, and then make sure that you have satisfactory answers ready for them. Obviously, the Bible will be your primary source of information. You might also want to peruse some books on apologetics in your church library or local Christian bookstore. Your first assignment: Find answers to these popular questions:

➤ How do you know that Christianity is right and other religions are wrong?

➤ How can you put your trust in Someone or something you can't see?

➤ How do you know the Bible is true?

➤ If God forgives sins, why can't we just do whatever we want after we become Christians?

perfect." Before you close this book in frustration and dismiss that goal as too lofty to even attempt, consider three things.

1. *We cannot achieve perfection.* As the popular bumper sticker says, "Christians aren't perfect—just forgiven." Passages such as 1 John 1:9 describe the availability of God's forgiveness for a reason: We need it! The fact that Jesus has freed us from slavery to sin doesn't prevent us from occasionally falling back into some old, damaging habits. Satan certainly doesn't stop his temptation of us when we accept Christ as Savior. If anything, he steps it up in order to make our Christian lives as ineffective as possible. In short, none of us is perfect.

2. *God knows that we cannot achieve perfection.* God isn't stupid, naive, deluded, or blinded by His love for us. Psalm 33:13–15 makes it clear that God knows exactly what we're doing, thinking, and feeling at all times. That means nothing we do comes as a surprise to Him. The Lord knows how much distance there is between us and perfection. He knew it when He gave the command to "be perfect" in Matthew 5:48.

3. *Those facts should not stop us from trying to achieve perfection.* Our failures are not the end of our quest to be perfect; they are the beginning. As followers of Christ, we have a responsibility to *continuously* strive to achieve His goal for our lives. When we fall, we shouldn't mope or moan about our imperfection or allow our failures to paralyze us. Instead, we must ask for God's forgiveness, get back up, and continue our quest for perfection.

We'll give the apostle Paul the final word in this chapter:

Not that I have already obtained all this, or have already been made perfect, but I press on to take hold of that for which Christ Jesus took hold of me. Brothers, I do not consider myself yet to have taken hold of it. But one thing I do: Forgetting what is behind and straining toward what is ahead, I press on toward the goal to win the prize for which God has called me heavenward in Christ Jesus. (Philippians 3:12–14)

Know What You Believe

How much do you know about God's expectations for His people? Here's a quiz to test your knowledge.

1. What does Jesus instruct every believer to do with his or her "light"?
    a. Use it sparingly so that it lasts a long time.
    b. Generate power for it through Bible study.
    c. Let it shine for everyone to see.
    d. Keep it hidden until He returns.

2. According to Jesus, what is the greatest commandment?
    a. "Love the Lord your God with all your heart and with all your soul and with all your mind."
    b. "Honor the Sabbath and keep it holy."
    c. "Love your neighbor as yourself."
    d. Jesus said that all of God's commandments are equally important.

3. Which of the following statements is not part of Jesus' teaching on mercy in Matthew 25:35–36?
    a. "I was hungry and you gave me something to eat."
    b. "I was in prison and you came to visit me."
    c. "I needed clothes and you clothed me."
    d. "I was trapped and you rescued me."

4. Which of the following steps is not part of active evangelism?
    a. Preparing ourselves to answer the questions of unbelievers
    b. Praying for someone who knows what they're doing to substitute for us
    c. Establishing personal relationships with unbelievers
    d. Communicating the truth about Jesus in a way that unbelievers can personally relate to

5. Which of the following is not one of the rewards for believers mentioned in Scripture?
   a. Crown of righteousness
   b. Crown of thorns
   c. Crown of glory
   d. Crown of life

Answers: (1) c, (2) a, (3) d, (4) b, (5) b

CHAPTER 13

Life in Providence

UNDERSTANDING GOD'S WILL

S N A P S H O T

"Hey, stranger."

Brady looked up from his scorecard. "Hey, Matt!" he said as he pulled up the hood of his windbreaker. "What brings you out on a day like this?"

Matt pulled a 3-wood from his golf bag and used it to knock some dirt loose from his spikes. "Well, I've been noticing a lack of frustration and irritation in my life lately," he said, "so I thought I'd do something about it."

Brady held up his scorecard and said, "Based on the round I just shot, I'd say you've come to the right place. By the way, how's the job search going?"

"Nothing to report yet," Matt replied. "But that's okay. I've still got six more weeks of unemployment checks coming."

SNEAK PREVIEW

1. God's directive will refers to the things He specifically causes to occur; His permissive will refers to the things He allows, but does not cause, to happen.

2. God's revealed will contains His commands and instructions–found in the Bible–regarding how we should live; God's secret will includes the unknowable decrees by which He governs the universe.

3. The best strategy for discovering God's will for your life is to obey His biblical commands, identify your spiritual gifts and abilities, and stay attentive to His leading.

"You seem to have a pretty good attitude about it," Brady noted.

"It's like you said at Bible study," Matt said. "God has a plan for my life. I'm just waiting to see what His will is."

"That's great!" Brady said.

"And, while I'm waiting, I figure I might as well have some fun," Matt continued.

"Have you had many interviews?"

"None, actually," Matt replied.

Brady shook his head and let out a low whistle. "Whew, tough job market. How many résumés have you sent out?"

Matt grinned and looked down at his shoes. "Let's just say I'm averaging one interview for every résumé I've sent."

Brady wrinkled his forehead. "Wait—you haven't sent out *any* résumés yet?" he asked.

Matt shook his head. "The way I see it, that would be like interfering with God's will."

Brady cocked an eyebrow at Matt but said nothing.

"Whoa, déjà vu," Matt said. "I got that same look from my girlfriend when I told her what I was doing."

"So you don't put much stock in that old saying, 'God helps those who help themselves'?" Brady asked.

"I figure I'm helping myself by being here," Matt pointed out. "Who knows what might happen during my round of golf today? It's possible that that guy on the putting green could be my next boss. Or maybe that guy on the tenth tee. After all, if something is God's will, it's going to get done whether I'm on a golf course or at a job interview, right?"

"Well . . . I guess that's one way of looking at it," Brady said slowly. Then he motioned toward Matt's golf bag. "But, if that's the case, why are you taking all of those clubs with you?"

Matt looked at his golf bag, then back at Brady. "What do you mean?" he asked. "It's a regulation set of clubs. Besides, on a day like today, I'm probably going to need every club in the bag just to break 90."

Brady shook his head. "Not if what you just said about God's will is true," he pointed out.

"Huh?"

"Think about it," Brady urged. "If it's God's will for you to shoot 89 today, it's going to happen whether you use one club or all fifteen. So you might as well just take a putter with you and save yourself some work. If that's how God's will works, you might as well milk it for all it's worth."

Matt frowned. "Or I could just grab a scorecard, write '89' on it, and go home," he said. "Suddenly I'm not in the mood for golf today."

* * * * * * * * * * * * * *

"Thy kingdom come, Thy will be done. . . ." Christians have been reciting that phrase from the Lord's Prayer for almost two thousand years. For two millennia, we've requested that the Lord accomplish His will in the world. But what is it, exactly, that we're asking for? What is God's will?

If you're a budding theologian, you might describe God's will as a logical extension of His perfections—specifically, His omnipotence, omniscience, and sovereignty. The facts are these:

➤ God is all-powerful; He can do anything that is within His nature.

➤ God is all-knowing; nothing escapes His notice and nothing is beyond His complete comprehension.

➤ God answers to and is dependent on absolutely no one.

When these attributes are applied to our world—and our lives—the result is a personal God who determines and approves every action necessary for accomplishing His perfect plan.

A Common Mistake

There is a tendency to approach the topic of God's will from an overly personal perspective. The question becomes not so much "What is God's will?" as it is "What is God's will for my life?"

And while there is certainly a personal element to God's will, it would be a mistake to focus solely on it. We need to get a sense of the "big picture" of God's will before we start trying to pick out personal details.

NOTABLE QUOTABLE

The end of life is not to deny self, nor to be true, nor to keep the Ten Commandments—it is simply to do God's will.

—HENRY DRUMMOND

Which Will It Be?

The first thing we need to understand is that "God's will" is a general phrase. Depending on who's keeping score, it can refer to any number of different aspects of His sovereignty, omnipotence, and other perfections. (For more information on God's perfections, head back to chapter 3.)

In order to understand God's will as completely as possible, we need to identify and explain a few of the key terms associated with it.

God's Directive Will

God's directive will refers to the things He specifically and intentionally brings to pass. Evidence of God's directive will can be found throughout Scripture. Here's just a sampling:

➤ In Genesis 1–2, God speaks the universe and the human race into existence.

➤ In Genesis 6–8, God sends a cataclysmic flood to wipe out the sinful human race. In the same passage, God arranges the construction of a giant ark to house the family of Noah, the only person in the world deemed "righteous" by God, and two representatives of every kind of animal in creation.

➤ In Exodus 3, God instructs Moses to lead the Israelites out of slavery in Egypt and to the land God promised them.

➤ In Judges 6–7, God instructs Gideon to lead a small band of Israelites in defeating the vast Midianite army.

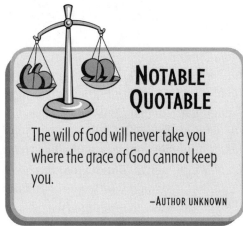

NOTABLE QUOTABLE

The will of God will never take you where the grace of God cannot keep you.

—AUTHOR UNKNOWN

➤ In the book of Jonah 1, God instructs His prophet Jonah to preach to the city of Nineveh and then uses the elements of nature to ensure Jonah's eventual obedience.

➤ John 3:16 tells us that God gave His Son as a means of salvation for the otherwise helpless human race.

In each situation, God determined that an occurrence should happen, and it happened. He directed each event and was personally responsible for it.

God's Permissive Will

God's permissive will refers to the things He allows—but does not *cause*—to occur. This would include:

➤ evil

➤ physical, mental, and emotional disabilities

➤ suffering

➤ tragedy

➤ sickness

➤ natural disasters

➤ injury

➤ death

We should point out that, in the Bible, God occasionally used natural disasters (such as the Flood in Genesis 7), sickness (such as the plague of boils in Exodus 9), and death (such as the plague of the firstborn in Exodus 11) as instruments of His judgment. However, He did not *create* evil or suffering. He's not *responsible* for them. He did not direct them to enter the world.

Of course, that still leaves us with an obvious question: Even if God isn't responsible for evil, suffering, and pain, why does He even permit them to exist? If He's all-powerful, why doesn't He just get rid of them?

Unfortunately, we have no satisfactory answers to those questions—at least, not ones our limited human intellect can comprehend. Perhaps when we get to heaven, God will help us understand this concept in its entirety. Until that time, though, we must focus on what we do know. Here are three truths about evil and pain in our world:

Fact #1: God is sovereign. Our heavenly Father ultimately has absolute control over everything. Evil could not exist without His permission. Evil didn't "sneak" its way into the world while God's head was turned. The forces of evil didn't overwhelm or outsmart Him. God is not powerless in the face of evil; neither is He incapable of stopping it.

Fact #2: God created humans with free will. As we explained in chapter 9, when God created humans, He didn't want creatures who would mindlessly obey Him only because they were "programmed" to do so. He wanted creatures who would *choose* to obey Him, out of love and gratitude. He wanted meaningful worship and obedience from His human creation. With the choice of obeying or disobeying Him comes the possibility of evil. Remember, any act of disobedience to God—anything that opposes Him and His Word—is evil.

Fact #3: God will ultimately do away with evil. We'll explore this truth in greater detail in chapter 15. For the purposes of this chapter, though, we need to point out that evil, suffering, and death are temporary entities, as far as Christians are concerned. Revelation 20:11–15 describes the "great white throne" judgment, when God will pass sentence on all evil and throw sin, death, and suffering—as well as anyone who rejects His gift of salvation—into the lake of fire for eternity.

God's Secret Will

Deuteronomy 29:29 provides a succinct explanation of God's secret will and His revealed will: "The secret things belong to the LORD our God, but the things revealed belong to us and to our children forever, that we may follow all the words of this law."

The secret things belong to the Lord. Those words read almost like a warning, don't they? God's secret will is not for us to know—at least, not prior to our arrival in heaven.

The apostle Paul acknowledged God's secret will in 1 Corinthians 4:19: "I will come to you soon, if the Lord is willing." James referred to it as well in his New Testament book: "Now listen, you who say, 'Today or tomorrow we will go to this or that city, spend a year there, carry on business and make money.' Why, you do not even know what will happen tomorrow. . . . Instead, you ought to say, 'If it is the Lord's will, we will live and do this or that'" (James 4:13–15).

Both writers simply acknowledged that they and their readers—and that includes us—have no power over any given situation, no say in any given matter. "God will do what God will do, and we must accept that" seems to be their attitude.

One aspect of God's secret will is His "master plan" for the universe, which would include everything from the innumerable implications of an individual's DNA code to the unknowable physical properties of black holes in space. Anything that is beyond the scope of science might be considered part of God's secret will.

Personal blessings and suffering might also be considered part of God's secret will. The fact is, we don't know why God chooses to bless certain people at certain times and why He allows other people to suffer at certain times. Prayer requests also fall into the "secret will" category. Generally speaking, we have no way of knowing why God responds in an obvious manner to some requests, yet remains silent in response to others.

JUST WONDERING

How should I respond to God's secret will?

The only response that really makes sense is acceptance. We may not understand why God does what He does; we may even get frustrated or discouraged about it. However, knowing what we know about God's omniscience, we can conclude that if something is part of God's plan, it will ultimately (a) work out for good, and (b) bring us fulfillment.

Trying to unlock, decipher, or guess at the details of God's secret will is a fruitless exercise at best and a dangerous distraction at worst. There are some things we are not meant to know. Period. What's more, we have enough information about God's *revealed* will to keep us busy for the rest of our lives.

God's Revealed Will

Fortunately for us, not all of God's will is secret. Otherwise, we'd be faced with the prospect of stumbling through our lives, cluelessly and hopelessly trying to guess at what might please God and never knowing for sure whether or not we're right.

Even more fortunate for us is the fact that God has given us much of His revealed will in written form. The Bible is the official document of God's revealed will. You don't have to look hard in its pages to find specific instructions as to what God wants and doesn't want us to do.

In the Old Testament, there are the Ten Commandments (Exodus 20:1–17):

1. Do not have any other gods before God.

2. Do not make or worship idols.

3. Do not misuse the name of the Lord.

4. Keep the Sabbath day holy.

5. Honor your father and mother.

6. Do not murder.

7. Do not commit adultery.

8. Do not steal.

9. Do not give false testimony.

10. Do not covet.

In the New Testament, there are the commands of Jesus and the exhortations of the epistle writers, including:

➤ "Love your enemies and pray for those who persecute you" (Matthew 5:44).

➤ "Do not worry about your life, what you will eat or drink; or about your body, what you will wear" (Matthew 6:25).

➤ "Go and make disciples of all nations, baptizing them in the name of the Father and of the Son and of the Holy Spirit, and teaching them to obey everything I have commanded you" (Matthew 28:19–20a).

NOTABLE QUOTABLE

The center of God's will is our only safety.

—BETSIE TEN BOOM

➤ "A new command I give you: Love one another. As I have loved you, so you must love one another. By this all men will know that you are my disciples, if you love one another" (John 13:34–35).

➤ "Do not use your freedom to indulge the sinful nature; rather, serve one another in love" (Galatians 5:13b).

➤ "Be joyful always; pray continually; give thanks in all circumstances, for this is God's will for you in Christ Jesus" (1 Thessalonians 5:16–18).

Put these and the many other commands and exhortations in Scripture together, and you get a pretty clear picture of the Christlike life that God wants from us—moral, loving, thankful, unselfish, and fully committed to Him. He has done us a big favor by revealing to us what attitudes, behaviors, and decisions please Him.

That's why any search for God's will must start with His "obvious" revelation. Obedience is Job One. Committing ourselves to understanding and obeying the commands of Scripture is not just a noble pursuit or a way to demonstrate Christlikeness; it's the key to unlocking God's will for our lives.

Getting Personal

The next question is obvious: How personal does God's revealed will get? In other words, how specific are His plans for our lives? Has He chosen one particular . . .

➤ college for us to attend,

➤ person for us to marry,

➤ career for us to pursue,

➤ house for us to buy,

➤ car for us to drive,

➤ group of friends for us to hang out with,

➤ pet for us to adopt, or

➤ church ministry for us to get involved in?

Some Christians believe that God has a detailed plan for every area of our lives. That doesn't mean we're irresistibly compelled to follow that plan, or that God will supernaturally prevent us from, say, buying the wrong car or getting involved in the wrong ministry. Instead, we suffer the consequences of our poor decisions. In other words, though we may be satisfied with the career we choose, if that career is not God's intended path for us, we won't be as fulfilled as we could be.

NOTABLE QUOTABLE

There are two kinds of people: those who say to God, "Thy will be done," and those to whom God says, "All right, then, have it your way."

–C. S. LEWIS

Some Christians believe that God gave us His Word as a blueprint for our lives but leaves the details to us. In other words, God expects us to weigh every decision we make against the commands of Scripture to make sure that it coincides with His revealed will. Then, as long as a life decision falls within the parameters of His Word, God will approve of it and bless it.

Some Christians take a middle position on the issue, suggesting that God has specific plans for certain areas of our lives but leaves other areas to our discretion—as long as our decisions align with His revealed will, of course.

The Pursuit of God's Will

Scripture is full of stories about people who received God's "call" and were shown His will for their lives.

➤ God appeared to Moses in the form of a burning bush and said, in effect, "Go to Egypt and tell Pharaoh to free My people from slavery."

➤ God, using the prophet Samuel, told David when he was just a young shepherd that one day he would be the king of Israel.

➤ God said to Jonah, "Go to Nineveh and warn the people about My impending judgment on them."

➤ God made known to John the Baptist from his earliest days that his job would be to prepare the way for the Messiah by preaching repentance to the people of Israel.

➤ Jesus instructed Peter and the rest of the disciples to follow Him—to go where He went, watch what He did, and listen to what He said.

Now those are some specific directions: "Go here and do this, and this will happen." Instructions don't come much clearer or easier to understand than those. That's why we must point out that while the biblical accounts of these characters may be inspiring and helpful to study, we must avoid the mistake of thinking of them as precedents for our own encounters with God's will.

There's a very strong likelihood that God will not reveal His plan (or will) for your life as dramatically as He did to Moses or as specifically as He did to Jonah. If you spend your life waiting for a "burning bush" encounter or a heavenly road map, you may be disappointed.

God has given—and will continue to give—each of us clues about His will for our lives. But He's not handing out those clues on flash cards. He expects us to put some effort into discovering His will.

ON A PERSONAL NOTE

If you're struggling with feelings of uncertainty regarding God's will, you may find it helpful to study God's leading in the lives of men and women of the Bible. Look at how God worked in and through the lives of people like Abraham, Moses, David, Esther, and Peter. You may gain some valuable insights into how He's working in your own life.

Gifted

One of the best places to direct our efforts in discovering God's will for our lives is in the area of spiritual gifts. In chapter 5, we mentioned that one of the Holy Spirit's ministries is distributing spiritual gifts to believers. Those gifts include:

➤ evangelism—sharing the gospel message in a way that people understand and respond to

➤ pastoring—leading, caring for, and protecting God's people

➤ serving—meeting people's physical and emotional needs

➤ teaching—explaining God's truth to people in ways that they understand and respond to

➤ faith—relying on God to have one's needs met and serving as an example to other believers of what faith can accomplish

➤ encouragement—spurring people on to achieve what God intends for them

➤ distinguishing spirits—being able to tell the difference between true and false teaching

➤ mercy—showing kindness and assistance to the needy

➤ giving—being generous with what you have

➤ administration—overseeing the daily operations of the church

➤ wisdom and knowledge—being able to understand God's truth and explain it to others

Some Christians may receive more gifts than others, but each of us possesses at least one or two spiritual gifts. Recognizing which gifts you've been given—and putting those gifts to use—is essential in discovering what God has planned for you. If

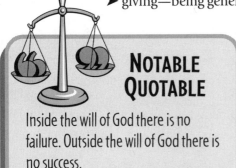

NOTABLE QUOTABLE

Inside the will of God there is no failure. Outside the will of God there is no success.

—BERNARD EDINGER

God has given you the ability to share the gospel effectively or the gift of selflessly serving others, there's a reason for it. As you learn more about your gifts by putting them to use, you may also gain insight into God's intentions for you.

In addition to your spiritual gifts, you have other God-given talents that come into play when you're searching for God's will. The fact is, God has wired you in a certain way for a reason. He's designed you to feel comfortable and thrive in certain settings.

Identifying those unique aspects of your personality can shed some light on what God may have in store for your career, your ministry, your social life, and your personal time.

ON A PERSONAL NOTE

If you're uncertain about which spiritual gifts you've been given, ask your friends and family members–the people who know you best–to offer their input. Chances are, they have noticed qualities, strengths, and abilities in you that you may not be aware of.

Three Search Helps

If you're serious about learning more about God's will and how it applies to your life, consider the following tips.

1. God's Will Is Understood Through an Intimate Relationship with Him.

God isn't a cosmic fortune-teller, offering peeks at His crystal ball to anyone who asks nicely. His revealed will and His plan for our lives are part of our larger relationship with Him.

Our primary purpose as Christians is not to figure out what lies ahead for us; it is to glorify God with our lives and to obey His commands and instructions. If we are faithful to Him, He will be faithful to us. Part of His faithfulness involves revealing what we need to know in order to make wise decisions.

We should point out that the key phrase in that last sentence is "what we need to know." That's what God reveals to us. He's not interested in sharing the complete details of our future with us. Think about it. If we knew our future, we would have no reason to rely on Him.

NOTABLE QUOTABLE

Though the sky fall, let Thy will be done.

–THOMAS BROWNE

Obviously, that's not what God wants. His desire is for us to draw closer to Him, to depend on Him to see us through each day. That's why He generally reveals His will for our lives a little at a time.

2. God's Will Is Often Most Clearly Seen in Retrospect.

Jesus' command in Matthew 6:34 is quite clear: "Do not worry about tomorrow, for tomorrow will worry about itself." God doesn't offer many previews of things to come. He wants our minds focused on the tasks at hand—that is, discovering and obeying His revealed will.

Though our forward view may be obscured, the view behind us can be awesome. Think about where you were a year ago, two years ago, or ten years ago—not just in your Christian walk but in your life. Then consider the following questions:

➤ When you were younger, what did you expect your life would be like at this point?

➤ How accurate have those expectations proved to be?

➤ What's been the most exciting change in your life over the past few years?

➤ What's been the most unexpected change in your life over the past few years?

➤ How would you describe your life's journey from where you were a few years ago to where you are now?

➤ What evidence have you seen of God's work in your life?

When you take time to examine your life's journey so far, you may be surprised to see God's fingerprints in places you never noticed them before—not only in the things that have happened but also in the things that *haven't* happened. The fact is, God closes as many doors as He opens. Depending on your circumstances, those closed doors might include a job interview that went wrong, a date that didn't work out, or a lease agreement that fell through.

Recognizing those closed doors and what they have meant to our lives is an important step in discovering God's will.

3. God's Will Isn't Always Pleasant.

Contrary to the wishful thoughts of believers and unbelievers alike, God's will for our lives does not necessarily involve . . .

➤ recognition,

➤ popularity,

➤ success,

➤ comfort, or

➤ happiness

. . . at least, not in the way we measure those things.

NOTABLE QUOTABLE

A man's heart is right when he wills what God wills.

–THOMAS AQUINAS

In fact, if you commit yourself to following God's will for your life, there's a very real chance that you will be overlooked, underestimated, dismissed, and ostracized. You will likely be placed in situations that make you uncomfortable—perhaps often. You may find yourself doing things you once considered beneath you. You will face struggles, setbacks, and challenges that will shake you to your core.

The Old Testament prophet Jonah would certainly testify to that. His story (in the book that bears his name) offers some gritty insight into what God's revealed will actually involves.

God instructed Jonah to go to the city of Nineveh and tell the Ninevites to repent. That's a pretty straightforward request for a prophet to receive from God. However, it presented all kinds of problems for Jonah. You see, Jonah hated Nineveh.

The anti-Ninevite prophet was afraid that if he preached repentance to the city, his enemies would turn from their wicked ways. He was afraid that if the Ninevites repented, God would not judge them. And that would have been a major blow to Jonah, because the destruction of Nineveh was probably right at the top of his wish list.

To say that Jonah was conflicted about God's plan would be an understatement. After being given three days to reconsider his attitude and prejudices—in the belly of a giant fish, no less—Jonah determined that he would rather die than do what God wanted, although he later repented and preached to Ninevah.

How do you think Jonah would respond to someone who said that God's will brings happiness, comfort, and pleasure?

For a more sobering example of the personal cost of following God's will, we need look no further than Jesus' ordeal in Gethsemane on the night before His execution. Jesus knew what lay ahead of Him. He knew He was going to have the weight of the world's sins placed on His shoulders. He knew He was going to be forsaken (temporarily) by His heavenly Father. He knew He was going to be savagely beaten and tortured, mocked and humiliated, and finally crucified by the very people He had come to save.

JUST WONDERING

How much should I listen to other people when it comes to discovering God's will for my life? Ultimately, you are the one responsible for carrying out God's will in your life. You are the one who will face the consequences for misunderstanding or ignoring that will. It's okay to seek input and advice from Christians you trust, but you don't automatically accept it. You have to make sure that their counsel is biblically sound and God-honoring.

In an anguished prayer to God just before His arrest, Jesus said, in effect, "Father, if there is any other way to accomplish Your plan of salvation, please let it happen." Then He immediately followed that request with this conclusion: "Yet not what I will, but what you will" (Mark 14:36).

All that ultimately mattered to Jesus was God's will. If that meant abandonment, ridicule, suffering, and death for Him, so be it.

Of course, we will never be faced with a situation as extreme as the one Jesus faced. Yet we are expected to place the same importance on God's will—regardless of the personal cost to us—as Jesus did.

The apostle Paul summarizes our responsibility in Philippians 2:5–8: "Your attitude should be the same as that of Christ Jesus: Who, being in very nature God, did not consider equality with God something to be grasped, but made himself nothing, taking the very nature of a servant, being made in human likeness. And being found in appearance as a man, he humbled himself and became obedient to death—even death on a cross!"

The Final Word

God has a plan for your life. How much of that plan you're privy to depends entirely on Him. For that reason, your best strategy for ensuring that God's will is accomplished in your life is to concentrate on understanding and obeying His revealed will in Scripture.

If you will follow, God will lead.

Know What You Believe

How much do you know about God's will? Here's a quiz to test your knowledge.

1. Which of the following is not an example of God's directive will?
   a. Satan tempting Adam and Eve to sin
   b. Moses leading the Israelites out of Egypt
   c. Gideon defeating the Midianite army
   d. Noah and his family surviving the flood

2. Which of the following statements do not figure into God's permissive will?
   a. God is sovereign.
   b. God will ultimately do away with evil.
   c. God created humans with free will.
   d. God has little interest in our daily activities.

3. Where is the best place to find God's revealed will?
   a. The mission field
   b. The church library
   c. The Bible
   d. The televangelist on channel 38

4. Why is it a fruitless exercise to try to unlock, decipher, or guess at the details of God's secret will?
   a. The Bible is full of stories of people who were struck dead for trying to unlock it.
   b. There are certain things that we are not meant to know. Period.
   c. According to theologians, God's secret will doesn't exist.
   d. God has hidden a lot of false clues in the universe to throw us off the track.

5. Which of the following is not true of God's will?
   a. It isn't always pleasant.
   b. It can't be understood outside of an intimate relationship with Him.
   c. It can be changed with a simple prayer.
   d. It is often most clearly seen in retrospect.

Answers: (1) a, (2) d, (3) c, (4) b, (5) c

Not Just a Sunday Morning Thing

UNDERSTANDING GOD'S PLAN FOR THE CHURCH

SNAPSHOT

"I don't understand why you still go to church," Greta said as she wiped off the seat of her exercise bike. "You found your man. You're engaged. Mission accomplished."

"Hey, what are you suggesting?" Amy asked playfully. "My church isn't some kind of meat market for Christian singles."

"You're telling me," Greta agreed. "I went there with you for two years and never even got a decent date from it."

"On behalf of the entire congregation, allow me to apologize," Amy said with a theatrical bow. "I'll talk to the church board about starting a 'hotties' ministry—some kind of outreach to good-looking, available men."

SNEAK PREVIEW

1. Jesus is the architect of the church; He built it to accomplish His work in the world until He returns.
2. The church has three primary responsibilities: worshiping God, nurturing believers, and evangelizing unbelievers.
3. The responsibility of individual believers to the church is to put our spiritual gifts to use for the benefit of the entire body of Christ.

"Now you're talking," Greta said. "At least it would give me a reason to start going to church again."

"As though things like worship and fellowship aren't reason enough?" Amy asked as she folded her sweats and put them into her bag.

"Oh, come on," Greta said. "If you could get people to tell you honestly why they go to church, I'll bet less than 25 percent of them would mention worship or fellowship."

"What other reasons would they give?" Amy asked.

"Tradition, for one," Greta replied. "I'll bet most of them would say they were taught that you're supposed to go to church on Sundays, so that's what they do. And I'll bet a lot of others would say they go just so they won't feel guilty on Monday for *not* going."

Amy stopped and looked Greta in the eyes. "I think you're choosing the wrong thing to be cynical about," she said with a firmness that surprised even her.

Greta's grin faded. "Are you saying that church is *really* that important to you?" she asked.

"Well, yeah," Amy replied. "And it's also really that important to *you*."

"You think so?"

"I do," Amy emphasized. "Our new pastor is doing a series on the body of Christ, and it's really opened my eyes about some things."

"New pastor, huh?" Greta asked.

"Yeah," Amy said. "I think you'd really like him."

"Why? Is he single?" Greta asked with a wink.

* * * * * * * * * * * * * *

Jesus described the church as an institution capable of withstanding the gates of hell (Matthew 16:18). The apostle Paul noted that "Christ loved the church and gave himself up for her" (Ephesians 5:25). And Colossians 1:24 refers to the church as the very "body" of Christ.

Clearly, the church holds a special place in the Lord's heart. If we're serious about understanding God, then we must understand the one institution that He sanctions and supernaturally empowers here on earth.

A Tale of Two Churches?

You'll notice that in the preceding two paragraphs, the article *the* precedes each reference to church. Yet if we were to write the sentence, "It's time for church" or "My church is having a bake sale," the article would disappear. The reason one reference to church has the article and the other doesn't is not a matter of grammar. It's a matter of meaning—we're talking about two different definitions.

The church refers to the entire body of Christ, the community of all true believers who have ever lived, including those who are now in heaven (Hebrews 12:23). This is also referred to as the "universal" or "invisible" church.

In contrast, *church* refers to a specific assembly of believers who meet together for a common purpose—in other words, the place Christians go to worship on Sunday. This is also referred to as the "local" or "visible" church.

To avoid confusion—and establish a workable definition for this chapter—we will suggest that *any* community of true believers may be correctly referred to as a church.

The Early Days

The idea of people coming together for a common experience of the Lord's work or blessing has a long biblical history. Passages such as Deuteronomy 4:10 (referring to God's command to "assemble the people before me") and Acts 7:38 (Stephen's reference to "the assembly in the desert") suggest that the Old Testament Israelites functioned as a kind of "church."

However, the church as we know it today got its start in and around Jerusalem in the months that followed Jesus' resurrection and ascension. Jesus' apostles, along with other men and women who had faithfully followed Him, began to meet together in their homes to pray, praise God, encourage one another, and spread the good news of Jesus to others.

That's not to suggest that the church has human origins. In Matthew 16:18, Jesus identifies *Himself* as the architect of the church. He "builds" it by calling people to Himself. Referring to the assembly of first-century believers in Jerusalem, Acts 2:47 says, *"The Lord* added to their number daily those who were being saved" (italics added).

What Is the Church, Anyway?

The best way to understand what Jesus had in mind for His church is to look at the metaphors used for its members in Scripture.

> ➤ Second Corinthians 6:18 suggests that the church is a family, made up of spiritual brothers and sisters.

> ➤ Ephesians 5:22–32 presents the church as the bride of Christ and compares its relationship to Jesus to a wife's relationship with her husband.

> ➤ First Corinthians 3:5–17 describes the church variously as "God's field," grown by the Lord Himself; "God's building," with Jesus Christ as its foundation; and "God's temple," the corporate dwelling place of the Holy Spirit.

> ➤ In John 15:1–8, Jesus refers to Himself as the "true vine" and the church as "branches," whose members receive nourishment and experience growth only through Him.

Perhaps the best-known metaphor for the church in all of Scripture is the apostle Paul's description of the "body of Christ" in 1 Corinthians 12:12–31 and Ephesians 4:4–16. We should point out that the two passages differ slightly in their portrayals of Christ's body. In 1 Corinthians 12, Paul presents the church as the *entire* body of Christ, with various believers functioning as "eyes," "hands," "feet," and "ears." The emphasis in that passage is that every part of the body is necessary and that no part is more important than another.

In Ephesians 4, Paul presents Christ as the *head* and the church as the rest of the body. The emphasis in that passage is that the church is under the leadership and direction of Christ.

Either way, the point of the "body of Christ" metaphor is clear. Members of the church, like parts of the body, are *interdependent*. We need each other in order to stay healthy and function as we're intended to.

ON A PERSONAL NOTE

Come up with your own metaphor for the church–either as it relates to Christ or as it relates to you. Think about what you would compare it to in order to explain it to someone who knew nothing about it. If you need some inspiration, check out the metaphors that Jesus and the apostle Paul came up with (in the passages listed above).

What's It For?

The next question we need to consider is what goals Jesus had in mind when He established His church. The Bible identifies three primary purposes for the body of Christ:

➤ an "upward" purpose to offer praise and worship to God

➤ an "inward" purpose to provide nurturing and fellowship to its members

➤ an "outward" purpose to minister to unbelievers through evangelism and mercy

In order to understand the church—and, in turn, understand God Himself—we must understand the importance of each of these purposes.

Praise and Worship

Ephesians 1:12 pinpoints the ultimate responsibility of all believers: "the praise of [God's] glory." Quite simply, we were created to bring glory and praise to God (see Isaiah 43:6–7). We were made to worship Him. The church offers us an opportunity to fulfill our responsibility with a community of believers.

Before we get too far into our discussion of worship, we should make sure that we have a common understanding of what it is. For the purposes of this chapter, we'll define worship as "the intentional act of glorifying God."

Passages such as 1 Corinthians 10:31 and 1 Peter 4:11 rightly suggest that we should glorify God in all that we do. However, that's not the kind of glorification we're talking about here. Worship, in the context of the church, involves coming together for the specific purpose of glorifying God.

JUST WONDERING

Why do most Christian churches today meet on Sunday?

First things first: Sunday is not the "Sabbath," the day the Lord declared holy in the Ten Commandments (Exodus 20:8). The Sabbath, which is still observed by many Jewish people today, is actually Saturday. Christians shifted their day of worship to Sunday shortly after Jesus' ascension. Some Bible scholars suggest that the early Christians chose Sunday as a symbolic gesture of dedicating the first day of every week to the Lord. Other scholars suggest that Sunday was chosen because it was the day on which Christ rose from the dead.

The apostle Paul paints a picture of worship in Colossians 3:16 that we, as members of the church, can and should use as a model in fulfilling our "upward" responsibility: "Let the word of Christ dwell in you richly as you teach and admonish one another with all wisdom, and as you sing psalms, hymns and spiritual songs with gratitude in your hearts to God."

Obviously, music and singing play a vital role in corporate (church) worship. So do prayer and Bible teaching. A church that neglects or overlooks one or more of these elements in its worship service does a disservice not only to its members but also to God.

The importance of worship can be seen in the specific reasons for it identified in Scripture. Let's take a look at three of them.

First, we worship because God deserves it. Why do we give standing ovations after great concerts or theatrical performances? Why do we jump out of our seats when we see a remarkable play in a ball game? Why do we high-five other fans when our favorite team pulls out an exciting, come-from-behind victory? Because the people who inspire them are worthy (if only momentarily) of our recognition and approval. We acknowledge the worth of the performers as effectively as we know how, whether it be through clapping, screaming, jumping up and down, or chanting in unison.

The same principle applies—on an infinitely grander scale—to our worship of God. True worship is the combination of a deep-down recognition of God's worthiness to receive our praise and glory, and a desire to express that praise and glory.

The Bible makes it clear that God alone is worthy of worship. In His second commandment to Moses, God forbids the creation of idols because, He says, "I, the LORD your God, am a jealous God" (Exodus 20:4). In Isaiah 48:11, He adds, "I will not yield my glory to another." So when the urge to worship strikes, there is only one true outlet for it.

> **NOTABLE QUOTABLE**
>
> If you do not join in what the church is doing, you have no share in this Spirit.
>
> —IRENAEUS OF LYONS

Second, we worship because God finds enjoyment in it. Psalm 149 offers a revealing look at worship. The first three verses are an exhortation to the children of God to carry out their responsibility before Him, to "rejoice in their Maker . . . [to] be glad in their King . . . dancing and [making] music to him with tambourine and harp" (verses 2–3). The fourth verse reveals why such exuberant worship is called for: "The LORD takes delight in his people."

Imagine that: The Lord takes delight in us, a bunch of imperfect, unprofessional, mistake-prone, tone-deaf (in some cases) worshipers. He finds pleasure in our efforts to glorify and praise Him. We can bring enjoyment to the Lord simply by worshiping to the best of our abilities!

How much more incentive could we possibly need to place worship—both personal and corporate—at the top of our priority list?

Third, we worship knowing that God blesses us as a result of it. James 4:8 promises that if we "come near to God"—in worship, for example—"he will come near" to us. The suggestion in the verse is that God makes Himself known in a special way to those who offer genuine worship.

Second Chronicles 20:1–30 records an incident that demonstrates just how seriously God takes worship of Him—and how He reveals Himself to true worshipers. Jehoshaphat, the king of Judah, received word that a massive army, made up of soldiers from Ammon, Moab, and Mount Seir, was descending on Judah. Jehoshaphat responded to the alarming news by assembling the people of Judah and Jerusalem . . . for a worship service.

After praising and glorifying God for His sovereignty and His work on behalf of His people in the past, Jehoshaphat brought to the Lord's attention the threat of the approaching army. God's response, in essence, was, "Don't worry about it."

So instead of preparing for battle, Jehoshaphat and the people of Judah continued to worship. Second Chronicles 20:21 says, "After consulting the people, Jehoshaphat appointed men to sing to the LORD and to praise him for the splendor of his holiness as they went out at the head of the army, saying: 'Give thanks to the LORD , for his love endures forever.'"

If that seems like an inappropriate time for corporate worship, check out the Lord's response: "As they began to sing and praise, the LORD set ambushes against the men of Ammon and Moab and Mount Seir who were invading Judah, and they were defeated" (2 Chronicles 20:22).

The people of Judah chose to worship God at a critical point in their nation's history, and they were rewarded for it with a major military victory, courtesy of God.

The good news for us is that the Lord continues to bless genuine worship today. He doesn't always do it in obvious ways, but He does it—and our lives become richer and more fulfilling because of it.

Nurturing and Fellowship

Passages such as 1 Corinthians 3:1–2 and Hebrews 5:11–14 make an important distinction between immature Christians who need "milk"—that is, the elementary truths of the Christian faith—and mature Christians who require "solid food"—that is, more advanced teaching. The strong emphasis in both passages is that there must be a natural progression, or maturation process, in Christians. Believers should not be content to exist on spiritual "milk" our entire lives; we must learn to digest "solid food" teaching.

The church obviously plays a significant role in the maturation process of Christians. As members of the body of Christ, we have a responsibility to nurture not only our own spiritual growth but also that of our fellow members. The apostle Paul describes the responsibility of the church as "admonishing and teaching everyone with all wisdom, so that we may present everyone perfect in Christ" (Colossians 1:28).

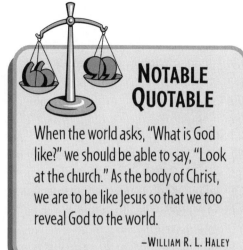

NOTABLE QUOTABLE

When the world asks, "What is God like?" we should be able to say, "Look at the church." As the body of Christ, we are to be like Jesus so that we too reveal God to the world.

–William R. L. Haley

The most obvious way a church can nurture spiritual growth in its members is to provide biblically sound teaching week in and week out. A less obvious way is to encourage mutual accountability among its members.

Proverbs 27:17 says, "As iron sharpens iron, so one man sharpens another." This principle is especially relevant when it comes to spiritual growth. When members of the body of Christ take a personal interest in each other's spiritual development, a "refining" process occurs. Having people to "answer to" regarding our personal Bible study and prayer habits, as well as our worship and ministry activities, can serve as powerful motivation for us to remain faithful in those areas.

The commitment to nurturing one another in the church results in fellowship. The need for fellowship among believers is strongly emphasized throughout the New Testament:

➤ "A new command I give you: Love one another. As I have loved you, so you must love one another. By this all men will know that you are my disciples, if you love one another" (John 13:34–35).

➤ "Each of you should look not only to your own interests, but also to the interests of others" (Philippians 2:4).

➤ "Warn those who are idle, encourage the timid, help the weak, be patient with everyone" (1 Thessalonians 5:14).

Fellowship isn't simply a "nice" thing to do; it's a vital part of our spiritual health. Without it, even our relationship with the Lord suffers.

ON A PERSONAL NOTE

If you're new to your church—or if you still feel like an outsider—there are some steps you can take to maximize your fellowship opportunities:

1. Hang around before and after the service. Learn to mingle. Get to know your fellow worshipers.

2. Get involved in ministry. Don't wait for an invitation; find a ministry in your church that will allow you to use your spiritual gifts and make your services available. You may be surprised by how quickly genuine fellowship develops among people who are working together for a common purpose.

3. Work toward deepening the relationships you make. By opening yourself up and taking a genuine interest in your fellow worshipers, you can establish God-honoring, mutually accountable relationships.

Likewise, fellowship isn't something best left to "others"—as in people who are naturally friendly or outgoing. Every member of the body of Christ has a responsibility to demonstrate love, concern, encouragement, and patience to as many other members as possible. Every member should offer forgiveness and even physical assistance whenever needed.

Genuine fellowship is the lifeblood of the church. It's our responsibility to make sure that it flows to every part of the body.

Evangelism and Mercy

Christ's command to His followers—His church—in Matthew 28:19 is crystal clear: "Go and make disciples of all nations." The church plays an integral part in carrying out His instruction through such activities as:

➤ providing consistent, biblically sound teaching on the responsibilities of believers regarding evangelism

➤ encouraging members to share their personal evangelism experiences with one another

➤ equipping believers to share their faith through practical evangelism courses

➤ organizing outreach events for unbelievers

➤ sponsoring missionaries

In addition to ministering to the spiritual needs of

unbelievers, the church also has a responsibility to minister to their physical and emotional needs. Obviously, Jesus didn't confine His healing and mercy to those who acknowledged Him as the Messiah. Luke 4:40 says that when crowds in Capernaum came to see Jesus, He laid His hands "on each one [and] healed them."

What's more, passages such as Luke 6:36 ("Be merciful, just as your Father is merciful") make it clear that Jesus expects the same kind of caring, generous, and hands-on approach from us. Remember, Jesus wasn't putting on a show for the entertainment of His followers; He was setting an example for us to follow. We, as members of the body of Christ, have a responsibility to show mercy because Christ Himself showed mercy.

A healthy church is one that continuously emphasizes all three purposes—worship, nurturing, and evangelism—and does not sacrifice one for the sake of the others.

No Ordinary Ordinances

Before we wrap up this chapter, we need to look at two essential aspects of church life: the ordinances of baptism and the Lord's Supper. Many Bible scholars suggest that the presence of these ordinances (or sacraments, as they're sometimes called) indicate a church's intent to function as a church. Baptism is the means for admitting people into the church; the Lord's Supper is the means by which people indicate their desire to remain part of the church.

Baptism

As we mentioned earlier, before Jesus ascended to heaven, He gave one final instruction to His

JUST WONDERING

What is tithing and why is it important?

Tithing is a way for believers to acknowledge the gifts that God gives us. We do this by giving a portion of them back to the Lord for use in His work. The word *tithe* means "one-tenth." For Christians, tithing involves giving at least one-tenth of our income back to God through "offerings" that are collected each week during Sunday morning services; some give more in gratitude. Most churches' operating budgets come from the tithes of members. However, the primary purpose of tithes is not to support the church but to demonstrate a God-honoring attitude toward our material blessings.

disciples: "Go and make disciples of all nations, *baptizing* them in the name of the Father and of the Son and of the Holy Spirit" (Matthew 28:19, italics added). The writer of the book of Hebrews identifies baptism as one of the "elementary teachings," or foundational truths, of the Christian faith (Hebrews 6:1–2). Jesus Himself began His public ministry by being baptized by John the Baptist.

Those three pieces of scriptural evidence should answer any questions about the importance of baptism. But what about its purpose? Why is baptism a vital part of the Christian faith and the body of Christ?

Specifically, baptism is an act of association, a way of identifying ourselves with Christ, His church, and His message. It's a public demonstration of our personal faith. Furthermore, God's Word links baptism symbolically to . . .

➤ repentance (Acts 2:38),

➤ the "washing away" of sins (Acts 22:16),

➤ unity with Christ (Romans 6:1–10), and

➤ evangelism (Matthew 28:19).

The first-century church practiced immersion, the act of baptizing a person by submerging him or her completely (but briefly) underwater. Many churches today continue the practice of immersion in their baptism services. Other churches practice affusion, in which water is poured on the person being baptized. Still other churches conduct baptism through sprinkling.

NOTABLE QUOTABLE

The duty of the church is to comfort the disturbed and to disturb the comfortable.

–Michael Ramsey

The Lord's Supper

This ordinance, also known as Communion, gives members of the spiritual body of Christ an opportunity to symbolically partake of the physical body of Christ. Jesus instituted the ordinance with His disciples at the Last Supper, just before His arrest. Matthew 26:26–29 describes it this way:

While they were eating, Jesus took bread, gave thanks and broke it, and gave it to his disciples, saying, "Take and eat; this is my body." Then he took the cup, gave thanks, and offered it to them, saying, "Drink from it, all of you. This is my blood of the covenant, which is poured out for many for the forgiveness of sins. I tell you, I will not drink of this fruit of the vine from now on until that day when I drink it anew with you in my Father's kingdom."

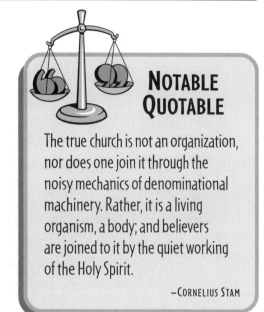

NOTABLE QUOTABLE

The true church is not an organization, nor does one join it through the noisy mechanics of denominational machinery. Rather, it is a living organism, a body; and believers are joined to it by the quiet working of the Holy Spirit.

—CORNELIUS STAM

By the way, if that passage (or portions of it) seems familiar, it may be because your pastor recites it during your church's observance of the Lord's Supper. Many pastors do.

According to Jesus, to eat the bread at Communion is to partake of His body; to drink the juice (or wine, in some instances) is to partake of His blood. The Lord's Supper gives believers the chance to . . .

➤ commemorate Jesus' sacrifice,

➤ think about what it involved for Him, and

➤ celebrate what it means to us—namely, the opportunity to be reconciled with God, to receive His forgiveness and salvation, and to spend eternity with Him.

In addition, acknowledging Christ as our spiritual "food" is a way of indicating that He is the One who sustains and nourishes us. Acknowledging that fact with a congregation of fellow believers is a way of building closeness and community.

Gift Exchange

One of the most common mistakes Christians make when it comes to fellowship and worship is to approach a church service like a critic approaches a movie or performance, praising the things we like and complaining about the things we don't. The mistake is one of perspective. You see, we're not part of the audience at church; we're part of the production crew. The responsibility for making a church "work" is ours.

Many Christians would ask, "What do I have to offer the church besides my attendance?" The answer is plenty, thanks to the Holy Spirit.

One of the ministries of the Holy Spirit is the distribution of "spiritual gifts"— God-ordained personal qualities and abilities—to believers. Romans 12, 1 Corinthians 12, and Ephesians 4 all contain lists of the various spiritual gifts the Spirit gives. In chapter 13 (and chapter 5 as well) we looked at eleven of these gifts, ranging from evangelism—the ability to communicate the truth about Jesus in a way that commands people's attention—to wisdom and knowledge—the ability to understand God's truth.

As noted in chapter 13, every believer receives at least one gift; some people receive more than one. We have no say in which gifts we receive, because the Holy Spirit assigns them according to His perfect wisdom.

His purpose in assigning our spiritual gifts is made clear in Ephesians 4:11–13: "It was he who gave some to be apostles, some to be prophets, some to be evangelists, and some to be pastors and teachers, to prepare God's people for works of service, so that the body of Christ may be built up until we all reach unity in the faith and in the knowledge of the Son of God and become mature, attaining to the whole measure of the fullness of Christ."

NOTABLE QUOTABLE

The church is so constituted that every member matters, and matters in a very vital sense.

– D. Martyn Lloyd-Jones

We're not given spiritual gifts for our own benefit or amusement; we're given them for the benefit of the body of Christ. When our individual gifts and abilities are put together with those of our fellow believers, the whole of the church becomes greater than the sum of its parts.

The flip side of that equation is that if we're not putting our talents and abilities to use in the church, we're squandering our God-given spiritual gifts. What's more, we're hurting the entire body of Christ!

One More Thing

As we wrap up this chapter, we're going to address a personal aspect of fellowship and worship—namely, finding the right church. If you're searching for a new (or first) church home, there are a few important questions that you'll need to consider:

➤ Is the church's doctrine biblically sound?

➤ Do you sense a welcoming, loving, positive attitude among the church members?

➤ Are you comfortable with the church's worship style?

➤ Does the church offer ministry opportunities that will allow you to use your spiritual gifts?

Keep in mind that there's no such thing as a "perfect" church. If you look hard enough, you'll always be able to spot flaws somewhere. Rather than continually searching for a "better" church than the one you're in, identify the specific elements that are most important to you—whether it's music, teaching, ministry opportunities, or fellowship—and find a church that offers them. Then learn to accept—or, better yet, work in love to change—the less-than-ideal qualities of your chosen church.

Know What You Believe

How much do you know about the body of Christ? Here's a quiz to test your knowledge.

1. According to Acts 2:47, what did Jesus do regarding the church in Jerusalem?
   a. Renamed it "The Fellowship Temple" to attract unsuspecting Jews
   b. Spewed it out of His mouth because the members were neither hot nor cold
   c. Added to their number daily those who were being saved
   d. Tore it down and rebuilt it in three days

2. Which of the following is not a biblical metaphor for the church?
   a. A groom
   b. A family
   c. A branch
   d. A field

3. What is the church's responsibility to Christians who require spiritual "milk"?
   a. To be a spiritual "refrigerator" in order to keep the milk "cold"
   b. To acquire a spiritual "cow" to continue providing the milk
   c. To nurture spiritual growth so that they may progress to "solid food"
   d. To keep them away from other believers as much as possible

4. Which of the following is not one of the spiritual gifts mentioned in Romans 12, 1 Corinthians 12, and Ephesians 4?
   a. Administration
   b. Intimidation
   c. Distinguishing of spirits
   d. Evangelism

5. Which of the following is not necessarily a question to consider when choosing a church to attend?
   a. Does the church offer ministry opportunities that will allow you to use your spiritual gifts?
   b. Are you comfortable with the church's worship style?
   c. Is the church's doctrine biblically sound?
   d. How much money does the pastor make?

Answers: (1) c, (2) a, (3) c, (4) b, (5) d

And in the End...

UNDERSTANDING GOD'S PLAN FOR THE FUTURE

SNAPSHOT

"Come on, Alec, join our pre-Bible study debate," Eric called out.

"What's the topic?" Alec asked, as he set down his Bible and took off his jacket.

"The worst judgment in Revelation," Eric replied.

"What do you mean by *worst*?" Alec asked.

"The scariest part of the book," Eric explained.

"The one thing you'd least like to experience," Caleb added.

"I said the sea turning to blood would be the worst," Eric explained. "Can you imagine what low tide would smell like, with all of that dried blood baking on the shore? Put that together with the dead fish that'll be floating everywhere and you're talking about a stench for the ages."

SNEAK PREVIEW

1. At an unknown time in the future, Jesus Christ will return for His followers, as He promised.
2. The end times will be marked by the rise of the Antichrist, the persecution of Israel, and a series of devastating judgments from God that will destroy a significant portion of the earth and its inhabitants.
3. At the final judgment, the righteous—those who believe in and follow Christ—will receive eternity in heaven; the unrighteous—those who reject Christ—will be condemned to eternal suffering in the lake of fire.

"Yeah, well, I'm from Jersey, so it's hard for me to get all worked up about bad smells," Alec replied. "I'd have to say the boils all over people's bodies would be the worst."

"Boils?" Caleb scoffed. "Come on, you pop 'em like pimples and it's over."

"What about the total darkness judgment?" Caleb asked. "Can you imagine what people's electric bills will be like?"

"Electric bills?" Eric asked incredulously. "We're talking about people who've been covered with nasty sores from head to toe, who then look out their windows and see that the sun is no longer shining. Do you really think they're going to be worrying about their utility rates at that point?"

"Well, it wouldn't be *just* the utility rates," Caleb replied. "If you've got darkness 24/7, that would mean people would basically be driving at night all the time. So you know car insurance premiums would skyrocket too."

"Leave it to a financial analyst to find economic horror in Revelation," Alec commented.

"I suppose you *could* make up for it by getting some prime coastline real estate cheap," Caleb reasoned. "What with all of the blood and everything."

"Revelation chapter twenty, verse fifteen." Eric, Caleb, and Alec turned and saw Chris standing in the doorway, reading from his Bible. "'If anyone's name was not found written in the book of life, he was thrown into the lake of fire.'"

Eric, Caleb, and Alec looked at each other and nodded sheepishly. "Well, when you put it *that* way—" Caleb began.

"I guess a judgment that lasts forever would be the worst," Eric acknowledged.

"I wish I would have thought of that one," Alec said.

Caleb nodded toward Chris. "That's why *he's* the Bible study leader and you're just a lowly group member," he explained.

＊ ＊ ＊ ＊ ＊ ＊ ＊ ＊ ＊ ＊ ＊ ＊ ＊

For many people, one of the biggest obstacles to understanding God is the pervasiveness of evil and suffering in the world. "Why doesn't God do something about it?" is a familiar refrain from believers and unbelievers alike.

Second Peter 3:9 tells us that God is "patient," not yet willing to call down His holy wrath on the world, because He wants to make sure that everyone who will believe and trust in Jesus has an opportunity to do so.

Yet despite the apostle Peter's emphasis on God's patience, there remains an inescapable, unavoidable, and inexorable fact: *God's judgment is coming.* The righteous will receive the eternal rewards promised to them, and the wicked will receive the punishment they deserve.

How and when these events will occur is the focus of *eschatology*, the theological study of the end times. In this chapter, we're going to sort out and explain the various events on tap for the final days of planet Earth. Specifically, we're going to focus on six topics:

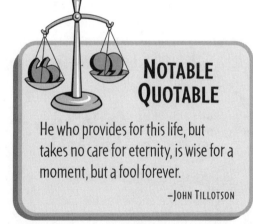

NOTABLE QUOTABLE

He who provides for this life, but takes no care for eternity, is wise for a moment, but a fool forever.

–John Tillotson

1. the Rapture of the church

2. the Tribulation

3. the second coming of Christ

4. the Millennium

5. the final judgment

6. eternity

Let's take a look at each one.

A Rapturous Review

Jesus is coming back. He made that quite clear to His followers while He was on earth. Here are just a few direct quotes from Him:

> ➤ "At that time the sign of the Son of Man will appear in the sky, and all the nations of the earth will mourn. They will see the Son of Man coming on the clouds of the sky, with power and great glory" (Matthew 24:30).

> "And if I go and prepare a place for you, I will come back and take you to be with me that you also may be where I am" (John 14:3).

> "You also must be ready, because the Son of Man will come at an hour when you do not expect him" (Luke 12:40).

That last passage raises an obvious question, one that's been asked by believers from the first century until today: When, exactly, is Jesus coming back?

In Matthew 24:36, Jesus revealed that the only person with the answer to that question is God the Father. And God isn't telling. His wisdom in maintaining strict secrecy regarding Christ's return becomes apparent when we consider the alternative.

Knowing the exact date of Christ's return would be a tremendous hindrance to our efforts to live by faith. If, for example, we knew for certain that Christ would return at 4:13 A.M. eastern standard time on April 24, 2065 (and we don't, so let's not start any rumors), those of us prone to procrastination would have little incentive to fulfill His commands and prepare ourselves (and others) for His return until a few weeks or so before "zero hour."

NOTABLE QUOTABLE

[The death of Jesus] means the verdict which God will pronounce over us on the day of judgment has been brought into the present. We therefore do not need to fear the Judgment Day.

—ANTHONY HOEKEMA

On the other hand, not knowing when He's coming—but knowing it could be anytime—gives us tremendous incentive to busy ourselves with God's work continuously. After all, who wants to be caught "loafing" when the Boss comes back?

Signs, Signs, Everywhere Signs

The Bible does offer some clues as to the timing of Jesus' return. Specifically, Scripture offers several signs that will mark the end of our present age. For example, in 2 Timothy 3:1–5, the apostle Paul offers a list of attitudes that will be prevalent during the "terrible times in the last days." Here's how Paul described people living in the end times:

- ➤ lovers of themselves
- ➤ lovers of money
- ➤ boastful
- ➤ proud
- ➤ abusive
- ➤ disobedient to their parents
- ➤ ungrateful
- ➤ unholy
- ➤ without love

- ➤ unforgiving
- ➤ slanderous
- ➤ without self-control
- ➤ brutal
- ➤ not lovers of the good
- ➤ treacherous
- ➤ rash
- ➤ conceited
- ➤ lovers of pleasure rather than of God

See anything familiar in that list, any prevailing attitudes or lifestyles in today's society? If so, perhaps you'll get a sense of just how imminent Jesus' return is. That's not to say that Jesus will return today, or tomorrow, or even a hundred years from now.

But He could.

In the Twinkling of an Eye

Regarding the specifics of the Rapture, we find much of our information in two passages of Scripture:

> Listen, I tell you a mystery: We will not all sleep, but we will all be changed—in a flash, in the twinkling of an eye, at the last trumpet. For the trumpet will sound, the dead will be raised imperishable, and we will be changed. For the perishable must clothe itself with the unperishable, and the mortal with immortality. When the perishable has been clothed with the imperishable, and the mortal with immortality, then the saying that is written will come true: "Death has been swallowed up in victory." (1 Corinthians 15:51–54)

> God will bring with Jesus those who have fallen asleep in him. According to the Lord's own word, we tell you that we who are still alive, who are left till the coming of the Lord, will certainly not precede those who have fallen asleep. For the Lord

himself will come down from heaven, with a loud command, with the voice of the archangel and with the trumpet call of God, and the dead in Christ will rise first. After that, we who are still alive and are left will be caught up together with them in the clouds to meet the Lord in the air. And so we will be with the Lord forever.
(1 Thessalonians 4:14–17)

Based on these passages (and a few others scattered throughout the Bible), we can conclude that the Rapture will involve, first, a triumphant return of the Lord. The description of an accompanying trumpet blast and a loud command indicate that Jesus' coming will be a spectacle of equal parts joy (for those who leave with Him) and terror (for those who realize they've missed the Rapture).

NOTABLE QUOTABLE

And at the end of the world, when the church of Christ shall be settled in its last, and most complete, and its eternal state, and all common gifts, such as convictions and illuminations, and all miraculous gifts, shall be eternally at an end, yet then divine love shall not fail but shall be brought to its most glorious perfection in every individual member of the ransomed church above.

—JONATHAN EDWARDS

The first ones to respond to Jesus' return will be dead believers ("those who have fallen asleep")—specifically, those who have died since the Day of Pentecost (Acts 2). They will be raised to meet the returning Lord.

After the dead in Christ have been raised, believers who are still alive will be instantly transported from the earth to the Lord's presence "in the air" without experiencing physical death. Jesus referred to the dramatic possibilities presented by the Rapture in Matthew 24:40–41: "Two men will be in the field; one will be taken and the other left. Two women will be grinding with a hand mill; one will be taken and the other left."

The resurrected dead in Christ and the raptured living believers will then return with Jesus to the heavenly realm, where they will be reunited with Christian loved ones who have died.

The Bible doesn't reveal how the world will react to such an unprecedented mass disappearance, but it seems reasonable to assume that the resulting chaos and confusion will pave the way for the next phase of God's plan for the earth.

The timing of the Rapture in relation to the other events of the end times is disputed by various groups of believers. We'll briefly explore some of the different views later in this chapter. It seems clear, though, that the removal of the church during the Rapture will set in motion events that will lead to the Tribulation, a period of unprecedented judgment and suffering on the earth.

Great Tribulation

Sixty-Nine, Going on Seventy

Most discussions of the Tribulation begin with Daniel's prophecy of seventy "sevens" in Daniel 9:20–27. To fully explain the prophecy would require another volume, so we'll provide a *Cliff's Notes* version of it. In an answer to one of his prayers, Daniel was told of a future period of time that would consist of seventy seven-year spans, a total of 490 years.

Based on the events described in the passage (and elsewhere), many Christians believe that sixty-nine of Daniel's seventy "sevens" have already passed. Furthermore, they believe that there is a "gap"— an indefinite amount of time set aside by God— between the sixty-ninth and seventieth sevens, and that that gap represents the age in which we now live.

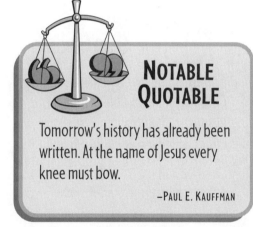

NOTABLE QUOTABLE

Tomorrow's history has already been written. At the name of Jesus every knee must bow.

–Paul E. Kauffman

During this gap, or interval period, God is at work developing the body of Christ—that is, the church. His work will continue until He deems it complete. At that time, He will usher in the seventieth "seven"—the period of Tribulation described so vividly in the book of Revelation. Like the other sixty-nine sevens in Daniel's prophecy, the seventieth one—the Great Tribulation—will last seven years.

Jesus pointed out (in Matthew 24:22) that the fact that the Tribulation lasts only seven years is a testament to God's goodness. If it were any longer than that, He indicated, no one would survive.

Little Horn Makes Big Noise

Passages such as Daniel 9:27 ("He will confirm a covenant for many for one 'seven'") and Daniel 7:24 ("After them another king will arise") suggest that the Tribulation will begin with the emergence of a world leader. This leader will make a name for himself by forging a seven-year covenant, or treaty, with Israel.

Israel, facing oppression from a coalition of world powers, will look to this new leader for alliance and protection. And they will get it—for a while. In the immediate wake of the treaty, life in Israel will be good. Under the new leader's regime, Old Testament worship practices will be restored. Most significantly, the temple will be rebuilt in Jerusalem.

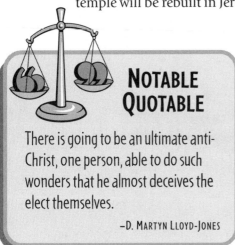

NOTABLE QUOTABLE

There is going to be an ultimate anti-Christ, one person, able to do such wonders that he almost deceives the elect themselves.

–D. Martyn Lloyd-Jones

Alas, though, the halcyon days will be short-lived. The Israelites will soon discover who it is they have aligned themselves with. In Daniel 7:8, he is referred to as the "little horn." In 2 Thessalonians 2:3, he is called "the man of lawlessness." In Revelation 11:7, he is named "the beast." But perhaps his best known appellation is found in 1 John 2:18: "the antichrist."

While the Antichrist is busy readying his agenda in Israel, two "witnesses" will emerge to challenge him. Revelation 11 tells us that these witnesses will be given an astonishing array of powers by God. Among other things, they will be able to destroy their enemies with fire, prevent rain from falling, turn water into blood, and bring plagues upon the earth at will.

The ministry of these two witnesses will last 1,260 days (Revelation 11:3). Based on months of thirty days, that works out to forty-two months, or three and a half years—exactly half of the Tribulation period. That's how long the witnesses will remain invincible.

When their work is done, God will allow the Antichrist to kill the witnesses. This will prove to be an extremely popular move with the people of the world, who will be glad to be rid of the witnesses, their frightening power, and their unpopular message.

After killing the witnesses, the Antichrist will display their bodies on the streets of Jerusalem. Revelation 11:9 suggests that for three and a half days people around the world will view (perhaps via satellite transmission) the bodies of the witnesses lying in the street. Verse 10 even goes so far as to say that people "will gloat over them and will celebrate by sending each other gifts."

The celebration won't last long, though. After three and a half days, with the world watching, God will resurrect the two witnesses and raise them to heaven. To put an exclamation point on His work, God will send a severe earthquake that will destroy one-tenth of the city of Jerusalem and kill 7,000 people (verses 11–13).

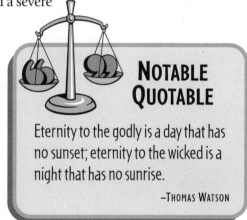

NOTABLE QUOTABLE

Eternity to the godly is a day that has no sunset; eternity to the wicked is a night that has no sunrise.

—THOMAS WATSON

About this same time, 144,000 converted Jews—that is, Jewish people who turned to Christ during the Tribulation (see Revelation 7 for details)—will be killed, further thinning the ranks of believers in the world.

Friends in Low Places

Knowing that his time is short, the Antichrist will step up his efforts and reveal his true intentions at the halfway point of the Tribulation. After dispensing with the two witnesses, he will turn his attention to the restored worship practices in Israel. Breaking his treaty with Israel, the Antichrist will set up *himself* as an object of worship.

If it seems unlikely that people would fall for such an obvious grab for power, consider that the Antichrist is not just any politician. For one thing, he will have the backing and power of Satan himself. Revelation 13:2 explains the scenario this way: "The dragon gave the beast his power and his throne and great authority."

Satan too will recognize that his time for thwarting God's work is running short. He will use the work of the Antichrist to accomplish his own purposes. (We should point out here that all of this will occur only because God will *allow* it to occur. God is sovereign. He will allow Satan and his followers a season to do their work, but His ultimate authority is never truly threatened or challenged.)

In addition to Satan's assistance, the Antichrist will also use a personal "setback" to achieve worldwide notoriety. Though the details of the event are sketchy, Revelation 13:3 tells us that the Antichrist will suffer what appears to be "a fatal wound." To the amazement of the world, though, the Antichrist will recover from the wound. It's unclear whether the Antichrist will actually die and be resurrected (as is suggested by the image in Revelation 11:7 of the beast rising out of "the Abyss") or whether he will be gravely wounded and recover. Either way, he will be miraculously restored to health.

The Antichrist's supernatural recovery will cause people to ask, "Who is like the beast? Who can make war against him?" (Revelation 13:4). He will then use their awe and fear to solidify his power and promote his agenda.

The Antichrist will also benefit from the efforts of a sinister assistant, alternately known as the " . . . beast of the earth" (Revelation 13:11) and the "false prophet" (Revelation 16:13). Like the two witnesses, the False Prophet will be able to call fire from heaven (Revelation 13:13) and perform other miraculous feats.

The False Prophet will use his powers to persuade people to worship the Antichrist. Revelation 13:14–15 tells us that he will commission a statue or idol of the Antichrist, and then bring that image to life through supernatural means. For those who still refuse to worship the Antichrist, the False Prophet will devise a more extreme plan.

Revelation 13:16–17 describes it this way: "He [the false prophet] also forced everyone, small and great, rich and poor, free and slave, to receive a mark on his right hand or on his forehead, so that no one could buy or sell unless he had the mark, which is the name of the beast or the number of his name." The False Prophet will institute a policy in which only people who swear their allegiance to the Antichrist—in the form of a permanent stamp—will be allowed to participate in the economic marketplace. Those who refuse the mark will be prohibited from buying anything—including food.

Pouring Judgments During the Tribulation

"For then there will be great distress, unequaled from the beginning of the world until now—and never to be equaled again." That's how Jesus described the Tribulation to His disciples in Matthew 24:21.

Though the work of the Antichrist will certainly be distressing, it's likely that Jesus was referring to the terrifying series of judgments that God will send to the earth during the Tribulation. The book of Revelation divides the judgments into three groups: the seven seal judgments, the seven trumpet judgments, and the seven bowl judgments.

Here's a brief overview of what each judgment will bring:

The Seven Seal Judgments

Descriptions of these judgments can be found in Revelation 6; 8:1–5. Here is a summary:

- *The first seal judgment.* A rider with a bow on a white horse is given a crown, and then sets out on a mission of conquest. Many Christians believe that this first judgment represents a general "spirit" of conquest, a desire to conquer people and lands that will mark the end times.

- *The second seal judgment.* A rider on a fiery red horse is given the power to remove peace from the earth. This represents a natural progression, since the spirit of conquest inevitably leads to warfare.

- *The third seal judgment.* A rider on a black horse is set loose. He holds a pair of scales in his hands. A voice from heaven suggests

JUST WONDERING

Where does the number 666 fit into all of this?
Revelation 13:18 refers to "the number of the beast," which is also "man's number," or "666." That's not to say that the mark of the beast will be three sixes across the hand or forehead. However, the number does play a part in the identification of the Beast. Some scholars have suggested that the number represents the unholy trinity of Satan, the Antichrist, and the False Prophet. (The number seven represents perfection in Scripture; the number six, which obviously falls one digit short, represents man.)

that a terrible famine will inflate the prices of food ten times their normal cost.

- *The fourth seal judgment.* A rider on a pale horse, identified as Death and followed closely by Hades, is given the power to kill over one-quarter of the earth's population by "sword, famine and plague, and by the wild beasts of the earth" (Revelation 6:8).

- *The fifth seal judgment.* The presence of "those who had been slain because of the word of God and the testimony they had maintained" (6:9) at the opening of the fifth seal suggests that believers already will have been martyred at some point during the Tribulation. God announces His intention to judge those who persecute believers.

- *The sixth seal judgment.* A massive earthquake strikes. The sun turns black. The moon turns bloodred. A meteor shower hits the earth. The skies roll back. Every mountain and island on earth is jolted out of place. People are so terrified that they cry out for the mountains to crush them rather than face any more of God's wrath.

- *The seventh seal judgment.* Silence envelops heaven for half an hour as the opening of the seventh seal begins the next series of judgments.

The Seven Trumpet Judgments

These judgments are described in Revelation 8:6–9:21; 11:15–14:20. Here is a summary:

- *The first trumpet judgment.* Hail and fire, mingled with blood, destroy one-third of the earth's trees and all of the grass.

- *The second trumpet judgment.* The description of "something like a huge mountain, all ablaze" (8:8) being thrown into the sea defies our complete comprehension. The effects of the collision will be obvious, though. One-third of the world's seas turn to

NOTABLE QUOTABLE

A continual looking forward to the eternal world is not a form of escapism or wishful thinking, but one of the things a Christian is meant to do.

–C. S. LEWIS

blood, one-third of all sea creatures are killed, and one-third of all ships are destroyed.

⚡ *The third trumpet judgment.* A blazing star called Wormwood crashes to earth, polluting one-third of the world's rivers and streams. The contamination of such a large percentage of the earth's freshwater results in many poisoning deaths.

⚡ *The fourth trumpet judgment.* One-third of the sun, the moon, and stars are darkened, creating havoc in the standard day-night cycle. Some Bible scholars have suggested that the twenty-four-hour day will be shortened to sixteen hours as a result of the fourth trumpet judgment.

⚡ *The fifth trumpet judgment.* A star crashes to the earth, opening "the Abyss" and unleashing nightmarish creatures that will afflict the earth for five months. The creatures are described as demonic "locusts" that are able to sting like scorpions. What's more, they are said to have the face of a human, the hair of a woman, and the teeth of a lion! Their sting is not fatal, but it is so intensely painful that people will try—in vain—to commit suicide to escape its agony.

⚡ *The sixth trumpet judgment.* A violent conflict, involving 200 million mounted troops, will wipe out one-third of the human population on the planet.

⚡ *The seventh trumpet judgment.* The final battle between good and evil commences. Knowing his time is short, Satan steps up his efforts to disrupt God's plan and oppress believers.

The Seven Bowl Judgments
You'll find the accounts of these judgments in Revelation 16.

⚡ *The first bowl judgment.* "Ugly and painful sores" afflict everyone who has the mark of the Beast on them. Revelation 16:11 suggests that the pain from these sores will continue even after the fifth bowl judgment. Rather than repenting for the actions that brought on the judgment, though, the suffering people curse God for their pain.

🗲 *The second bowl judgment.* The sea turns to blood, killing all marine life. In a sense, this is a completion of the second trumpet judgment, in which one-third of the seas turn to blood and one third of all sea creatures are killed.

🗲 *The third bowl judgment.* The rivers and natural springs of the world turn to blood, contaminating the earth's drinking water.

🗲 *The fourth bowl judgment.* The heat of the sun's rays is intensified, causing sunlight to scorch people's skin. Victims continue to curse God rather than repent.

🗲 *The fifth bowl judgment.* Complete darkness envelops the Antichrist's kingdom. The continuing pain of the sores in the first bowl judgment cause people to gnaw their tongues in agony.

🗲 *The sixth bowl judgment.* The Euphrates River dries up, allowing the armies of the world to converge on Armageddon for one final battle.

🗲 *The seventh bowl judgment.* An earthquake of unprecedented magnitude divides Jerusalem into three parts, causes other cities to collapse completely, flattens the earth's mountains, and sinks the world's islands. Hailstones weighing one hundred pounds batter the earth.

These judgments are arranged in chronological order. You'll notice that they increase in frequency, if not severity, as the Tribulation draws to a close. By the time the last judgment is over, those people who are left on earth will be ready to take out their pain, fear, and frustration on God Himself.

The Second Coming of Christ

The Final Showdown

In the face of these tragedies and his own relentless persecution of the Jewish people, the Antichrist will see his power base begin to crumble. The first strike against him will come in the form of an attack by the northern army of Magog. (Ezekiel 38 predicts the battle.) The Antichrist and his army will be able to withstand their enemy, but only for a short time.

Another strike will occur in the wake of the sixth bowl judgment, the drying up of the Euphrates River. With no natural water boundary to stop them, an army led by "kings from the East" (Revelation 16:12) will attack Israel. In the midst of that battle, yet another army will invade. This one, however, will come from heaven, and it will be led by Jesus Christ Himself.

When Christ Appears

Revelation 19:11–16 describes the awesome spectacle of the Lord's return: "I saw heaven standing open and there before me was a white horse, whose rider is called Faithful and True. With justice he judges and makes war. His eyes are like blazing fire, and on his head are many crowns. He has a name written on him that no one knows but he himself. He is dressed in a robe dipped in blood, and his name is the Word of God."

The apostle John continues concerning the Lord's armies and His power: "The armies of heaven were following him, riding on white horses and dressed in fine linen, white and clean. Out of his mouth comes a sharp sword with which to strike down the nations. 'He will rule them with an iron scepter.' He treads the winepress of the fury of the wrath of God Almighty. On his robe and on his thigh he has this name written: King Of Kings and Lord Of Lords."

ON A PERSONAL NOTE

Many believers (and unbelievers) have found the wildly popular *Left Behind* series to be a helpful, if fictional, introduction to the events described in the book of Revelation. Written by Tim LaHaye and Jerry Jenkins, the series depicts life on earth after the Rapture and during the Tribulation. Though the authors' interpretations of some Scripture passages have been disputed, the series has proven to be an effective tool in encouraging people to think about what is to come. If you're interested in reading the books for yourself, you'll find copies at just about any large bookstore in your area—if not in your local library.

This will be the climactic showdown of good versus evil. For every person who has ever asked, "When is God going to do something about all the evil in the world?" Jesus will provide a definitive answer. The carnage of this battle, which is commonly referred to as "Armageddon," will be staggering. Revelation 14:20 describes a scene in which the blood of the dead runs as high as a horse's bridle over an area of about 180 miles.

When it's over, the armies of the earth will be defeated, the Antichrist and False Prophet will be thrown into the lake of fire, and Christ will stand victorious as the King of Kings and Lord of Lords.

Christ's victory at Armageddon will mark the end of the Tribulation period and will usher in His millennial reign.

The Millennium: One Hundred Righteous Decades

Simply put, the Millennium will be earth's finest hour—or, more accurately, earth's finest thousand years. (The first seven verses of Revelation 20 affirm—no less than six times, actually—that the Millennium will be an actual one-thousand-year period of time.) Christ will establish His kingdom on earth—in Jerusalem, to be specific—and, with His perfect wisdom, justice, compassion, and love, will rule over everyone and everything. His Word will be law. His plans will be fulfilled. His followers will prosper.

JUST WONDERING

Who will be on earth during the Millennium?

Those who survive the Tribulation will become subjects in Christ's kingdom in their physical bodies. Resurrected Christians will also be subjects, but in their resurrection bodies. Unlike their never-dead fellow subjects, the resurrected inhabitants of the kingdom will not require food, drink, rest, or shelter.

As if the prospect of Jesus as supreme commander-in-chief of earth weren't tantalizing enough, there are a couple of other factors that will make the Millennium especially noteworthy. First, there's the fact that Satan will be out of the picture for the duration of Christ's earthly reign. Revelation 20:2 says that Satan will be "bound . . . for a thousand years." He will not be allowed to deceive or tempt in Christ's kingdom.

Second, there's the possibility of personally participating in Christ's kingdom. David will be a part of it (Ezekiel 37:24–25). So will the twelve apostles (Matthew 19:28). Passages such as Revelation 5:10 and Revelation 20:4 indicate that Christians who remain faithful to Christ and His work throughout their lives will be rewarded with a position of honor and importance in His kingdom.

The Millennium will be a time marked by unprecedented peace throughout the world. It will also be a time of perfect justice. Sin will still exist, despite Satan's absence. However, with Christ in charge, it will be dealt with decisively and immediately. Isaiah 35:1–7 suggests that the earth will be amazingly prosperous during the Millennium, providing abundant vegetation and harvest.

The Final Judgment

Here Comes the Judgment
Revelation 20:7–10 tells us that after the Millennium, Satan will be turned loose for one final attempt at thwarting God's plans. After deceiving the nations, he will assemble a massive army for one last assault on God and His people. The campaign will be stopped by fire from heaven that consumes the entire army. Satan will then face his final judgment.

After countless millennia of evil, wickedness, lies, temptation, perversion, and destruction, Satan will be thrown into the "lake of burning sulfur," joining the already-sentenced Antichrist and the False Prophet. In the final reference to Satan in Scripture, Revelation 20:10 makes special note of the fact that he "will be tormented day and night for ever and ever."

After Satan's sentencing, the scene shifts to the judgment of the dead before the Lord's "great white throne" (Revelation 20:11). The evidence for this final judgment will be indisputable; the sentence will be immediate. Those whose names are not written in the Book of Life—those who refuse the salvation offered by Jesus' sacrifice—will be thrown into the lake of fire.

Judgment for Believers Too
The unsaved are not the only ones who will be judged in the end times. Although biblical scholars disagree on the actual number of judgments that will occur, God's Word makes it clear that believers will be judged as well.

That's not to say that our eternal destiny is in question. In John 5:24, Jesus says, "I tell you the truth, whoever hears my word and believes him who sent me has eternal life and will not be condemned; he has crossed over from death to life."

Instead, the judgment of believers will focus on our faithfulness in obeying God's instructions. In 2 Corinthians 5:10, the apostle Paul tells the Corinthian believers, "For we must all appear before the judgment seat of Christ, that each one may receive what is due him for the things done while in the body, whether good or bad." The verdict of the judgment will determine the degrees of "reward" that believers will experience in heaven.

This Must Be Heaven

Verses that affirm that heaven is the final destination of all believers are plentiful in Scripture. Verses that describe what heaven is like are considerably rarer. That's what makes the apostle John's description of the "new heaven" in Revelation 21 so fascinating. John essentially provides an eyewitness account of the place. Yet the vision he sees is so overwhelming and so beyond his realm of context that his description of it is barely comprehensible.

Here are some of the features of heaven that John identifies in Revelation 21:

➤ a crystalline and golden appearance

➤ an equilateral cube design in which each side measures about 1,400 miles long

➤ a twelve-layer foundation, with each layer inlaid with jewels

➤ walls made of jasper two hundred feet thick

➤ three solid pearl gates in each of the four walls, with each gate named for a tribe of Israel

➤ a river that flows from God's throne

➤ streets made of transparent gold

➤ a sea of glass

No physical description can do justice to heaven. Perhaps, then, the best way to communicate what it will be like is to quote the voice that comes from the throne of God, as recorded in Revelation 21:3–4: "Now the dwelling of God is with men, and he will live with them. They will be his people, and God himself will be with them and be their God. He will wipe every tear from their eyes. There will be no more death or mourning or crying or pain, for the old order of things has passed away."

We will never be able to fully comprehend the grandeur and magnificence of our eternal home until we are able to enjoy it for ourselves.

A Barrelful of Isms

As we mentioned at the beginning of the chapter, not all Christians hold the same views regarding the end times. In fact, there are a handful of different approaches to eschatology. In this chapter, we've presented the "pretribulation premillennial" view. In a nutshell, this view holds that the Rapture will occur before the seven-year Tribulation period—which means believers who are alive at that time will be spared the judgments and suffering of the Tribulation—and that Jesus' second coming will occur before the Millennium. In other words, there are two returns of Christ, separated by a period of seven years.

Other believers subscribe to one of the following views regarding the return of Christ:

➤ midtribulational premillennialism

➤ posttribulational premillennialism

ON A PERSONAL NOTE

Picture your friends, loved ones, and acquaintances standing before the great white throne of God, awaiting final judgment (as described in Revelation 20:11–15). As far as you know, how many of them will discover too late that their names are not written in the Book of Life? What can you do to make sure that they have all the information they need before they face that situation? Brainstorm some specific faith-sharing strategies to reach the unsaved people in your life.

➤ postmillennialism

➤ amilliennialism

➤ reverse postmillennialism with a double-toe loop and triple salchow

Okay, we made that last one up. Granted, at first glance, these terms may seem like things you'd find only on a theologian's Scrabble board. Actually, though, the names are pretty self-explanatory. The first two positions aren't very far removed from the "pretrib" (that's how all cool theologians refer to it) position we covered in this chapter.

The basic difference is that *midtribulational premillennialists* believe that the Rapture will occur at the midpoint of the Tribulation—that is, after three and a half years. *Posttribulational premillennialists* believe that the Rapture will occur after the seven years of tribulation have ended. In other words, they believe that Christians will endure the judgments of the Tribulation. They also view the Rapture and the Second Coming as a single event.

Postmillennialists, on the other hand, believe that the preaching of the gospel and the work of the Holy Spirit will eventually cause the world to become "Christianized." At some point in the future, they contend, the earth will enjoy a period of peace and righteousness. They believe that one day Jesus' Great Commission in Matthew 28:19 ("make disciples of all nations") will be accomplished. This, they believe, will mark the beginning of the Millennium.

That's not to say that postmillennialists believe everyone in the world will be a Christian during the Millennium. However, postmillennialists believe that Christian virtues and values, such as love and obedience, will be the rule rather than the exception. As a result, sin will become much less prominent.

Postmillennialists do not believe that the Millennium will necessarily last for one thousand years. In fact, many believe that it will last much longer than that. Some believe it will begin gradually; others believe it will have a specific and obvious starting point.

Amillennialists discount the idea of a future earthly kingdom. Some amillennialists believe that biblical accounts of the Millennium refer to events that are being fulfilled by the church on earth. Others believe that they refer to events that are being fulfilled by the saints in heaven now.

One More Thing

If the biblical descriptions cited in this chapter seem somewhat vague and impenetrable to you, well . . . welcome to the world of eschatology. God apparently doesn't want us to know many of the details of what the future holds. He's given us enough clues to respond to and anticipate, but not so many that we can say with confidence exactly what things will be like during the "end times."

Before we wrap up this chapter, we need to offer a quick reminder of why God gives us information about the future to begin with. First Thessalonians 4:18 offers this instruction: "Encourage each other with these words."

Despite the accounts of judgments and suffering in the book of Revelation, our efforts to understand God's future for the world should fill us with encouragement and comfort. The fact is, our God is in complete control of the future, and Christ is coming again. No matter what happens to us on earth, the promise of eternal life in heaven is guaranteed.

Know What You Believe

How much do you know about end-times events? Here's a quiz to test your knowledge.

1. Which of the following will not occur at the Rapture?
   a. The dead will rise from their graves.
   b. A trumpet will sound.
   c. An earthquake will level Jerusalem.
   d. Believers will be "caught up" to the clouds.

2. Which of the following is not another name for the Antichrist?
   a. Little horn
   b. The man in black
   c. The Beast
   d. The man of lawlessness

3. Which of the following is not one of the trumpet judgments described in the book of Revelation?
   a. One-third of the sun, moon, and stars are darkened.
   b. One-third of the world's seas turn to blood.
   c. One-third of the earth's population is killed.
   d. One-third of all cities are condemned and torn down.

4. Which of the following is not one of the descriptions of the returning Christ in Revelation 19:11–16?
   a. Riding a white horse
   b. Eyes blazing like fire
   c. Dressed in a robe dipped in blood
   d. Long hair flowing majestically in the breeze

5. Which of the following is not an actual theological position regarding the end times?
   a. Ultramillennialism
   b. Amillennialism
   c. Postmillennialism
   d. Premillennialism

Answers: (1) c, (2) b, (3) d, (4) d, (5) a

The Ball's in Your Court

RESPONDING TO WHO GOD IS

SNAPSHOT

"Don't get me wrong," Charlie said as he threw two quarters into the toll basket and pulled away. "I *like* talking to you about God. I think it's an interesting topic, and it makes the commute go faster. I'll even admit that I've learned some things from you."

"But?" Mark prompted.

"But that doesn't mean I want to change my life because of it," Charlie said.

"Why not?" Mark asked.

Charlie seemed surprised by the question. "Why *not?* Well, for one thing, I don't have time right now. Things are crazy at the office these days. Plus, my girlfriend's complaining that I don't spend enough time with her. I just don't have room in my schedule for anything else."

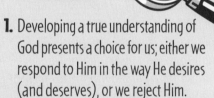

SNEAK PREVIEW

1. Developing a true understanding of God presents a choice for us; either we respond to Him in the way He desires (and deserves), or we reject Him.

2. The best way to respond to what we know about God is with acceptance, reverence, humility, obedience, gratitude, confidence, and excitement.

3. Any risks or inconveniences involved in pursuing an active relationship with the Lord are dwarfed by the rewards of remaining faithful to Him.

287

"I see," Mark replied. "So, how soon do you think you could pencil in the Supreme Being of the universe?"

"Do I detect a little sarcasm in your voice this morning?" Charlie asked.

"No, I'm just curious about your priorities," Mark replied.

"What about them?" Charlie asked.

"Last week you said you believe that what the Bible says about God is true," Mark pointed out.

"I do," Charlie emphasized. "Just like you do."

"So you believe that God is the Creator of the world, the most powerful Being in the universe, and the One who knows everything there is to know about everything."

"Yes, yes, and yes," Charlie replied.

"And you're aware that He has plans for your life?" Mark continued.

Charlie nodded his head thoughtfully for a moment and said, "Yeah, I guess so."

"Well, then, how in the world does that become a back-burner issue in your life?" Mark asked.

Charlie shrugged. "Like I said, I have other things going on right now," he explained.

"But think about the things you *do* find time for," Mark urged. "Golf. Softball. The football pool at work. Renting videos."

"You're saying those things are wrong?" Charlie asked.

"No, I'm saying those things are *unimportant*," Mark emphasized. "It's like getting a phone call from the president of the United States and then putting him on hold for a couple hours while you call around for movie times."

Charlie paused for a moment to consider the analogy. "Okay," he said slowly. "So you think my priorities are out of whack."

"I think it doesn't matter what *I* think," Mark replied.

"Okay," Charlie said, "then does *God* think my priorities are out of whack?"

"You've got Him lined up behind golf and your football pool!" Mark pointed out. "What do *you* think He thinks about it?"

* * * * * * * * * * * * * *

If the title of this book were, say, *The World's Easiest Guide to Understanding Cubist Art,* we could fill it with biographical sketches of noteworthy artists, scholarly examinations of their techniques and influences, and representations of their work, and be done with it. If it were *The World's Easiest Guide to Understanding the Civil War,* we could confine our discussion to "who did what to whom when, where, and why."

Those approaches are insufficient, however, when the topic is "understanding God." Coming to grips with the reality of the Deity isn't simply an intellectual pursuit. It can't be—at least, not from a Christian perspective.

To understand God—even in the limited way dictated by our finite minds—is to be presented with a choice. We must either acknowledge Him for who He is—and adjust our lives accordingly—or reject Him. There is no middle ground where God is concerned. Remaining noncommittal is the same as rejecting Him.

To put it another way, a head knowledge of God's . . .

- ➤ revelation,
- ➤ attributes,
- ➤ covenants,
- ➤ triunity,
- ➤ laws,
- ➤ Word,

- ➤ creation,
- ➤ salvation,
- ➤ work in people's lives,
- ➤ expectations,
- ➤ will, and
- ➤ plan for the future

. . . demands a heart response from us.

ON A PERSONAL NOTE

Here's a Bible study idea: Investigate the way God responds to various people in the Bible, and come up with a recommendation of the best way for us to approach God, based on the positive biblical encounters that you find. Here's a list of passages to get you started: Genesis 4:2b–5 (Cain's sacrifice versus Abel's sacrifice); Genesis 18:16–33 (Abraham's "bargaining" for Sodom); 1 Samuel 1 (Hannah's pleading for a son); Psalm 51 (David's prayer for forgiveness). For each passage, ask yourself:

➤ What is it about the interaction that God responded to?

➤ What can I learn from this interaction?

➤ What changes do I need to make in the way I approach God or interact with Him?

Incorporate any strategies, principles, or attitudes you discover into your own prayer life.

As we wrap up this book, let's take a look at how we should respond to what we know about God.

Response Number One: Acceptance

If you've made it this far in the book, you're probably more than familiar with the biblical instructions for accepting God's gift of salvation:

➤ "Repent and believe the good news!" (Mark 1:15).

➤ "Believe in the Lord Jesus, and you will be saved" (Acts 16:31).

Of course, simply being familiar with the instructions isn't enough. You've got to personally apply them to your life. If you haven't specifically and purposefully repented of your sin and placed your trust in Christ, now is the time to do so. Take a few minutes to offer a genuine, heartfelt prayer to God in which you confess that you are a sinner, ask Him to forgive your sin, and commit yourself to turn away from sin and to Christ.

If you're unsure of what to say, here's a sample prayer that you can either repeat verbatim or modify to fit your personal situation:

Dear God,

I have sinned against You and I need Your grace. Please forgive me for my sin so that I may be righteous in Your eyes. Your Son gave His life to save me, and now I give my life to Him. I ask that You send Your Holy Spirit to change my life. In Jesus' name I pray. Amen.

To sincerely and genuinely offer a prayer that includes these elements is to be saved. Now you too have a relationship with God and the promise of eternal life.

Salvation is only the beginning, though. As Acts 16:31 suggests, God expects us to accept His Son not only as Savior, but as *Lord* as well. Making Jesus Lord means accepting . . .

➤ His leadership as the direction of our lives,

➤ His will as our own, and

➤ His life as our model.

NOTABLE QUOTABLE

The difference between "involvement" and "commitment" is like an eggs-and-ham breakfast; the chicken was "involved"–the pig was "committed."

–AUTHOR UNKNOWN

Romans 8:5 explains the transformation that's involved this way: "Those who live according to the sinful nature have their minds set on what that nature desires; but those who live in accordance with the Spirit have their minds set on what the Spirit desires." We're talking about a monumental shift in focus here.

Responding to God with *acceptance* means that we no longer live to please ourselves or to do what's "right for us." Instead, it means that we make a conscious, continuous effort to do what pleases God. Rather than making decisions based on how much fame, money, or freedom they will give us, we base our life choices on the criteria outlined in 1 Corinthians 10:31: "So whether you eat or drink or whatever you do, do it all for the glory of God."

Responding to God with acceptance also means committing ourselves to honor Him in . . .

➤ the things we say,

➤ the way we work,

➤ the way we treat others,

➤ the way we treat our bodies,

> the morals we live by,

> the way we spend our free time

. . . as well as *everything* else we do. If that seems like a life-changing, never-ending proposition to you, you're absolutely right.

Response Number Two: Reverence

In Exodus 3:5, Moses was instructed to remove his sandals before he approached the burning bush. In Leviticus 16:1–25, one room of the Jewish tabernacle was declared off-limits—upon penalty of death—to everyone but the high priest, who was allowed to enter it only once a year and only after painstaking preparation and cleansing. In 1 Chronicles 13:9–10, a man named Uzzah died because he touched the ark of the covenant.

The common factor in these three biblical accounts is God's *holiness*. Moses was required to go shoeless because the ground around the burning bush was holy. The forbidden room of the tabernacle, which represented God's throne, was called "the Most Holy Place." The ark of the covenant was holy—and untouchable—because it symbolized God's presence among His people.

We mention these events not to familiarize you with obscure Old Testament worship regulations, but to remind you of who it is we're talking about.

God isn't some kindly, well-meaning, grandfatherly figure prone to homilies and gentle warnings about the importance of staying on the right path. He's not Someone who can be listened to or ignored, with little consequence either way.

The God we are striving to understand is the One who . . .

> sent ten devastating plagues to the people of Egypt (Exodus 7:14–12:30),

> collapsed the waters of the Red Sea on top of Pharaoh's army (Exodus 14:5–31),

> opened up the earth to swallow Korah and his band of rebels (Numbers 16:28–35), and

> blinded the entire Aramean army (2 Kings 6:8–23).

That's not to say that we should walk around in fear of being swallowed by the earth or struck with a plague. We should, however, give God the respect and reverence that His holiness, power, and majesty dictate. In other words, we are to treat Him the way He deserves to be treated.

God gives us an idea of the way we should approach Him in Malachi 2:5. Holding up His covenant with Levi as a model, God says, "He revered me and stood in awe of my name." If we don't show reverence to God and stand in awe of His name every time we approach Him in prayer or study His Word, we're doing something wrong.

Response Number Three: Humility

Along with maintaining an accurate perception of who God is and what He's like, we must also maintain an accurate sense of who we are. Talk of God's love, His plans for our lives, and His desire for a personal relationship with us may start to fill our heads with delusions of grandeur, if we're not careful. In extreme cases, we may even begin to believe that we deserve to be loved by God and enjoy a personal relationship with Him.

Let's be clear here: The only thing we deserve from God is His eternal wrath. Romans 3:23 declares that each and every one of us has failed to live up to God's standard. Ephesians 2:8–9 tells us that God's *grace* is the only reason we aren't treated the way we deserve to be treated by Him.

The fact that we are able to . . .

> ➤ rest assured in our salvation,

> ➤ call God "Father,"

> ➤ take our needs and requests to Him, and

> ➤ experience His work in our lives

. . . should be a source of constant amazement to us.

David had the right idea in Psalm 8:3–4. You can practically feel the astonishment in his words when he wrote, "When I consider your heavens, the work of your fingers, the moon and the stars, which you have set in place, what is man that you are mindful of him, the son of man that you care for him?" To put it another way, David was asking, "What is a sovereign, all-powerful Deity like You doing hanging out with an undeserving, insignificant person like me?"

The Bible leaves little doubt as to God's feelings about humility:

➤ "You save the humble but bring low those whose eyes are haughty" (Psalm 18:27).

➤ "He guides the humble in what is right and teaches them his way" (Psalm 25:9).

➤ "For the LORD takes delight in his people; he crowns the humble with salvation" (Psalm 149:4).

➤ "For whoever exalts himself will be humbled, and whoever humbles himself will be exalted" (Matthew 23:12).

➤ "Humble yourselves, therefore, under God's mighty hand, that he may lift you up in due time" (1 Peter 5:6).

NOTABLE QUOTABLE

The reason why God is so great a lover of humility is because He is the great lover of truth. Now humility is nothing but truth, while pride is nothing but lying.

–VINCENT DE PAUL

The choice is ours: We can either approach God with a spirit of humility or we can be humbled by Him. One way or the other, though, we *will* find our proper place before the Lord.

Response Number Four: Obedience

First John 2:3–6 sets the bar for people who desire to understand God: "We know that we have come to know him if we obey his commands. The man who says, 'I know him,' but does not do what he commands is a liar, and the truth is not in him. But if anyone obeys his word, God's love is truly made complete in him. This is how we know we are in him: Whoever claims to live in him must walk as Jesus did."

It's one thing to *declare* God to be sovereign or to nod our heads in vigorous agreement when someone mentions His omniscience or omnipotence. It's quite another thing to live in a way that demonstrates our beliefs. According to biblical criteria, a person who claims to believe in God's authority, wisdom, and power, but refuses to live according to His will or Word, doesn't *really* believe.

Lip service just doesn't cut it with God; He demands action. That's why James wrote, "Do not merely listen to the word, and so deceive yourselves. Do what it says" (James 1:22).

Obedience has been God's primary demand for His human creation since the earliest days in Eden. You could argue that almost every major event in Scripture is somehow tied to the issue of obedience or disobedience to God. Adam and Eve were kicked out of the garden because of their disobedience. Noah survived the Flood because of his obedience. The Israelites prospered when they obeyed God and suffered when they didn't. Daniel was sentenced to death in the lion's den because he obeyed God—and was protected by God from the lions for the same reason.

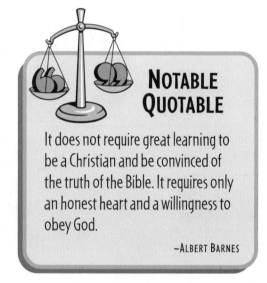

NOTABLE QUOTABLE

It does not require great learning to be a Christian and be convinced of the truth of the Bible. It requires only an honest heart and a willingness to obey God.

–ALBERT BARNES

Beyond the illustrations of God's rewards for obedience and punishment for disobedience are His instructions and promises scattered throughout Scripture:

➤ "You must obey my laws and be careful to follow my decrees. I am the LORD your God. Keep my decrees and laws, for the man who obeys them will live by them. I am the LORD" (Leviticus 18:4–5).

➤ "But from everlasting to everlasting the LORD's love is with those who fear him, and his righteousness with their children's children—with those who keep his covenant and remember to obey his precepts" (Psalm 103:17–18).

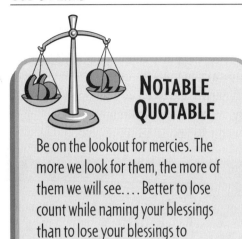

NOTABLE QUOTABLE

Be on the lookout for mercies. The more we look for them, the more of them we will see.... Better to lose count while naming your blessings than to lose your blessings to counting your troubles.

–MALTBIE D. BABCOCK

➤ "Blessed rather are those who hear the word of God and obey it" (Luke 11:28).

➤ "Jesus replied, 'If anyone loves me, he will obey my teaching. My Father will love him, and we will come to him and make our home with him. He who does not love me will not obey my teaching. These words you hear are not my own; they belong to the Father who sent me'" (John 14:23–24).

➤ "This is love for God: to obey his commands" (1 John 5:3a).

Here's what it comes down to. If we're not going to respond to God with obedience, we need not bother showing Him acceptance, reverence, or humility. Those attitudes, while positive and pleasing, are meaningless apart from a genuine commitment to align our actions with God's instruction.

Response Number Five: Gratitude

The necessity of responding to God with gratitude has very little to do with good manners or politeness. On the other hand, it has everything to do with awareness and recognizing the truth about our situation. The truth is that our family, friendships, health, talents, ability to think and reason, and even our sense of humor are gifts from God. So too are our peace of mind and spiritual growth—every good thing in our lives comes from the Father (see James 1:17).

As the old hymn says, He is the One "from whom all blessings flow." That's a fact, an indisputable truth for all believers. What's more, that fact puts the proverbial "ball" in your court.

Either you're the type of person who recognizes God's blessings or you're not. It's that simple. If you truly recognize them, you can't help but respond to them with gratitude. If you don't recognize them . . . well, that says more about you than you probably care to acknowledge. (Think about how *you* react to ungrateful people.)

The Bible certainly advocates an "attitude of gratitude." Second Samuel 22 records David's song of praise and gratitude to God for rescuing him from the hands of his enemies. You can get a sense of the genuineness of David's expression just by looking at his words:

➤ "The LORD is my rock, my fortress and my deliverer" (verse 2).

➤ "The cords of the grave coiled around me . . . . In my distress I called to the LORD" (verses 6–7).

➤ "He rescued me because he delighted in me" (verse 20).

Exodus 15 contains a similar song of praise by Moses. Then there's the Old Testament prophet Daniel, who was charged with the responsibility of interpreting King Nebuchadnezzar's dream. Because Daniel was an Israelite captive in Babylon, this was a high-pressure assignment for him. Daniel 2:19 tells us that one night, God revealed the interpretation of the king's dream to Daniel.

ON A PERSONAL NOTE

Write your own song of praise to God. Look at the examples of David in 2 Samuel 22 and Moses in Exodus 15. Notice how specific they are in their expressions of gratitude, the way they single out individual events and blessings for special mention. Write a list of specific things that God has done in your life. Then express your thankfulness for them in a format similar to the ones used by David and Moses. Don't worry about trying to rhyme your song "lyrics"; just express your thoughts and feelings as creatively as possible.

You'd think that Daniel's first reaction would have been to rush into the king's chamber and give him the good news, or perhaps to write down the details of the interpretation so that he wouldn't forget it. Instead, Daniel offered an immediate prayer of praise to the Lord for His work. As far as Daniel was concerned, everything could wait except the gratitude.

It's no coincidence that Daniel, a man eager to express his gratitude and praise, was used mightily by God. We can learn from Daniel's example by demonstrating eagerness and immediacy in our own responses of gratitude to the Lord.

Lamentations 3:22–23 assures us that we will never run out of things to show gratitude for because God's blessings (or "compassions") are "new every morning." As far as we're concerned, then, every day is Thanksgiving where the Lord is concerned.

Response Number Six: Confidence

Hebrews 4:16 gives all believers permission to "approach the throne of grace *with confidence*, so that we may receive mercy and find grace to help us in our time of need" (italics added).

Yes, we are to show reverence to God always. Yes, we must never forget who He is and who we are. Having said that, though, we must also remember that we need never wring our hands, wondering if we're imposing on God or wasting His time with unimportant requests. He has given us immediate and complete access to Him whenever we need it.

NOTABLE QUOTABLE

Faith is a living, daring confidence in God's grace, so sure and certain that a man would stake his life on it a thousand times. This confidence in God's grace and knowledge of it makes men glad and bold and happy in dealing with God and with all His creatures; and this is the work of the Holy Ghost in faith. Hence a man is ready and glad, without compulsion, to do good to everyone . . . in love and praise of God.

—Martin Luther

The reason is simple: We're family. The fact that we become the adopted children of God when we believe in His Son (Ephesians 1:3–6) gives us the privilege of approaching Him as a child would approach a loving father.

Jesus also encouraged a spirit of boldness in believers who take their requests to God. Look at His words in Matthew 7:7–8: "Ask and it will be given to you; seek and you will find; knock and the door will be opened to you. For everyone who asks receives; he who seeks finds; and to him who knocks, the door will be opened." Then Jesus gave the reason we can ask boldly—the care of our loving Father: "Which of you, if his son asks for bread, will give him a stone? Or if he asks for a fish, will give him a snake? If you, then, though you are evil, know how to give good gifts to your children, how much more will your Father in heaven give good gifts to those who ask him!"

That's not to say that God is an indulgent Father who spoils His children by granting their every request. We can rest assured in the fact that God will answer our every prayer. We must keep in mind, though, that "No" is as valid an answer as "Yes" is.

Our confidence springs from the fact that God is concerned about our *needs*. We can take them to Him anytime, anywhere, knowing that He will listen and act, according to His will. (Lest we become overconfident, we should point out that God is *not* concerned about our ideas and plans for getting our needs met. Our invitation to approach God's throne with confidence does not give us the right to tell Him what we think should be done.)

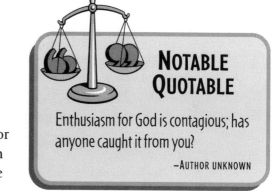

NOTABLE QUOTABLE

Enthusiasm for God is contagious; has anyone caught it from you?

–AUTHOR UNKNOWN

Our response of confidence should extend not only to our personal interaction with God, but to the way we live our lives as well. Romans 8:31 issues the challenge: "If God is for us, who can be against us?" In other words, if we have a genuine understanding of God and a personal relationship with Him, who can oppose us or stand in our way?

The confidence that comes from an intimate alliance with God means that we can approach every interaction, decision, and confrontation with a peace of mind and a sense of boldness, knowing that nothing can supersede Him and His will for us.

Response Number Seven: Excitement

The more we learn about God and the more we begin to understand His work and will, the more we should want to "spread the wealth" of knowledge to others. The fact is, all of us know dozens of people who could benefit from hearing about God's love, forgiveness, power, and wisdom.

Consider the way people in the Bible responded to their discovery of God's work and power. Mark 1:40–45 tells the story of a man who was miraculously healed of leprosy by Jesus. Though Jesus urged the man to keep quiet about what had happened (perhaps because He didn't want to draw too much attention to His healing ministry at the expense of His teaching), the man couldn't contain himself. "He went out and began to talk freely, spreading the news" (verse 45). Matthew 9:27–31 tells a similar story of two blind men who were healed by Jesus. Again Jesus urged them not to tell anyone about their healing. Like the former leper, though, "they went out and spread the news about him all over that region" (verse 31).

We have no such command to keep quiet. In fact, several passages in Scripture encourage us to spill the beans about what we learn and experience of God and His work.

➤ "My mouth will speak in praise of the LORD. Let every creature praise his holy name for ever and ever" (Psalm 145:21).

➤ "I will tell of the kindnesses of the LORD, the deeds for which he is to be praised, according to all the LORD has done for us—yes, the many good things he has done for the house of Israel, according to his compassion and many kindnesses" (Isaiah 63:7).

➤ "I tell you, whoever acknowledges me before men, the Son of Man will also acknowledge him before the angels of God. But he who disowns me before men will be disowned before the angels of God" (Luke 12:8–9).

➤ "We proclaim to you what we have seen and heard, so that you also may have fellowship with us. And our fellowship is with the Father and with his Son, Jesus Christ" (1 John 1:3).

Our excitement about God is an accurate gauge of our understanding of Him. The more we understand about Him, the greater our excitement will be. Conversely, a lack of excitement about God and His work indicates a lack of understanding of Him.

One More Thing

Perhaps the best way to wrap up this chapter—and this book—is to quote 1 Corinthians 2:9: "No eye has seen, no ear has heard, no mind has conceived what God has prepared for those who love him."

Understanding God is not an easy task. In fact, you'll discover it's a lifelong pursuit that requires diligent effort and continuous sacrifice on your part. Whatever inconveniences are involved in pursuing an active relationship with God, however, are dwarfed by the rewards that come from a genuine realization of who He is and what He's like.

Know What You Believe

How much do you know about responding to God? Here's a quiz to test your knowledge.

1. Which of the following is not a recommended response to understanding God?
   a. Confidence
   b. Secrecy
   c. Gratitude
   d. Obedience

2. Which of the following is not an example of responding to God with acceptance?
   a. Treating our free time as an opportunity to honor Him
   b. Treating others according to His instructions in Scripture
   c. Treating our bodies in a way that pleases Him
   d. Treating Satan as though he doesn't exist

3. Strictly speaking, what do we *deserve* from God?
   a. Eternal wrath
   b. Long life
   c. Protection from evil
   d. Assistance in understanding Him

4. What has been God's primary demand for His human creation since the earliest days in Eden?
   a. Animal sacrifice
   b. Obedience
   c. Good grooming
   d. Bible study

5. What did the leper and two blind men who were healed by Jesus do—against Jesus' wishes—after their healings?
    a. They became Pharisees.
    b. They wrote songs about Jesus.
    c. They spread the news about what had happened to them.
    d. They pretended to still be afflicted in order to make money begging.

Answers: (1) b, (2) d, (3) a, (4) b, (5) c

Index

The World's Easiest Guide to ...

Family Relationships

Gary Chapman has gathered treasured and time-tested insights from his previous books—*The Five Love Languages, Loving Solutions, Five Signs of a Loving Family, The Other Side of Love,* and *Toward a Growing Marriage*—to create an easy-to-use, comprehensive guide to family relationships. These insights provide the tools for successful relationships for those whose marriages are in trouble and for those raising their children as single parents.

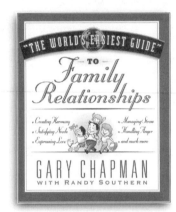

ISBN: 1-881273-40-7

Understanding the Bible

For every person who loves and values Bible reading, there are dozens of others who think of the Bible as a thick confusing, mysterious book. Whichever group you belong to, *The World's Easiest Guide to Understanding the Bible* should lessen the mystery and increase your mastery of Scripture by making you a better detective. You'll learn to put the events of the Bible into context, observe Bible passages, make valid deductions, and arrive at personal applications that are both significant and satisfying.

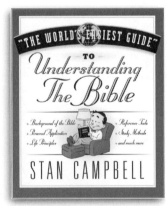

ISBN: 1881273-23-7

The World's Easiest Guide to ...

New Believers

Living a Christian life is a daunting proposition—wouldn't it be great if you had a guidebook that explained clearly and concisely what you need to know and do in order to experience all that God has in store for you? *The World's Easiest Guide for New Believers* tackles the basic issues of Christianity and offers practical, easy-to-understand answers to the questions that make up the foundation of our faith.

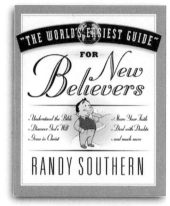

ISBN: 1-881273-64-4

Finances

Are your finances just too hard to manage? Here, at last, are easy answers for the financially challenged! You probably would agree that it's easy to get into debt, easy to put off your retirement planning, and easy to live without a detailed budget. Suddenly your financial future doesn't look at all like your original plans. Now there is and easy and comprehensive guide that even a beginner can understand.

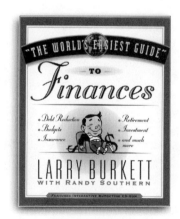

ISBN: 1-881273-38-5

MOODY
PUBLISHERS
THE NAME YOU CAN TRUST.

1-800-678-6928 www.MoodyPublishers.com

WORLD'S EASIEST GUIDE TEAM

ACQUIRING EDITOR:
Mark Tobey

COPY EDITOR:
Jim Vincent

BACK COVER COPY:
Julie-Allyson Ieron, Joy Media

COVER DESIGN:
The Smartt Guys

INTERIOR DESIGN:
The Smartt Guys

PRINTING AND BINDING:
Von Hoffman Graphics, Inc.

The typeface for the text of this book is
Giovanni